Left: richly decorated conservation shophouses.

Atlas

Below: a sculpture by the Singapore River, depicting early life on the banks.

3

Singapore

Singapore is an eclectic, unique city. Although a tiny island nation, it boasts large attractions and achievements. Its multi-racial people celebrate a multitude of cultures and traditions, yet they are worldly and efficient. Visitors are attracted not by the city's wealth or social wisdom, but by the simple joys of its food, shopping, nightlife and ethnic neighbourhoods.

Singapore Facts and Figures

Population: 4.8 million
Area: 710.3 sq km (274.2 sq miles)
Population density: 7,022 per sq km (18,189 per sq mile)
Average daily temperature: 24–33°C (75–91°F)
Crime rate (per 100,000 population): 670
Number of airlines served: 84
Number of taxis: 24,300
Number of visitors in 2009: 9.7 million

Orientation

Conservation has become a priority in this city. If a building is of architectural or historical significance, it tends to be conserved, restored and adapted for new use rather than destroyed. The results are apparent – in the Civic District, Chinatown, Little India, Kampong Glam and old residential neighbourhoods. The gentrification, apart from giving the city added charm, has also helped Singaporeans develop a sense of their own history.

Downtown Singapore remains largely arranged according to the original town plans Sir Thomas Stamford Raffles had implemented in 1819. The colonial hub of the city, today's Civic District, is still the heart of the administration, as it was in Raffles' time. The clamour of Chinatown and the hum of business in the Central Business District around Raffles Place have not diminished. The Malay-Muslim area of Kampong Glam and the predominantly Hindu Little India retain their ethnic feel and laid-back air. Chic Orchard Road, although a plantation area in colonial times, has been transformed into one of Asia's premier shopping belts. The addition of new casino complexes — diplomatically called Integrated Resorts (IRs) — has endowed the Marina Bay area and Sentosa islands) with new lease of life.

Singapore packs in quite a bit given its miniscule size. Once you've covered the city centre, venture out to the suburbs. Here you'll find the housing heartlands interspersed with quirky attractions and pockets of green, where time has stood still and there is precious space for Singapore's residents to take in fresh air.

A Melting Pot

The *lingua franca* is English, but on the streets you will see Chinese, Malay, Indian, Eurasian and Caucasian faces. Mosques, churches, and Hindu and Chinese temples often stand side by side, and local cuisines borrow ideas and ingredients from one another.

On the surface, the city may appear Westernised, but in reality, Asian precepts still temper ideals of personal freedom, and respect for one's elders ranks high. Society and public discourse are kept on a tight rein compared to the West, and there are fines for littering, spitting and other social misdemeanours. The result, however, is an uncommonly efficient city, with the cleanest streets outside of Switzerland.

Below: Indians form one of the communities in polyglot Singapore.

Singapore is also one of the safest cities in the world. So if you see a little alleyway that looks promising, go ahead and explore it. Downtown is easy to get around on foot, by bus or by Mass Rapid Transit (MRT) trains. Taxis are comfortable, inexpensive and especially good for journeys to the suburbs.

Eat, Shop, Drink and Be Merry

Singaporeans tend to be a little competitive, thanks to a healthy *kiasu* (meaning 'afraid to lose' in the Hokkien dialect) attitude. But they play as hard as they work. Engage Singaporeans as they indulge in their favourite pastimes and you'll see their cheerful, outgoing sides. Without a doubt, the nation's favourite activity is eating. The island's cultural diversity has given it an extraordinary array of food options; as a result, this city never stops eating, even in the wee hours of the morning.

Shopping ranks only a close second as Singaporeans' favourite diversion. Many indefatigable locals have been known to trawl Orchard Road at the weekends, mall by mall.

This city, once derided as boring, is also learning to take itself less seriously. Its nightlife scene swings with cool bars and clubs that operate 24/7. The new integrated resorts have opened up a whole new smorgasbord of entertainment options and if the vibrant arts calendar is anything to go by, the city's appetite for culture just keeps on growing.

Highlights

▲ **The Esplanade – Theatres on the Bay** The city's swankiest performance venue is as renowned for its acoustics as for its unconventional architecture.

▲ **Clarke Quay** An entertainment hub with the trendiest bars, clubs and restaurants, set in pretty converted colonial-era godowns.

▲ **VivoCity** Singapore's largest mall fulfils every one of your consumption fantasies.
▼ **Night Safari** A great after-hours alternative.

▲ **National Museum of Singapore** Newly refurbished treasure house of history.
▶ **Sentosa** Excellent excursion with beaches, historical sights and kid-friendly entertainment.

Singapore River

The Singapore River has been Singapore's commercial lifeline for more than a century. This was where Sir Thomas Stamford Raffles, founder of modern Singapore, and early immigrants first landed. The mangrove swamps and floating skulls deposited by pirates are long gone, as are the coolies, junks and warehouses. Its quays are now lined by colourful conservation shophouses, and its surroundings speckled with stately colonial-era buildings, theatres and museums. A walk along the Singapore River is really a stroll down memory lane, enlivened by sights and monuments that reflect the city's rich historical past.

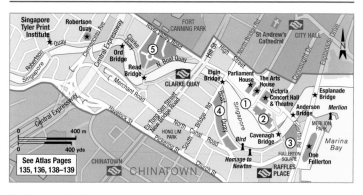

Raffles' Landing Site

The river's place in history is amply demonstrated by the **Raffles' Landing Site** ① and the sights around it. A white marble statue of Raffles marks the very spot on the northern bank where he stepped ashore on 28 January 1819.

Behind the statue sits a clutch of cultural institutions housed in colonial-era buildings. **The Arts House**, a multidisciplinary performing arts centre, occupies the premises of the old Parliament House. Members of Parliament now parley at the **new Parliament House** next door. The **Asian Civilisations Museum** ② exhibits fine Asian artefacts in the neoclassical Empress Place Building, which overlooks the river.

Beside the Empress Place Building are the **Victoria Theatre** and **Victoria Concert Hall**, both built in the 1880s to commemorate Queen Victoria's Diamond Jubilee. In front stands an 1887 bronze statue of Raffles.

Running along the river is a leafy, breezy promenade that makes for a nice stroll. The path leads to **Cavenagh Bridge** and **Anderson Bridge**.

SEE ALSO DANCE, P.47; FILM. P.61; MONUMENTS, P.78, 80, 81; MUSEUMS AND GALLERIES, P.82; MUSIC, P.91; THEATRE, P.121

Left: a picture with the water-spewing Merlion is a must for many visitors.

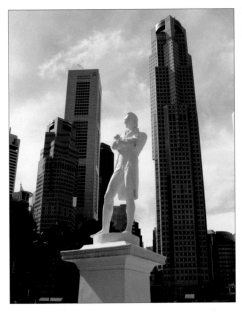

Left: a statue of Raffles marks his landing spot.

When urban renewal fever gripped Singapore in the 1970s, the lighters were banned from the river, flotsam and jetsam were cleared and the shophouses refurbished. Even with its popularity as a drinking hole overshadowed by Clarke Quay *(see below)* today, a good number of executives from the surrounding office towers still unwind at its pubs and restaurants.

Clarke Quay

Upriver from Boat Quay, on the northern bank, is **Clarke Quay** ⑤. This former warehouse district is another example of successful regeneration. It is now the city's hottest after-hours destination, sizzling with well-heeled, fashionable people in the flashy clubs and restaurants housed in its restored 19th-century godowns.
SEE ALSO ARCHITECTURE, P.26

Robertson Quay

The quiet residential enclave of **Robertson Quay** lies further upstream. Its pretty courtyard awakens in the evening, when the surrounding bars and restaurants open for business. Several arts organisations, including the **Singapore Tyler Print Institute**, have also made the quay their base.
SEE ARCHITECTURE, P.30; MUSEUMS AND GALLERIES, P.88

A handful of sculptures dot the Singapore River area. Of note are Fernando Botero's *Bird* and Salvador Dali's *Homage to Newton* outside and at the atrium of UOB Plaza respectively. Along the river there are also delightfully life-like bronze sculptures by local artists, which are part of a series called 'People of the River'. They depict life in Singapore's early days.

The Fullerton Area

The grand building across Cavenagh Bridge is the former General Post Office, restored to its current incarnation as the five-star **Fullerton Hotel** ③. For a study in architectural contrast, take the underpass beneath The Fullerton to the glass-and-steel **One Fullerton**, a restaurant hub on the waterfront. Close by is the

Right: Boat Quay is a lively riverside dining and drinking venue.

Merlion Park, where the kitschy Merlion pours its heart out into the Marina Bay. This half-fish, half-lion creation is the city's tourism mascot.
SEE ALSO ARCHITECTURE, P.28; HOTELS, P.70; MONUMENTS, P.80

Boat Quay

Boat Quay ④ runs along the southern bank between Cavenagh Bridge and Elgin Bridge. For a century until the late 1960s, it reverberated with the clamour of coolies loading and unloading cargo between lighter boats and quayside shophouses.

Marina Bay

The Singapore River empties into the Marina Bay, an artificial inlet formed by reclaimed land, which has become the heart of the city's redevelopment. At the heart of this new hub is the Marina Bay Sands, one of Singapore's two new Integrated Resorts (IRs). Surrounding it are the 101-hectare Gardens by the Bay, the Singapore Flyer (the island's answer to the London Eye) and the Marina Bay Street Circuit, which hosts the Singapore Grand Prix. It is dominated by the Esplanade – Theatres on the Bay, the pride and joy of Singapore's arts scene, and is home to Suntec City and Marina Square – self-contained retail and business cities.

nights. Walk along the **Marina Bay Promenade** just outside; this is one of the best spots to view the CBD skyline. The **Makansutra Gluttons Bay**, to the Esplanade Theatres' right, is popular for after-performance suppers.
SEE ALSO ARCHITECTURE, P.27; DANCE, P.47; FOOD AND DRINK, P.65; MUSIC, P.90; THEATRE, P.121

Marina Square and Suntec City

On the same side of the bayfront as the Esplanade Theatres is **Marina Square**, a huge mall linked to several of the city's top hotels – **Ritz-Carlton Millenia**, **Mandarin Oriental** and **Pan Pacific**.

Suntec City ②, a massive shopping and business development, is also connected to Marina Square. Retail options abound in the oversized **Suntec City Mall**, noted for its gigantic **Fountain of Wealth** ③ – the world's largest.
SEE ALSO HOTELS, P.71; MONUMENTS, P.79; SHOPPING, P.115, 116

Singapore Flyer

On the eastern tip of the bayfront turns the **Singapore Flyer** ④. Enjoy a jaw-dropping panorama of the bay from the world's highest observation wheel at 165m (541ft).
SEE ALSO WALKS AND VIEWS, P.131

Esplanade Theatres

Whatever your opinion of the **Esplanade – Theatres on the Bay** ① – looming on the waterfront with its spiny hedgehog-like profile – there's no denying the role of this S$600 million arts centre as a symbol of the city's aspiration to be Asia's arts hub. The

audacious structure has been a magnet for artistic creativity since it opened in 2002, showcasing a finely tuned repertoire of performing arts from Singapore and abroad.

The adjoining **Esplanade Mall** houses an array of restaurants and quirky shops, busiest on performance

Left: the spiny Esplanade –
Theatres on the Bay makes a
bold statement.

hospitality complex, boasts
two 2,000-seat theatres, three
hotel towers, convention facilities, restaurants helmed by
celebrity chefs and a museum
combining the themes of art
and science. The first phase
of its operations was rolled
out in May 2010, with the
casino and a few restaurants
open to the public. Its second
phase, including the **SkyPark**
and additional retail joints, is
slated to open in summer
2010, at time of press.

It will be anchored by the
S$5 billion **Marina Bay Sands**
⑤, said to be the most expensive ever built by the American
casino-resort giant Las Vegas
Sands. Complementing the
resort are the extension of the
CBD, named **Downtown@
Marina Bay**, luxury apartments and 101-hectare (250-
acre) waterfront gardens
called **Gardens By the Bay**.

A 280-m (918-ft) vehicular
and pedestrian bridge, whose
design is inspired by the double helix, will connect the two
sides of the bay. Viewing platforms along the path will
allow superb bay vistas.

Esplanade Park

If the weather is pleasant, it is
worth making a detour to the
left of the Esplanade Theatres,
where a string of modest
memorials stand, set in tree-
lined open spaces. These
include the **War Memorial**, in
the park of the same name, a
tribute to the countless civilians who died in World War II.

The **Esplanade Park,**
stretching along Connaught

Drive, is dotted with monuments like the Victorian-style
Tan Kim Seng Fountain,
built to mark the merchant's
£13,000 contribution in 1857
to build the town's public
water works. Further along,
the **Cenotaph** pays homage
to the soldiers who died in
the two World Wars.
SEE ALSO MONUMENTS, P.79, 81

The New Marina Bay

The southernmost area bor-
dering the sea is a hotbed of
construction activities for
what has been billed as 'the
centrepiece of Singapore's
redevelopment'.

No urban planning initiative
in Singapore has generated as
much buzz as the new
Marina Bay development, the
subject of an impassioned
public debate because it will
house one of Singapore's two
new casinos in this squeaky
clean city. Additionally, this
'integrated resort', a mega
leisure, entertainment and

Below: the Suntec City Mall's
Fountain of Wealth.

The **Marina Barrage**, built
across the Marina Bay, is a
clever addition to the island's
reservoir stores. This unique
three-in-one project encom-
passes a dam that acts as a
tidal barrier to prevent flooding
during high tides. A freshwater
reservoir sits behind the dam,
while a 12-storey-high fountain
has been built over a spot
where undersea pipes continu-
ously drain water from the
reservoir for storage elsewhere. The reservoir's stable
water level allows for a variety
of water activities and events.

The Civic District

Roughly the area north of the Singapore River and between the City Hall and the Dhoby Ghaut MRT stations, the Civic District is where many colonial-era buildings stand. In his original town plan, Sir Stamford Raffles assigned the area north of the river to the British, ordering the building of offices, banks, hotels, churches and clubs there. He also built his house on the top of Fort Canning Hill. The city is today still governed from the colonial nucleus Raffles established, although many of the historical buildings have been restored and adapted for functions that are completely different from those in the past.

Above: the famous Singapore Sling was created at the Raffles.

City Hall

The expanse of green called the **Padang** ① ('field' in Malay), adjacent to the Esplanade Park, and the two leisure clubs flanking the field, the **Singapore Recreation Club** and the **Singapore Cricket Club**, used to be a focal point of the colonials for sport and social activities. The Padang, then known as the Esplanade, was earmarked in Raffles' town plan as a recreation area, and it remains so today as the site of cricket and rugby matches and public events.

Across St Andrew's Road from the Padang are a cluster of stately government build-ings that are also centre-pieces in Singapore's architectural landscape. Capped by a green dome and fronted by stout Corinthian columns is the **old Supreme Court**. It is now emptied of its law courts, which have moved to the glass-and-steel **new Supreme Court** behind it.

Next to the old Supreme Court is the stoic **City Hall**, once Singapore's most important government build-ing. Both the old Supreme Court and the City Hall are being converted into Singa-pore's **National Gallery**, which will open in 2010.
SEE ALSO ARCHITECTURE, P.26, 29, 30; PARKS AND GARDENS, P.101

Raffles City and Raffles Hotel

Standing above the City Hall MRT station amid verdant greenery is the gleaming white **St Andrew's Cathedral** ②, a gazetted monument that dates back to 1862.

The church spire rises tall, but not as high as the 72-storey **Swissôtel The Stamford**, formerly Southeast Asia's tallest hotel. It is linked to the **Raffles City**, another of the city's stylish malls, designed by I.M. Pei.

CityLink Mall extends from the City Hall MRT station to Suntec City *(see p.8)*. This subterranean retail corridor, with over 50 stores, restau-rants and cafés, is a great rainy day route.

Left: the Raffles Hotel, grande dame of Singapore's hotel scene.

On Armenian Street is the **Peranakan Museum**, which offers a treasure trove of rare and typically intricate Peranakan (Straits Chinese) artefacts. Finding favour with stamp hobbyists is the **Singapore Philatelic Museum** at the top of Armenian Street.

Fort Canning Park ⑦ is uphill from the philatelic museum. Well-marked paths weave through its lush greenery, and the **Battle Box**, an underground war bunker used in World War II, adds interest for history buffs.
SEE ALSO MUSEUMS AND GALLERIES, P.82, 83, 85, 87, 88; PARKS AND GARDENS, P.100

Hill Street

At the foot of the hill runs Hill Street, lined by a few architectural highlights. At the corner with Coleman Street are the atmospheric **Armenian Church** and the **Central Fire Station**, which also has the **Civil Defence Heritage Gallery** on site. With its 911 technicoloured window shutters, the **MICA Building** is hard to miss.
SEE ALSO ARCHITECTURE, P.26, 29; CHURCHES, MOSQUES AND TEMPLES, P.40; MUSEUMS AND GALLERIES, P.84

Making a stop at the **Raffles Hotel** ③ on Beach Road is de rigueur for many tourists, who come to admire its colonial-era architecture, sip a Singapore Sling, relax in its leafy courtyard or shop for luxury items at the **Raffles Hotel Shopping Arcade**.

Nostalgia continues across from the Raffles at the **Mint Museum of Toys**, a gem of a repository on Seah Street.
SEE ALSO CHURCHES, MOSQUES AND TEMPLES, P.43; HOTELS, P.71, 72; MONUMENTS, P.80, MUSEUMS AND GALLERIES, P.85; SHOPPING, P.116

Churches Past and Present

At the corner of North Bridge and Bras Basah roads are two churches, both significant in history but now offering contrasting facets. **Chijmes** ④, a former convent school with a chapel, has been converted into a collection of restaurants and shops. The **Cathedral of the Good**

> Enjoy a Singapore Sling at the Long Bar of the Raffles Hotel, where it was first concocted in 1910. The fruity gin-based drink packs a punch.

Shepherd is a tranquil place of worship offering Roman Catholic service, built in 1846 in the design of a crucifix.
SEE ALSO CHURCHES, MOSQUES AND TEMPLES, P.41; MONUMENTS, P.78

Museum District

The Civic District is the city's museum district. The **Singapore Art Museum** ⑤ on Bras Basah Road has regular exhibitions of works from its permanent collection of 4,000 Southeast Asian paintings. A stone's throw away on Stamford Road is the recently rejuvenated **National Museum of Singapore** ⑥, displaying a collection of Singapore treasures in a handsome neoclassical building.

Below: St Andrew's Cathedral.

Chinatown and the Central Business District

The area south of the Singapore River comprises two distinct districts – Chinatown and the CBD. It may seem odd that this city, with a predominantly Chinese population, has a Chinatown. But this can be traced to Raffles' original town plan, which assigned the different races to various districts. Immigrants from China huddled in Chinatown then, living in dark and cramped quarters in the shophouses. Closer to the river, within the CBD's glass-and-steel maze, are historical and cultural gems worth visiting.

See Atlas pages 138–139

Chinatown

Today's Chinatown is hemmed in by soaring high-rises, but vestiges of the traditional can still be seen. Conservation shophouses house decades-old businesses, which stand shoulder to shoulder with even older places of worship. Medical halls dispense traditional herbal cures, and families flock to restaurants for dim sum at the weekends.

Exotic sights and smells still dominate. There are rare Asian ingredients and frogs to be skinned in the fresh-produce market. At certain times of the year, the streets are filled with the pungent aroma of durians (a thorny Southeast Asian fruit).

SOUTH BRIDGE ROAD

Chinatown has its fair share of Chinese temples, but it also has some of the most well-known places of worship of other faiths, such as the **Sri Mariamman Temple** ① and **Jamae Mosque** along South Bridge Road.
SEE ALSO CHURCHES, MOSQUES AND TEMPLES, P.41, 43

CHINATOWN STREETS

The heart of Chinatown embraces **Pagoda, Temple, Trengganu, Smith** and **Sago streets**. In the evenings, vendors of the **Chinatown Night Market** set up stalls along these streets, selling tourist souvenirs and Chinese trinkets. After browsing at the

night market, have supper at the hawker stalls which line the open-air **Chinatown Food Street** on Smith Street.

The former Chinese opera house of **Lai Chun Yuen** stands at the corner of Trengganu and Smith streets. The hardships of early residents are showcased in the excellent **Chinatown Heritage Centre** ②, which occupies three shophouses on Pagoda Street.

The ostentatious **Buddha Tooth Relic Temple and Museum** ③, which claims to hold a sacred Buddha's tooth, stands between Sago Street and Sago Lane.

The pedestrian bridge extending from Pagoda Street across New Bridge Road and

Below: Chinatown's shops are fascinating to browse.

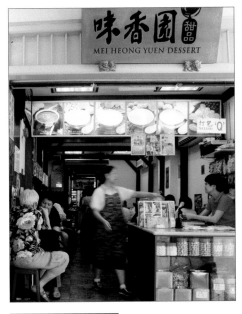

MEI HEONG YUEN DESSERT

Left: Chinatown is full of places to stop for a bite.

CBD is another conservation zone. **Ann Siang Road and Club Street** used to hum with the activities of Chinese clan associations but are now taken over by posh restaurants and boutiques.

The area boasts the **Singapore City Gallery**, which charts the city's urban development, and the **Fuk Tak Chi Museum**, which displays articles donated by early Chinatown residents.

Telok Ayer Street is a street for the faithful, lined by the **Thian Hock Keng Temple** ④, **Al Abrar Mosque** and **Telok Ayer Chinese Methodist Church**. At the street's southern end, the **red dot design museum** in the red dot Traffic building stages industrial-design exhibitions.
SEE ALSO CHURCHES, MOSQUES AND TEMPLES, P.40, 45; MUSEUMS AND GALLERIES, P.84, 86, 88

Sago Street is lined with age-old shops. **Fong Moon Kee** (No.16) sells traditional healing oils. **Leung Sang Hong** (No.18) has delicious Chinese pastries.

Eu Tong Sen Street leads to **Yue Hwa**, a one-stop emporium for all things Chinese.
SEE ARCHITECTURE, P.29; CHURCHES, MOSQUES AND TEMPLES, P.40; MUSEUMS AND GALLERIES, P.83; SHOPPING, P.115, 116

Tanjong Pagar

To best appreciate the architectural flourishes of Chinatown's Chinese Baroque-style shophouses, walk around the **Tanjong Pagar Conservation District**, along Tanjong Pagar, Duxton, Craig and Neil roads. The European-style **Jinriksha Station** at the corner of Tanjong Pagar and Neil roads, where rickshaw pullers used

to congregate, offers a contrast in architectural style.

Nearby in the former red-light district of **Keong Saik Road**, splendid shophouses have been converted into hip boutique hotels and bars.

The **Baba House** is further along on Neil Road. It boasts most of its original mouldings and intricate tile work. Rece-ntly restored and redecorated, it offers a fascinating glimpse into old Peranakan life.
SEE ALSO ARCHITECTURE, P.28, 30; MUSEUMS AND GALLERIES, P.83

Ann Siang Road and Club Street

Between Chinatown and the

Central Business District

Singapore's financial boom-town centres on **Raffles Place** ⑤, an open-air plaza surrounded by skyscrapers, including OUB Centre, **UOB Plaza** and **Republic Plaza**.

In the shadow of the I.M. Pei-designed **OCBC Centre** is the incense-filled **Wak Hai Cheng Temple**, built by Chinese Teochew immigrants to give thanks to the gods for their safe passage between China and Singapore.
SEE ALSO ARCHITECTURE, P.29, 30, 31

Right: roof detail at the Thian Hock Keng Temple.

Orchard Road and Surroundings

O rchard Road is to Singapore what Fifth Avenue is to New York – one seemingly interminable line of smart boutiques, shopping malls and hotels stretching from one end of a very long road to the other. But there is more to this former plantation area than just retail glamour and enchantment. The fashion strip also has a few leafy parks, a presidential palace, sidewalk cafés and a charming enclave filled with some of Singapore's finest examples of Chinese Baroque-style shop- and terrace houses.

Dhoby Ghaut

The Dhoby Ghaut MRT station marks the top end of Orchard Road, around where shopping centres like **Plaza Singapura** and **Park Mall** stand. Park Mall, on Penang Road and named after Fort Canning Park behind it, is a favourite hunting ground for furniture shoppers.

A detour from Penang Road up Clemenceau Avenue leads to Tank Road, where three institutions stand in testimony of Singapore's polyglot character: the Roman Catholic **Church of the Sacred Heart**, the Chinese-style **Teochew Building** and the Hindu **Sri Thandayuthapani Temple** ①.

At the corner of Clemenceau Avenue and Penang Road is the former **House of Tan Yeok Nee**, one

of the only two southern Chinese-style courtyard houses left in Singapore, now home to a business school.

Just beyond Plaza Singapura on Orchard Road is the **Istana**, the official residence of Singapore's president, set amid manicured lawns. **Istana Park** opposite is a pleasant patch of landscaped greenery with a café.

SEE ALSO ARCHITECTURE, P.28; CHURCHES, MOSQUES AND TEMPLES, P.44; MONUMENTS, P.80

The Main Stretch

Orchard Road gets its name from the nutmeg and pepper orchards that once blanketed the area in the 1840s. The only glimpses of this rural past are the roads named after plantation owners, such as Scotts, Cairnhill and Cuppage.

Cuppage Terrace, a strip of restored shophouses housing pubs and eateries, sits behind **Centrepoint**, a mall well loved by Singaporeans. Its anchor tenant is **Robinsons**, a large department store that offers some of the best service in the city. Next door is **Peranakan Place**, a complex of ornate shophouses. At its shaded terrace café, relax with an ice-cold drink, before exploring the lovely Chinese Baroque-style terrace houses further up the slope on **Emerald Hill** ②.

Across the road are two spanking new malls. **313@ Somerset** is popular with young women, while beside it is the **Orchard Central**, which suffers from an odd layout where escalators bypass several floors. Its

Left: taking a break from shopping on Orchard Road.

Many alfresco cafés along Orchard Road are located on the street level, fantastic spots from which to people-watch.

Scotts Road

Scotts Road, extending from the main stretch, is home to upscale hotels and eclectic malls. On one side is **Shaw House**, with plenty of eateries and cineplexes, the youngster hangout **Pacific Plaza**, and the striking red duty-free store **DFS Galleria**. On the other side of the street is **Far East Plaza**, popular with teens looking for affordable street-wear. Perched at the top of a gentle rise is the castle-like **Goodwood Park Hotel** ④.
SEE ALSO HOTELS, P.73; MONU-MENTS, P.80; SHOPPING, P.114, 115

rooftop, however, offers several dining options with fabulous views of Orchard Road.

Cross Cairnhill Road to **The Heeren Shops**. It enjoys a younger clientele, as does **Orchard Cineleisure**, a complex of cineplexes and games arcades at the corner of Orchard and Grange roads. The malls that follow cater to a decidedly more upmarket crowd. Beside Orchard Cineleisure is the recently

revamped **Mandarin Gallery**, full of posh boutiques, eateries and designer labels. **The Paragon** is another haven of designer goods, while the massive **Ngee Ann City** offers an impressive mix of high street labels and designer shops, as well as an impressive food hall in its basement. **Wisma Atria** is also a popular fashion destination. The darling of Singapore shopping, however, is the new, outré and sprawling **ION Orchard** ③ on the corner of Orchard and Paterson roads.

Across Mount Elizabeth Road from The Paragon is the comparitively dowdy **Lucky Plaza**, nevertheless a favourite with tourists for its electronics goods. Adjacent to it is the home-grown retail darling of **TANGS** department store.
SEE ALSO ARCHITECTURE, P.27; SHOPPING, P.114, 115, 116

Left: Chinese Baroque-style houses on Emerald Hill.

Lower End of Orchard

Back on Orchard Road, **Wheelock Place**, a complex designed by architect Kisho Kurokawa, houses the American bookstore **Borders**. More elegant designer boutiques are found in the **Hilton Hotel Shopping Gallery**, **Palais Renaissance** and **Forum The Shopping Mall**.
SEE ALSO LITERATURE, P.77

Tanglin Road

Tanglin Road, often regarded as an extension of Orchard Road, offers a change of pace from frenetic shopping action. You can wind down in the lush **Singapore Botanic Gardens** ⑤ or relax in **Tanglin Village** ⑥ further west. Also known as the Dempsey Road area, Tanglin Village is now flourishing with stylish cafés and restaurants. Antiques and home décor shops here specialise in Asian furnishings.
SEE ALSO PARKS AND GARDENS, P.101

15

Little India and Kampong Glam

Perhaps the most colour- and scent-saturated areas in Singapore, Little India and Kampong Glam still bustle with traditional businesses and religious centres. Beginning first as a camp for Indian convict workers, Little India's abundant grass and water later made it an ideal cattle-breeding ground. Kampong Glam had a more idyllic beginning as the location of the palace of Sultan Hussein, the Malay ruler who ceded the island to the British. A walk through these areas is a trek through Singapore's past.

Little India comes alive in October or November for the annual Deepavali light-up. Twinkling fairy lights and colourful decorations adorn the streets, and the Deepavali bazaar, selling snacks, religious paraphernalia and home décor items, is always worth a browse.

On Syed Alwi Road is the sprawling **Mustafa Centre** ③, a 24-hour shopping complex that is hugely popular with bargain hunters.

SEE ALSO CHURCHES, MOSQUES AND TEMPLES, P.40, 42, 43, 44; FOOD AND DRINK, P.65; SHOPPING, P.114

Kampong Glam

To the east of Little India is **Kampong Glam**, which means 'village of the *gelam* tree' in Malay. Malays used to use the bark of the *gelam* tree to caulk boats, although it would be difficult to find this tree here today.

The first Arab settlers, along with the Bugis, Javanese, Boyanese and people from the Riau Islands, turned Kampong Glam into a commercial hub. Today the area still draws those in search of bargains, but beyond that, Kampong Glam is also a lovely enclave that offers plenty to see on a

Little India

Serangoon Road is the main thoroughfare that runs through Little India. Its side-streets, such as Campbell Lane, Dunlop Street and Buffalo Road, are lined with brightly-lit shops spilling over with spices, fabrics, floral garlands and glittering jewellery. A landmark at the junction of Serangoon and Bukit Timah roads is **Tekka Centre** ①, a bustling fresh-produce market worth a look.

Although Little India is the hub of the Hindu community,

religious centres of various faiths call the area home. Also marvellous examples of various architectural styles, these places of worship include the **Abdul Gaffoor Mosque** on Dunlop Street, and **Sri Veeramakaliamman Temple** ② and **Sri Srinivasa Perumal Temple** along Serangoon Road. The stunning **Sakya Muni Buddha Gaya Temple** and the ornately decorated **Leong San See Temple** also attract the Chinese faithful to the area.

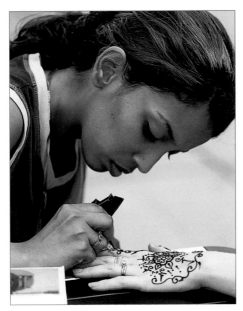

Left: a henna tattooist in Little India.

now converted into the **Malay Heritage Centre**. The **Malabar Muslim Jama-Ath Mosque**, at the corner of Jalan Sultan and Victoria Street, and the **Hajjah Fatimah Mosque**, off Beach Road, are two of the prettiest mosques in the city.

SEE ALSO CHURCHES, MOSQUES AND TEMPLES, P.41, 43, 44; MUSEUMS AND GALLERIES, P.85; WALKS AND VIEWS, P.128

Bugis

Above the Bugis MRT station is another shopping hub with the overcrowded **Bugis Street Market** and the **Bugis Junction** mall, featuring a glass-covered retail 'street' with boutiques and cafés.

Nearby **Waterloo Street** is a hive of activity with Buddhist worshippers, medicine sellers and fortune tellers crowding the entrance to the **Kwan Im Tong Hood Cho Temple** ⑥. Hindu devotees congregate at **Sri Krishnan Temple** on its right.

At the junction of Waterloo Street and Middle Road is the **Sculpture Square**, dedicated to three-dimensional art.

SEE ALSO CHURCHES, MOSQUES AND TEMPLES, P.42; MUSEUMS AND GALLERIES, P.87; SHOPPING, P.115

leisurely stroll. Lately it has even earned a reputation as Singapore's coolest neighbourhood, where boutiques and antiques shops sit side by side with Middle Eastern restaurants and cosy bistros, all set in restored two-storey shophouses. Many of these houses were built in the Early Shophouse style in the 1840s, resembling unadorned dollhouses with their squat upper levels and simple lines.

Batiks, linens and baskets of every shape, size and colour are sold on **Arab Street** ④. **Bussorah Street** holds a treasure trove of shops selling Asian and Muslim-inspired crafts. At the end of the street is the golden-domed **Sultan Mosque** ⑤.

Dotting the Kampong Glam area are several other cultural sights. At the centre is **Istana Kampong Gelam**, the former royal palace built in the 1840s,

Below: religious posters in Little India *(left)*; shopping in Kampong Glam *(right)*.

Sentosa and the Southern Islands

Get away from the urban sprawl and head offshore for a spot of island hopping. The most popular of Singapore's offshore islands is Sentosa, the site of the country's other new major 'integrated resort'. Younger adults love it for its beautiful beaches and laid-back bars, while families visit for its child-centric attractions. Several other islands lie within easy access of the mainland, ranging from tiny specks like Sisters' Islands to larger gems like St John's Island.

Admission fees to Sentosa (depending of mode of transport) apply and include access to all park areas and beaches, unlimited rides on the light rail, buses and beach trams on Sentosa.

across the 710-m (2,329-ft) causeway that links Sentosa to Singapore island.

However, for a more exciting start to your trip, hop on the recently upgraded cable car ride that floats 60m above the harbour into the island. Cable cars depart from HarbourFront Tower 2 and The Jewel Box on Mount Faber. The lofty ride offers a bird's-eye view of the city and the port.

Sentosa

Sentosa, located to the south of the main Singapore island, was once known as Pulau Blakang Mati ('island at the back of death' in Malay), in reference to the frequent fatal disease outbreaks on the island. It was also a refuge for pirates in the 19th century before the British used it as a military fortress. When the British pulled out their troops in 1968, the island was turned into a leisure playground and renamed Sentosa ('isle of peace and tranquillity').

Recent redevelopment has seen Sentosa re-emerge as the latest lifestyle enclave away from the city. Sentosa Cove, an upmarket residential project, now boasts swish multi-million-dollar homes by the water. **Resorts World Sentosa**, the first integrated resort to open in Singapore, is headlined by the Universal Studios theme park and a glitzy casino.

GETTING THERE
From the HarbourFront Cen-tre, take a taxi or bus, or walk

Below: a Sentosa Express train passes the Sentosa Merlion.

Left: Sentosa's *Songs of the Sea* multimedia display.

water World ③, a small but excellent oceanarium with a submerged acrylic tunnel.
SEE ALSO CHILDREN, P.38

BEACHES

The best beaches are on Sentosa. Sun worshippers gravitate to the soft, clean sands of **Palawan Beach** and **Siloso Beach** ④, both of which have cool bars and watersport equipment for hire. Siloso Beach is also the site of *Songs of the Sea* ⑤, a multimedia spectacle combining shooting jets of water, fire and laser lights, which is a fine end to an excursion on Sentosa. **Tanjong Beach** is a more peaceful spot.
SEE ALSO BEACHES AND ISLANDS, P.34; CHILDREN, P.38

Southern Islands

Beyond Sentosa is an archipelago of tiny islands. These include **Kusu Island**, a place of both rest and worship, **St John's Island**, a holiday haven with an easygoing air, and **Sisters' Islands** and **Pulau Hantu**, both popular for diving.
SEE ALSO BEACHES AND ISLANDS, P.35

Below: some of the realistic waxworks at Fort Siloso.

The quickest way into the island is to take the light rail **Sentosa Express** from VivoCity shopping mall on the main island. Once on the island, you can walk or take the shuttle bus or tram services to the various attractions.

IMBIAH LOOKOUT

A whole day should be set aside for Sentosa. There are plenty of attractions, and choosing the right ones can make all the difference.

Many of Sentosa's attractions are grouped in a cluster named the **Imbiah Lookout**, near the Imbiah Station. A number of sights here provide wonderful vistas of Singapore's skyline and the nearby islands. These include the 131-m (430-ft) -high **Tiger Sky Tower** and the 37-m (121-ft) -high **Sentosa Merlion** statue. From the summit of **Mount Imbiah**, a former gun battery, enjoy views of the nearby Indonesian islands.

The Imbiah Lookout's best attraction is **Images of Singapore** ①, a waxwork museum. Sentosa's other major historical display is **Fort Siloso** ②, located on the western tip, which was originally built in the 1880s for Singapore's defence.
SEE ALSO MUSEUMS AND GALLERIES, P.84

SENTOSA FOR CHILDREN

Sentosa has plenty of sights to keep children entertained. The **Butterfly Park** and **Insect Kingdom**, with some 1,500 fluttering butterflies and over 3,000 mounted bugs, also includes some of the world's rarest creepy crawlies.

Near the Butterfly Park is the **Sentosa Luge & Skyride**, where you ascend on a gondola and slide downhill in a luge. The **Sentosa 4D Magix** theatre thrills with four-dimensional visual entertainment. Another attraction the little ones will love is the **Under-**

19

Southern and Western Singapore

Southern Singapore is the gateway to the leisure resort of Sentosa and also harbours the world's busiest port, the Port of Singapore. It has also gained cachet of late as a bona fide entertainment destination with the opening of several nightlife venues and the city's largest shopping mall, VivoCity. Western Singapore, although designated as the country's industrial zone with factories and petroleum refineries, is also the location of a major recreation zone with sprawling green spaces and theme parks.

constructed the serpentine road up to the summit. The **Jewel Box** on the hilltop is a dining and drinking venue with the best views, especially at night. From here, you can also board a cable car to Sentosa.

SEE ALSO NIGHTLIFE, P.94; WALKS AND VIEWS, P.131

HarbourFront Precinct

At the base of Mount Faber is the **HarbourFront Centre**, where cable cars en route from Mount Faber pick up passengers to Sentosa. The nearby **Singapore Cruise Centre** receives passenger ships. Next to the HarbourFront Centre is Singapore's largest mall **VivoCity** ②, a shopping experience that spans over 102,000sq m (1,097,918 sq ft) with covetable retail and dining options. The **Sentosa Express** light rail to Sentosa stops at the third level. An

Mount Faber

Begin exploring the west coast from the south at **Mount Faber** ①, off Kampong Bahru Road. This bluff is covered by one of the oldest rainforests in Singapore, with various vantage points looking out to the harbour. The name Mount Faber is in fact a misnomer, as the hill is only 110m (361ft) high. Formerly called Telok Blangah Hill, it was renamed in 1845 after Captain C.E. Faber of the Madras Engineers, who

Below: the twinkling Jewel Box, which offers fantastic views.

For a taste of the high life, dine 70m above sea level in a cable car. 'Sky Dining' is available nightly, during which guests are served a three-course Western dinner accompanied by views of the twinkling skyline. For bookings, call 6337 9688 or check www.mountfaber.com.sg.

Left: kitschy Haw Par Villa is a unique theme park.

Biodiversity Research here displays specimens of rare plants and animals.
SEE ALSO MUSEUMS AND GALLERIES, P.86

Holland Village

Holland Village, close to Buona Vista MRT station, is a villagey enclave with two-storey shophouses, well loved by expatriates and locals for its good cafés, watering holes, fashion boutiques and art galleries. **Chip Bee Gardens** here is the locale of several of Singapore's top restaurants.

Jurong

Further west, in the industrial zone of Jurong, lie a few gardens that are good for a tranquil stroll, and some theme attractions. The **Singapore Science Centre** and adjacent **Omni Theatre** on Science Centre Road provide educational entertainment that is welcomed by families. Close by on Yuan Ching Road are the **Chinese and Japanese gardens** with serene Asian-style landscaped gardens.

Just off the Ayer Rajah Expressway is the **Jurong BirdPark** ⑥, where many of its 9,000 birds fly free.
SEE ALSO CHILDREN, P.37, 39; PARKS AND GARDENS, P.100

overhead bridge joins the mall to the red-brick **St James Power Station,** a massive nine-venue nightclub housed in a former coal-fired power station.
SEE ALSO NIGHTLIFE, P.95; SHOPPING, P.116, TRANSPORT, P.123

Pasir Panjang Road

At the western end of the harbour, off Pasir Panjang Road, is **Labrador Park** ③, a World War II site offering tours of its hidden war tunnels.

Also in the vicinity is another World War II site, **Reflections at Bukit Chandu.** It pays tribute to the Malay Regiment who fought Japanese troops at the Battle of Pasir Panjang in 1942.

Haw Par Villa ④, on Pasir Panjang Road, is a collection of macabre statues illustrating stories and the various stages of Hell in Chinese mythology. The **Hua Song** **Museum,** which chronicles the history of the Chinese diaspora, is also here.
SEE ALSO CHILDREN, P.36; MUSEUMS AND GALLERIES, P.84, 85, 87

NUS Museums

Along Kent Ridge Crescent is the National University of Singapore (NUS), which houses the first-rate **NUS Museums** ⑤, with three galleries offering insights into Chinese, Asian and local art. The **Raffles Museum of**

Right: at the NUS Museum.

21

The East Coast

The East Coast offers a melange of different lifestyles. Friendly Geylang Serai is the heart of Malay history and culture, while in Katong, there are glimpses into the Peranakan and Eurasian ways of life. The East Coast Park lures watersport enthusiasts, romancing couples and family picnickers from all over the island with its sun, sand and sea, and day trippers set off to rural Ubin island on an idyllic boat ride from the Changi Coast. Perhaps due to its restful and breezy atmosphere, the east also has a host of alfresco cafés and restaurants in its various neighbourhoods, from Siglap and Joo Chiat to Changi Village and the East Coast Park.

Above: many visit Singapore's East Coast for its excellent dining options.

Geylang

Geylang is Singapore's red-light district, but is worth a visit for its more salubrious facets. Food-mad Singaporeans swarm to this gourmet heaven with a high density of well-known eateries.

Its ethnic flavour is the strongest in **Geylang Serai** ①, roughly the section of Geylang Road between Jalan Eunos and Aljunied Road. The area was named after the *serai* (lemon grass) fields that once covered it. By the early 20th century, flamboyantly decorated shop- and terrace houses, similar to those found in Chinatown and Kampong Glam, had taken over. Many of these, conserved and refurbished, are found in the lanes between Geylang Road and Sims Avenue.

The best time to visit Geylang Serai is the Ramadan fasting month that leads up to Hari Raya Puasa every year. The streets are ablaze with blinking lights, and a boisterous open-air, night-time bazaar offers Malay snacks, colourful apparel, home furnishings and fascinating fodder for photographers.

At other times, a more subdued cultural experience awaits in the Malay shops and restaurants, and at the **Malay Village**, opposite the Paya Lebar MRT station.
SEE ALSO MUSEUMS AND GALLERIES, P.85

Katong

Opposite the Malay Village is the **Joo Chiat** area, which like **Katong** ② further south, is a stronghold of the Eurasian and Peranakan communities. Katong, which used to be by the coast, gets its name from a now-extinct species of sea turtle. Many wealthy English,

> Katong's favourite stalwart is **Chin Mee Chin Confectionery** (204 East Coast Road; tel: 6345 0419), where two generations of Katongites have snacked on their toasted buns with *kaya* (coconut and egg jam) and old-fashioned cakes. The staff and menu of the confectionery have not changed since it opened in the 1960s.

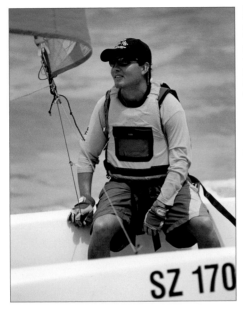

SEE ALSO BEACHES AND ISLANDS, P.32; FOOD AND DRINK, P. 64; RESTAURANTS, P.113

Left: sailing is a popular sport at the East Coast.

Seafood Centre to hawker fare at the **East Coast Lagoon Food Village**. A few kilometres west is **Marine Cove**, a restaurant hub.

Changi

Before the Changi Airport opened in the early 1980s, laid-back **Changi Village** ④ was the only reason to venture to the far-eastern coast. The shops in this slice of old Singapore, such as George Photo and the Salvation Army Thrift Shop, are tinged with nostalgia.

The **Changi Village Food Centre**, serving local fare, is often a refuelling stop for day trippers to **Pulau Ubin** ⑤, who take boats from the nearby Changi Point Ferry Terminal.

A footbridge leads to **Changi Beach Park**, a small, quiet beach popular with picnickers and anglers. The stretch of sea is dotted with dinghies and keelboats from the nearby sailing clubs.

Near the Changi Airport on Upper Changi Road North is the historic **Changi Chapel and Museum** ⑥, dedicated to the memories of World War II POWs.

SEE ALSO BEACHES AND ISLANDS, P.32, 33; FOOD AND DRINK, P.64; MUSEUMS AND GALLERIES, P.83

Pasir Ris

Pasir Ris Park, on the north-eastern coast, offers another pleasant stretch of beach. The **Escape Theme Park** is ideal for families and energetic children, while the adjacent **Wild Wild Wet** water theme park promises more thrills.

SEE ALSO BEACHES AND ISLANDS, P.33; CHILDREN, P.36

Portuguese and Chinese settlers were once owners of plantations beside the sea.

The Peranakan and Eurasian influence is discernible today in the antiques shops and restaurants. But perhaps the finest clues to the area's Peranakan heritage are the florid Chinese Baroque-style terrace houses along **Joo Chiat Road** and **Koon Seng Road**.

SEE ALSO ARCHITECTURE, P.28; WALKS AND VIEWS, P.129

Siglap and East Coast Park

Continuing east along Upper East Coast Road brings you to **Siglap**, a residential enclave peppered with alfresco cafés and wine bars.

South of Siglap, the **East Coast Park** ③ stretches more than 10km (6 miles), where people jog, rollerblade and indulge in watersport.

Dining options are plentiful here, from Singapore-style seafood at the **East Coast**

Below: boats from the Changi Point jetty depart for Ubin island.

Central and Northern Singapore

Central and Northern Singapore are a paradox. The two areas have some of the country's most heavily populated housing districts, yet at the same time hold most of its pockets of nature, including three of the four gazetted reserves and two open-concept zoos set in lush greenery. In fact, these parts of the island offer such large tracts of tropical forest and mangrove swamp that getting close to nature here is as much a part of the Singaporean lifestyle as eating and shopping.

The four gazetted nature reserves in Singapore are the **Central Catchment Nature Reserve**, **Bukit Timah Nature Reserve**, **Sungei Buloh Wetland Reserve** and **Labrador Nature Reserve**. Together they comprise more than 3,340 hectares (8,235 acres) of untouched greenery – which is by no means a small number in land-scarce Singapore.

Temples and Memorials

With Central Singapore home to a large proportion of the population, it is no surprise it is also the locale of a few of the country's most important Chinese temples. **Lian Shan Shuang Lin Monastery** ①, better known as Siong Lim Temple to locals, is located in Toa Payoh, one of Singapore's oldest housing estates, about 5km (3 miles) north of Orchard Road. A number of its buildings are noted for carvings and sculptures crafted by artisans from China.

A few kilometres north of Shuang Lin Monastery is the **Kong Meng San Phor Kark See Temple**, located on Bright Hill Drive. Built in 1980, it is the largest Buddhist temple in Singapore.

The national monument of **Sun Yat Sen Nanyang Memorial Hall** ② lies further south. This two-storey Victorian-style bungalow, built in 1900, was gifted to Dr Sun, the leader of China's nationalist movement. The museum chronicles his revolutionary activities. SEE ALSO CHURCHES, MOSQUES AND TEMPLES, P.42; MUSEUMS AND GALLERIES, P.88

Central Catchment Nature Reserve

West of the Kong Meng San Phor Kark See Temple is a lush expanse known as **MacRitchie Reservoir Park**, which forms the **Central Catchment Nature Reserve** ③, one of the four gazetted nature reserves in Singapore, together with the Pierce Reservoir Park and the Upper Seletar Reservoir Park further north.

A highlight worth exploring in the reserve is the **Treetop Walk**, an excursion on a suspension bridge that allows memorable views of the rainforest canopy. SEE ALSO WALKS AND VIEWS, P.130

Bukit Timah Nature Reserve

To the west of MacRitchie is the **Bukit Timah Nature Reserve** ④, located in the geographic centre of Singapore, 12km (7.5 miles) from the city. Most of Singapore's

Left: the Kranji War Memorial is dedicated to the fallen of World War II.

SEE ALSO CHILDREN, P.37, 39; PARKS AND GARDENS, P101

Kranji

The peaceful, solemn **Kranji Commonwealth War Cemetery**, further west on Woodlands Road, is the final resting place of two presidents and Allied soldiers who were killed in World War II. In its middle is the War Memorial, engraved with names of over 24,000 men who died in the Asia Pacific battles.

The **Sungei Buloh Wetland Reserve** ⑦, on the extreme northwestern tip, is a favourite with birders and trekkers. Mangroves thrive here, as do freshwater flora like water lilies and lotuses. The abundant birdlife, such as plovers, egrets and sandpipers, can be observed along its boardwalk and trails.

Over the last few years, Kranji has been developed as a rustic getaway from Singapore's urban sprawl. Called **Kranji Countryside**, a slice of this rural area now boasts various organic, goat, egg and frog farms and an aquarium that are worth a day trip.
SEE ALSO PARKS AND GARDENS, P.100; WALKS AND VIEWS, P.131

forest was heavily logged until the mid-19th century. In 1883, in response to research by the Straits Settlement government on climatic changes arising from deforestation, the Bukit Timah Nature Reserve was established.

With its moist, dark greenery overlaid by the buzzing of cicadas, this isolated patch of land seems almost surreal in this concrete jungle of a city.
SEE ALSO WALKS AND VIEWS, P.128

Mandai

About 15km (9 miles) northeast of the Bukit Timah reserve is the much-lauded **Singapore Zoo** ⑤ on Mandai Lake Road. The world's first night wildlife park, the **Night Safari** ⑥, is next door with nocturnal animals in recreated habitats.

West of the zoo is the **Mandai Orchid Garden** on a hillside, covered with orchids in all shapes and shades.

Below: admiring nature from the Treetop Walk at the Central Catchment Nature Reserve *(left)* and the boardwalk at the Sungei Buloh Wetland Reserve *(right)*.

25

Architecture

Singapore has seen numerous buildings come and go. A common lament is the lack of sentimentality shown towards old buildings, which get razed in favour of modernisation. In all fairness, in such a land-scarce city, redevelopment is par for the course. But look closer and you'll find a good number of old buildings that have stood their ground over generations. To date, the Preservation of Monuments Board has listed 55 buildings as national monuments. Singapore's architecture is much like its population – a melting pot of ethnicities, styles and sensibilities that invariably find their own harmony.

Central Fire Station

62 Hill Street; tel: 6332 2996; www.scdf.gov.sg; gallery Tue–Sun 10am–5pm; free; MRT: City Hall or Clarke Quay; map p.136 A1

The oldest fire station in Singapore is housed in this distinctive red-and-white 'blood and bandage' building completed in 1901. Its architecture is Edwardian England, a departure from the usual Palladian and classical styles prevailing in Singapore at the time. The 'blood' is the exposed brick, while the 'bandage' refers to the brick covered in white-washed plaster. The building also holds the **Civil Defence Heritage Gallery**.
SEE ALSO MUSEUMS AND GALLERIES, P.84

City Hall

St Andrew's Road; MRT: City Hall; map p.136 A1

Completed in 1929, this was once Singapore's most important government building, featuring Grecian architecture, dignified columns and a grand staircase. It has seen numerous ceremonies in history, including the World War II surrender of the Japanese on its steps in 1945, the declaration of Singapore's city status by King George VI and governor Sir Franklin Gimson in 1951, and the proclamation of self-government by Lee Kuan Yew in 1959. Lee later declared the nation's independence on the very same steps in 1963.

Together with the old Supreme Court (*see p.30*), the City Hall will be home to the National Art Gallery from 2013.

Clarke Quay

River Valley Road; MRT: Clarke Quay; map p.135 E1

Clarke Quay was named after the second governor of the Straits Settlement, Lieutenant-General Sir Andrew Clarke. Until the 1970s, it hummed with activity as bumboats carried cargo from ships to the warehouses on its banks. Today it has a hum of a different kind, with trendy bars, clubs and restaurants nestled in the restored warehouses lining its lanes. But look a little closer and discover some of its history. For instance, at its

Left: restored warehouses at Clarke Quay.

Left: colourful and ornate terrace houses.

1903, is particularly outstanding – it features a grand Chinese entrance that was carefully restored by craftsmen from China.

Esplanade – Theatres on the Bay

1 Esplanade Drive; tel: 6828 8222; www.esplanade.com; free; MRT: City Hall; map p.136 B1

The design of this landmark – which people either love or hate – with its distinctive facade of sharp-edged metal sunshades, has been mired in controversy since the model was first unveiled in 1992. Michael Wilford, the British architect who designed the edifice, quit the project in 1995 over unexplained differences, leaving home-grown company DP Architects to complete the job. The result is a glazed building that is protected from the tropical sun and heat by triangular aluminium sun shields. The shields are set to open or close at varying angles, depending on the angle of

southern end, on the wall of the last shophouse is a sign proclaiming that it was once Whampoa's Ice House. A wealthy Chinese landowner, Whampoa gifted the land where the Singapore Botanic Gardens sits today to the British, who gave him the land at Clarke Quay in return.

Emerald Hill and Peranakan Place

Orchard Road, between Midpoint Orchard and Centrepoint; MRT: Somerset; map p.135 D3–4

This area was once settled by the Peranakan people, or Straits-born Chinese, whose unique culture evolved through intermarriage between Chinese immigrants and local Malay women in the 17th century. Peranakan Place is a complex of ornate Peranakan-style shophouses that have been transformed into a commercial hub. Its shady terrace café is popular with tourists for its drinks and a great place to watch Orchard Road go by.

Up the slope on Emerald Hill is a collection of lovely old restored terrace houses

> Once dilapidated and shunned, many shop- and terrace-houses are much sought-after properties today because of their unique facades and historical value. Strict guidelines govern the restoration of these houses, many of which have been turned into chic restaurants, bars and boutique hotels, as well as offices for advertising and publishing firms.

that once belonged to wealthy Peranakan families. The 30 or so homes along the slightly curved road were built between 1901 and 1925 in the Chinese Baroque style, typified by ornamental mouldings, shuttered wooden windows, pastel colours and colourful ceramic tiles. These houses were also the first to be given conservation status in 1981, which means the owners cannot alter their facades. Look out for the four terrace houses numbered 39 to 45, with forecourts and gates and topped with ornate Chinese roofs. No.45, designed by M.T. Moh in

Below: the spiky facade of the Esplanade Theatres.

the sun's rays. And so arose the building's myriad nicknames, everything from 'fish scales' and 'bug eyes' to what most people seem to have settled on, the 'Durian'.
SEE ALSO DANCE, P.47; MUSIC, P.90; THEATRE, P.121

The Fullerton Hotel

1 Fullerton Square; tel: 6733 8388; www.fullertonhotel.com; MRT: Raffles Place; map p.139 D4

This grand building was built in 1924. Named after Sir Robert Fullerton, the first governor of the Straits Settlements, it was Singapore's largest and is now a wonderful example of the Edwardian Baroque neoclassical style that once dominated the Civic District. Before it was artfully renovated for an astounding S$400 million and reopened as a hotel in 2001, it was the heart of social, official and commercial life, having housed the Singapore Club, the Chamber of Commerce and the General Post Office. The hotel, whose central atrium was created by punching out several floors and the old ceiling, is deceptively contemporary within its stately walls.
SEE ALSO HOTELS, P.70

House of Tan Yeok Nee/Chicago Graduate School of Business

101 Penang Road; MRT: Dhoby Ghaut; map p.135 E3

Today unceremoniously called the Chicago Graduate School of Business, this building has a fascinating history. The eponymous Teochew cloth peddler turned wealthy gambier and pepper merchant built this elegant house in 1885. Over the years, the mansion has variously served as the residence of a station master

Above: the Fullerton's stately walls belie its contemporary interior.

and a bishop, a boarding school for girls, accommodation for Japanese army officers in World War II and the Salvation Army headquarters. It is a rare example of a southern Chinese-style courtyard house, with a grand entrance and sloping roofs with spiral ornamentation. The national monument, after undergoing extensive restoration work, was taken over by the school in 2000. It is not open to visitors but there's nothing against a potential student wandering in.

Jinriksha Station

Corner of Tanjong Pagar and Neil roads; MRT: Chinatown or Tanjong Pagar; map p.138 B2

In land-scarce Singapore, providing housing for the masses means building upwards. More than 80 percent of Singaporeans own and live in high-rise flats built by the Housing and Development Board. In many other parts of the world, public housing is associated with poverty and social unrest, but not in Singapore. In fact, its public housing programme is one of its finest achievements, with other fast-growing countries seeking to emulate its success.

An eye-catching triangular edifice built in 1903 in the classical style, Jinriksha Station is crowned by a square tower with an octagonal cupola. It served as the main station for *jinriks* (two-wheeled rickshaws pulled by men), which first arrived in Singapore in the 1880s from Shanghai. They were the main means of transport in Singapore in the early 1900s. The rickshaw coolies found it convenient to live around the station, renting bed space in tiny Chinatown cubicles.

Joo Chiat Road and Koon Seng Road

MRT: Paya Lebar; bus: 40, 43, 76 or 135

The Joo Chiat area was once home to Peranakan familes. They have since moved away, but the area still retains traces of its Peranakan heritage, such as the beautifully restored Chinese Baroque shop- and terrace houses along **Joo Chiat Road** and **Koon Seng Road**. Built in the 1930s, in what has come to be known as the Late Shophouse Style (the most florid of all shophouse styles), they feature richly decorated facades and ornate details that testify to the wealth of the original homeowners.

Lai Chun Yuen

36 Smith Street;
MRT: Chinatown; map p.138 B3

Built in 1887, this restored three-storey building, with gleaming wooden floors and carved banisters, was formerly called Lai Chun Yuen, a Cantonese opera house that packed in the fans in its heyday. Famous opera stars performed here in the 1920s. If there is a faint similarity between the facade of the theatre and that of the Raffles Hotel, it is because both were designed by R.A.J. Bidwell. It was restored in 1988 and bought over for a cool S$50 million by a Taiwanese business-man, who then donated it to the Buddhist relief organisa-tion Tzu Chi. The building was returned to the owner in 2007 and will be renovated into a boutique hotel.

MICA Building

140 Hill Street; MRT: Clarke Quay or City Hall; map p.136 A1

The MICA Building, built in 1934, is also commonly known as the Old Hill Street Police Station, which once occupied the premises. The more delicate features of this classical Renaissance-style building with horseshoe arches are now rather

overwhelmed by its startling multicoloured shutters – there are 911 altogether – but experts agree that it is one of the city's premier examples of British colonial architecture.

After undergoing extensive restoration, the building reopened in 2000 and today houses the offices of the Ministry of Information, Communication and the Arts, the National Arts Council and the National Heritage Board. The **ARTrium** courtyard on the ground level is occupied by a number of art galleries.
SEE ALSO MUSEUMS AND GALLERIES, P.89

New Supreme Court

1 Supreme Court Lane; tel: 6336 0644; MRT: City Hall or Clarke Quay; map p.136 A1

Designed by the renowned architect Lord Norman Foster, the new Supreme Court building houses Singa-pore's main law courts. The civil courts are located on lower floors and the criminal courts are above. Singa-pore's highest court, the Court of Appeal, is symboli-cally raised above the other courtrooms, occupying the dramatic aluminium steel-and-glass-clad disc on top. The architect intended the disc,

Above: the MICA Building.

on par with the dome of the old Supreme Court *(see p.30)*, as the latter's modern interpretation. With its palette of materials, including glass and stone, the building allows light to filter through it by day and emits a warm lantern-like glow by night.

There is a a a public **observation deck** (free) on the 8th floor with excellent views of the Singapore River. On the ground level is the **Supreme Court Gallery**, which traces Singapore's legal history (Mon–Fri 8.30am–6pm, Sat 8.30am–1pm; free).

OCBC Centre

65 Chulia Street; MRT: Raffles Place; map p.139 C3

This 52-storey monolith had the honour of being the first foreigner-designed sky-scraper after independence. The city's tallest building when it was completed in 1976, it is a fine example of architect I.M Pei's vision of the modern brutalist style, which is often defined by the use of concrete and repetitive angular configuration. Designed to symbolise per-manence and strength, this stoic building bears three dis-tinctive tiers separating strik-ing windows that resemble

Below: the old (left) and new (right) Supreme Courts.

Left: Republic Plaza is among the tallest buildings in Singapore.

The tower tapers upwards, a design that ensures stability against gales. And despite the forest of skyscrapers around the building, the top floors enjoy unobstructed sea views, made possible by the unconventional strategy of turning the building's axis on the upper floors 45 degrees from that of the ground floor.

Robertson Quay

MRT: Clarke Quay, then taxi; bus: 32, 54, 64, 123, 139, 143 or 195; map p.135 D1

Robertson Quay lies upriver of Clarke Quay. In the old days, European and Chinese merchants used this part of the river mostly for storing goods. Although a few warehouses still exist along Rodyk Street, Robertson Quay has been taken over by some of Singapore's most exclusive riverside apartments. A number of restored 19th-century warehouses are now occupied by bars, clubs and the **Singapore Tyler Print Institute**.

SEE ALSO MUSEUMS AND GALLERIES, P.88

button pads. Because of these windows and its slim profile, it has earned the nickname of 'the Calculator'.

Old Supreme Court

St Andrew's Road; MRT: City Hall or Clarke Quay; map p.136 A1

Completed in 1939, the old Supreme Court was the swansong of Frank Dorrington, then chief architect of the Public Works Department. The imposing edifice is most notable for its Corinthian and Ionic columns and green copper dome, as well as its pediment, which is ornamented by a tympanum sculpture crafted by the Milanese sculptor Cavalieri Rudolfo Nolli. The centre figure of the sculpture is Justice, distinguished by the scale she is holding. Flanking her are figures representing a lost soul, the law, gratitude, prosperity and abundance.

The law courts have all moved to the glass-and-steel new Supreme Court located just behind (*see p.29*). Together with the City Hall (*see p.26*) next door, the old Supreme Court is awaiting its new lease of life in 2013 as Singapore's National Art Gallery.

Republic Plaza

9 Raffles Place; MRT: Raffles Place; map p.139 D3

Architect Kisho Kurokawa's clever ways around the design constraints for the Republic Plaza won him a top architectural award, the World Best Architecture 1997 Award from FIABCI. Built at a height of 280m (918ft), the maximum allowed by Singapore's aviation regulations, the Republic Plaza is one of the three tallest skyscrapers in Singapore – the other two are OUB Centre and UOB Plaza One (*see opposite*).

Tanjong Pagar Conservation District

Tanjong Pagar, Craig, Neil and Duxton roads; MRT: Chinatown or Tanjong Pagar; map p.138 B2

Once a Malay fishing village, the land around Tanjong Pagar was turned into a nutmeg plantation in the 1830s. The area then became a thriving commercial hub, but by the 1960s, it fell into disrepair, and would have met the wrecker's ball if the authorities had not started its massive conservation drive. Tanjong Pagar soon became an archetype for

From the 1960s to the 1970s, anything that stood in the way of economic progress, including colonial-era buildings, was razed. By the 1970s Singapore had achieved prosperity, but was criticised for its lack of character and culture. In the 1980s the government began to restore older buildings, focusing on four conservation areas, namely Boat Quay, Little India, Kampong Glam and Chinatown/Tanjong Pagar. More areas have been added since, but many still feel that the preservation efforts have come too late.

Above: 'five-foot-ways' front many conservation houses.

how the remainder of historic Singapore would be restored.

The 190 shophouses were renovated for 'adaptive reuse' as restaurants, shops and offices. The first units were put up for tender in 1987 and almost overnight Tanjong Pagar became hot property for creative people, who were drawn by its traditional architectural elements.

The two- and three-storey narrow yet deep structures typically feature ornate plaster facades, wooden window shutters and stairways, high ceilings and 'five-foot-way' footpaths, which are so named because they always measure 5ft (1.5m) wide.

The area takes on a magical glow at night when the lights come on and people unwind in the pubs and restaurants.

Thong Chai Medical Institute

50 Eu Tong Sen Street; MRT: Clarke Quay; map p.138 C4
The former Thong Chai Medical Institute was built in 1892 as a free hospital.

Right: Salvador Dali's *Homage to Newton* at the UOB Plaza.

Modelled after a southern Chinese palace with two inner courtyards, it is distinctive for its ornately decorated ridges and green-tiled gabled roofs shaped like clouds. The building is now a national monument, although it also serves as the headquarters of an American company.

UOB Plaza

80 Raffles Place; MRT: Raffles Place; map p.139 D4
Completed in 1992, the twin towers of UOB Plaza are the most well-known icons of Singapore's CBD skyline, designed by Japanese architectural maestro Kenzo Tange. His concept was built on that of the original octagonal 38-storey UOB Building designed by Lim Chong Keat. Taking the sculptural concept a step further, Tange added more storeys that are turned at 45 degrees relative to one another, rendering the building's chiselled look.

The ground floor is hollowed out as an atrium, which connects the Singapore River and Raffles Place. Salvador Dali's large bronze statue *Homage to Newton* stands in the middle of the atrium, overlooking the constant stream of smartly dressed executives. The buzz, especially at lunchtime, is quite incredible.

Beaches and Islands

With its urban sprawl, it is often easy to forget that Singapore is a tropical island. There are beaches aplenty, good for walks, picnics and watersport, while the outlying islands are lovely respites from the shopping malls, office buildings, museums and shiny restaurants. You can spend the night on most of the islands, although accommodation is the bare basics on the smaller ones, while the larger ones like Sentosa boast plush retreats that are a mere bus or boat ride away from the main island.

Changi Beach Park

Along Changi Coast Road; free; bus: 2, 29, 59 or 109

A short walk from Changi Village Food Centre (see p.64) is the Changi Point Ferry Terminal, which offers a boat service to Pulau Ubin (see opposite). This ferry terminal is also the start of the **Changi Point Coastal Walk**, a 2.6-km (1.6-mile) boardwalk, heading west, which offers pleasant views of the sea, Pulau Ubin and Malaysia. A footbridge in the opposite direction leads to Changi Beach Park, a short but pleasant stretch of sand

Look out for the **Changi Beach Massacre Site** along Changi Beach, marked by a storyboard. This was where 66 male civilians were killed by a Japanese firing squad in World War II.

with views across the water to Malaysia and Pulau Tekong. Changi Beach is not as popular as the East Coast Park and therefore far less crowded.

East Coast Park

Along East Coast Park Service Road; free; MRT: Bedok, then bus: 401

The visitor's first encounter with Singapore starts with the lush east coast as one travels into town from the Changi Airport. The area could be described as Singapore's 'riviera', with coconut groves and sandy beaches on one side of the coastal highway, and expensive condos on the other.

East Coast Park stretches for more than 10km (6 miles) along the coast between the Changi Airport and Marina Bay. Fringed with casuarinas and coconut palms, the park affords superb views of ships anchored in the Straits of Singapore. The sea breeze blows gently and it's often peaceful enough for birds to flock to special tall-grass sanctuaries found along the coastline.

The park is the playground for residents living in the eastern part of the island. Tai chi practitioners can be seen exercising in the park as early as 6am, together with joggers and cyclists. Picnic tables and barbecue pits are set up under the trees, and

Below: rollerblading at the East Coast Park.

Left: locals enjoying the beach.

has maps and leaflets that detail Ubin's flora and fauna and things to do. It's best to see the island on a bicycle, which can be rented from shacks in the main village, where there are also seafood restaurants.

Ubin has vast tracts of secondary jungle and mangrove swamp that sustain a wide variety of animals, such as long-tailed macaques and monitor lizards and birds like sunbirds, kingfishers and brahminy kites.

A walk in the swamp or forest may reveal unexpected surprises, such as sightings of oriental whip snakes curled up on trees and fruit bats rustling in the evenings. There are also wild orchids and flowers to be found and, if one is lucky, carnivorous pitcher plants with trapped insects.

Below: cycling on Pulau Ubin.

happy campers pitch their colourful tents. The park is especially packed at weekends as Singaporeans escape to the beach, but on weekdays the beach and picnic areas are blissfully quiet.

Swimming is pleasant here; just don't expect crystal-clear waters and powdery white sand, although the water and beach are clean. Watersport and other recreational facilities are available along the beach. And like everywhere else in Singapore, there are plenty of food options, from burgers and pizzas to local seafood at the **East Coast Seafood Centre**.

SEE ALSO RESTAURANTS, P.113

Pasir Ris Park

Along Pasir Ris Drive 3; free;
MRT: Pasir Ris
The idyllic Pasir Ris Park is another pleasant stretch of beach, overlooking Pulau Ubin just across the water. Part of the park, near car park C (entry via Pasir Ris Green), encloses a reserve that protects a 6-hectare

(14.8-acre) mangrove swamp, where many migrating birds feed and build their nests.

A wooden boardwalk leads across the mudflats and brackish ponds, with signboards that provide details about the flora and fauna. Nature lovers will also enjoy Sungei Api Api nearby. This river is one of the few remaining natural rivers in Singapore and about 26 species of mangrove have been identified in this swamp.

If flora and fauna does not interest you, then spend a lazy afternoon relaxing on or swimming by this undulating sand stretch. A string of pubs, cafés and restaurants are also located here.

Pulau Ubin

Off Singapore's northeastern tip;
free; boat from Changi Point
Ferry Terminal
Ubin island measures just 8km (5 miles) across and 1.5km (1 mile) wide. An information kiosk run by the National Parks Board (tel: 6542 4108; daily 8.30am–5pm)

Accommodation is available at the **MCC Ubin Resort**, which offers cottage-style rooms and outdoor activities (tel: 6388 8388; www.marinacountryclub.com.sg). You can also pitch tents on **Jelutong**, **Noordin** and **Mamam beaches**.

CHEK JAWA WETLANDS

Call it nature's outdoor classroom if you will. Thanks to passionate nature lovers, the Chek Jawa wetlands, located on Pulau Ubin's southeastern coast and discovered only in 2000, has been saved from reclamation. The vast expanse of sand and mudflats is so fertile it has created an astonishingly diverse ecosystem found nowhere else in Singapore. The wetlands with several habitats – seagrass bed, rocky shore, sand bar, mudflats and mangrove forest – teems with endangered flora and fauna.

> Guided tours of Chek Jawa are conducted at low tides by the National Parks Board and must be booked in advance. Schedules are posted on www.nparks.gov.sg; for more information, call tel: 6542 4108.

Visitors can now enjoy the wildlife of Chek Jawa along a boardwalk and from a floating pontoon and viewing tower.

Sentosa's Beaches

Southern Sentosa; tel: 1800-736 8672; www.sentosa.com.sg; entrance charge to Sentosa; MRT: HarbourFront, then Sentosa Express from VivoCity or cable car from HarbourFront Centre; cable car from Mount Faber

If you disregard the views of ships in the distance, Sentosa's beaches are probably Singapore's finest stretches of sand, running some 3km (1.8 miles) along the southern shore of the resort island, interspersed with scenic saltwater lagoons and coconut groves.

Watersport enthusiasts should head for **Palawan Beach** or **Siloso Beach**, where windsurfers, canoes and pedal boats can be hired. Beach volleyball has attracted a lively crowd of bikini-clad girls and bare-chested young men, especially at weekends. Throughout the year, events like sand-sculpting competitions, jazz evenings and bazaars keep the beaches a hotbed of activity, while beach bars and clubs like the

Above: imbibing the good life on Siloso Beach.

Ibizan import **Café del Mar** and the home-grown Coastes have turned Sentosa into a nightlife destination.

The *Songs of the Sea* multimedia show comes on nightly at Siloso Beach. At Palawan Beach, you can also climb on its **suspension bridge** to get to the southernmost point of Continental Asia.

If you prefer peace and quiet, head for **Tanjong Beach** at the eastern end of the island. A beach tram plies all three beaches daily from 9am to 7pm.

SEE ALSO CHILDREN, P.38; NIGHTLIFE, P.95

Below: Sentosa has the best beaches in Singapore; Siloso Beach is perfect for a game of volleyball.

Southern Islands

South of Sentosa; tel: 1800-736 8672; www.sentosa.com.sg; ferry from Marina South pier

The archipelago of tiny islands that lie beyond Sentosa range from uninhabited coral outcrops to popular weekend retreats.

GETTING THERE

The ferry to Kusu and St John's islands departs at 10am and 2pm Mon–Sat and at 9am, 11am, 1pm, 3pm and 5pm on Sun and public holidays, from the **Marina South Pier** (tel: 6534 9339; www.islandcruise.com.sg). To get to the pier, take bus 402 from the Marina Bay MRT station. The last ferry departs St John's at 3.15pm Mon–Fri and at 6.15pm on Sun and public holidays, and leaves Kusu at 3.45pm Mon–Fri and at 5.50pm on Sun and public holidays.

Sisters' and Hantu islands are not served by regular ferries, so you will have to hire a boat at the Marina South Pier. An alternative way to see the harbour and islands is on the *Cheng Ho*, a replica Chinese junk that cruises around the southern islands with a brief stopover at Kusu (tel: 6533 9811; www.watertours.com.sg).

If you are visiting Sisters' and Hantu islands, be sure to pack a picnic as the islands do not offer food or drinks or facilities of any sort. Camping is allowed on Sisters' and Hantu islands, but a permit from Sentosa is required. Bungalows on St John's Island can be booked with Sentosa as well.

KUSU ISLAND

Kusu Island, also called Turtle Island, is a place of both relaxation and worship. Legend has it that two ship-

Above: a Chinese pavilion on Kusu Island.

wrecked sailors – one Malay, one Chinese – were saved when a giant turtle transformed itself into an island. Each man gave thanks according to his own belief, and so today the Taoist **Tua Pek Kong Temple** with its turtle pool and the Muslim *keramat* (shrine) on the hill are popular pilgrimage sites, especially during the ninth month of the lunar calendar, usually straddling October and November.
SEE FESTIVALS AND EVENTS, P.59

PULAU HANTU

Many of the southern islands are enveloped by coral reefs, including Pulau Hantu, or Ghost Island, to the northwest of Sentosa. Named so because it is said to be haunted by the spirits of two ancient warriors who fought to their deaths here, Hantu is regarded as one of Singapore's best diving spots. Contact The Hantu Blog, a non-profit environmental group that raises funds by organising monthly dive trips to Hantu (www.pulauhantu.org).

ST JOHN'S ISLAND

Also called Pulau Sakijang Bendera, this was where Raffles anchored before meeting the Temenggong,

or Malay chief, on the Singapore River in 1819. The island served as a quarantine centre for immigrants until the 1950s when it was used as a holding centre for political detainees. In 1975 St John's was turned into a holiday resort with lagoons, shady paths and picnic spots, making it a popular weekend getaway.

SISTERS' ISLANDS

Pulau Subar Darat and Pulau Subar Laut are the two small islands collectively known as Sisters' Islands. With one of Singapore's richest coral reefs, they are an ideal venue for diving. The currents can get pretty strong, so take care when swimming.

Below: terrapins are released at the tortoise sanctuary on Kusu Island for good luck.

35

Children

If nothing else, Singapore is one of the world's most family-friendly places. Movies are censored and rated, shopping malls offer road shows with popular television and cartoon characters almost all year round, and incentives like the Baby Bonus are dished out to willing parents. In the same vein, the city's attractions offer all things educational and entertaining for children of all ages. The island resort of Sentosa is an obvious choice, but there are also a number of quirky tours and amusement parks as well as exceptional zoos. Some of them are so good that adults will find them hard to resist.

Escape Theme Park

1 Pasir Ris Close; tel: 6581 9112; www.escapethemepark. com.sg; Sat–Sun and public and school holidays 10am–8pm; entrance charge; MRT: Pasir Ris, then free shuttle bus

Welcomed by parents with indefatigable children, this park has gravity-defying rides, bumper boats, go-karts, dodgem cars and a haunted house to keep kids amused.

Haw Par Villa

262 Pasir Panjang Road; tel: 6872 2003; daily 9am–7pm; free; MRT: Buona Vista, then bus: 10, 20, 188 or 200

Also known as Tiger Balm

Adjacent to the Escape Theme Park is the **Wild Wild Wet** theme park (1 Pasir Ris close; tel: 6581 9128; www.wildwild wet.com; Mon, Wed–Fri 1–7pm, Sat–Sun and public and school holidays 10am–7pm; entrance charge), with four-storey-high water slides and massive wave pools. Younger children can muck about in a shallow splash area.

Gardens, this theme park houses a collection of rather grotesque statues that illustrate Chinese mythological stories and notorious crimes from Singapore's history.

These gaudy exhibits are the only remaining collection of this genre in Asia, and for this reason, are a must-see.

Haw Par Villa ('villa of the tiger and the leopard') was built by Aw Boon Haw ('Gentle Tiger') for his brother Aw Boon Par ('Gentle Leopard') in 1937. The Aw brothers were philanthropists who made their fortune with Tiger Balm, the cure-all that is now world famous. When Boon Par died in 1945, Boon Haw turned Haw Par Villa into public property as a way of preserving Chinese culture.

The 1,000 statues and 150 tableaux may be too gory for some, but they are meant to impart lessons of morality. Don't miss the **Ten Courts of Hell,** showcasing the methods of torture meted out to wrongdoers, such as disembowelment and immersion in boiling oil.

The **Hua Song Museum** is located here.
SEE ALSO MUSEUMS AND GALLERIES, P.84

Left: thrills at the Escape Theme Park.

Left: the little ones will have a splashing good time in Singapore.

world, this 20-hectare (49-acre) park attracts well over a million visitors each year. A relaxing way to explore the park is by the **Panorail** (daily 8.30am–5.45pm; separate charge), which affords panoramic vistas.

The park is split into various themed areas. These include the **Penguin Parade**, which is a re-created Antarctic habitat for penguins and puffins; the **Flamingo Lake** with delicate pink flamingos; and the walk-in **Waterfall Aviary**, where over 100 species of Southeast Asian birds fly almost free in a simulated rainforest. The **Lory Loft** is another walk-in free-flight aviary resembling Australia's rural landscape.

Also unique is the **World of Darkness**, a nocturnal bird house with a reversed lighting system such that when it is day outside, it is night inside. Residents here include the snowy owl, tundra and buffy fish owl.

Included in the entrance charge is admission to the highly entertaining bird shows. Check the information board for schedules.

Jacob Ballas Children's Garden

Singapore Botanic Gardens, 1 Cluny Road; tel: 6471 7361; www.sbg.org.sg; daily 8am–7pm; free; MRT: Orchard, then taxi; bus: 7, 105, 123 or 174

If your kid needs to get in touch with the great outdoors, this children's park at the Botanic Garden's Bukit Timah Core might just do the trick. Children up to the age of 12 will be treated to adventures in the **A-Maze-ing maze garden**, learn about photosynthesis at the **Magic of Photosynthesis** interactive exhibit, and hang out at the tree house and suspension bridge in the **Fantastic Forest**, among other themed attractions.
SEE ALSO PARKS AND GARDENS, P.101

Jurong BirdPark

2 Jurong Hill; tel: 6265 0022; www.birdpark.com.sg; daily 8.30am–6pm (last admission 5.30pm); entrance charge; MRT: Boon Lay, then bus: 194 or 251

Home to 9,000 birds of 600 species from all over the

Night Safari

80 Mandai Lake Road; tel: 6269 3411; www.nightsafari.com.sg; daily 7.30pm–midnight (last admission 11pm); entrance charge; MRT: Ang Mo Kio, then bus: 138 or MRT: Choa Chu Kang, then bus: 927

Next door to the Singapore Zoo, the Night Safari is the world's first night wildlife park, with over 920 nocturnal animals awake and active in 41 realistic re-created habitats with clever unobtrusive lighting resembling moonlight.

Below: the Night Safari's open concept allows gentle animals to wander freely.

From 7.30pm, a series of trams (separate charge) with witty guides aboard takes about 45 minutes to encircle the eight themed zones on a 3.2-km (2-mile) track.

Deer and other small animals wander freely by the tram. You can disembark to take a closer look at the animals in their open enclosures by following one of the three walking trails. Visitors are separated from the larger animals by natural barriers such as moats, vegetation and near-invisible wires. Flash photography is not allowed.

Don't miss the interactive **Creatures of the Night** show (daily 7.30pm, 8.30pm and 9.30pm) featuring nocturnal animals such as the puma, leopard cat and spotted hyena.

Sentosa

South of Singapore island; tel: 1800-736 8672; entrance charge to Sentosa; opening times and entrance charges for attractions vary; MRT: Harbour-Front, then Sentosa Express from VivoCity or cable car from HarbourFront Centre; cable car from Mount Faber

Sentosa has a plethora of sights to keep children entertained all day. Here is a selection of some favourites.

4D MAGIX

Imbiah Lookout; tel: 6274 5355; www.sentosa4dmagix.com.sg; daily half-hourly shows 10am–9pm; entrance charge

At Southeast Asia's largest four-dimensional theatre, enjoy an engaging multi-sensory experience complete with images leaping out at you and precisely timed environmental effects like water sprays and blowing wind.

DOLPHIN LAGOON

Palawan Beach; tel: 6275 0030; www.underwaterworld.com.sg; daily 9am–9pm; entrance charge includes admission to Underwater World

The endangered Indo-Pacific humpbacked pink dolphins here endear themselves to the crowd with their antics. 'Meet the Dolphin' shows take place daily (11am, 3pm and 5.45pm). In addition, up to eight people can sign up to swim with the dolphins (Thur–Tue 9.45am). Advance reservations are required.

LUGE & SKYRIDE

Near Sentosa Express Beach Station; daily 10am–9.30pm; entrance charge

Riders ascend a slope by chairlift and hurtle down in a luge, a part go-kart, part-toboggan, at a speed that suits their fancy.

SONGS OF THE SEA

Siloso Beach; daily 7.40pm and 8.40pm; entrance charge

End your visit to Sentosa with the spectacular *Songs of the Sea*, a mesmerising night show with a live cast, dazzling pyrotechnics, brilliant computer imaging, bursts of fire and great music, which will draw oohs and ahhs from the kids.

UNDERWATER WORLD

Northwestern Sentosa; tel: 6275 0030; www.underwaterworld.com.sg; daily 9am–9pm; entrance charge includes admission to Dolphin Lagoon

The oceanarium's highlight is the 83-m- (272-ft-) long acrylic tunnel with a travellator, which leads under a huge tank containing over 2,500 sea creatures – think bright, luminous reef dwellers, sinister stingrays and sharks. Stone fish, sea urchins and moray eels lurk behind the rocks and amid colourful corals.

Left: chairlifts carry lugers uphill before they speed back down them at the Sentosa Luge & Skyride.

Don't miss the Living Fossils exhibit at the Underwater World, where about 20 fish have been tagged with microchips. When a tagged fish passes by a sensor, visitors can read facts about it, such as its name, species and origins, on a touchscreen.

Above: catch animals in lively action at feeding time at the zoo.

There are also 'touch pools' and aquariums of jelly fish, sea dragons and other colourful marine life.

Throughout the day, you can watch these denizens of the deep being hand-fed by divers. The more adventurous can 'Dive with the Sharks' while intrepid scuba-certified divers can sign up for the 'Extreme Bull Shark Encounter'. The shark-shy can instead 'Dive with the Dugong'. Extra charges apply for these special encounters and advance reservations are essential.

Singapore Science Centre

15 Science Centre Road; tel: 6425 2500; www.science.edu.sg; Tue–Sun 10am–6pm; entrance charge; MRT: Jurong East, then bus: 66 or 335

Inquisitive minds will find the 1,000 interactive exhibits in the Science Centre's 15 galleries a thorough joy.

Highlights include the **Genome Exhibit**, where DNA structures and their functions are explored through three-dimensional exhibits. There are optical illusions in the **Mind's Eye** gallery, and kids will find the **Kinetic Garden**, with sculptures and water features, especially engaging.

The adjacent **Omni-Theatre** presents several wide-screen Omnimax movies each day (10am–8pm; separate charge) on a five-storey-high hemispheric screen with sound from 72 amplifiers.

Singapore Zoo

80 Mandai Lake Road; tel: 6269 3411; www.zoo.com.sg; daily 8.30am–6pm (last admission 5.30pm); entrance charge; MRT: Ang Mo Kio, then bus: 138 or MRT: Choa Chu Kang, then bus: 927

Spread over 28 hectares (69 acres), the zoo stands out in nearly every category by which animal collections are judged: variety of wildlife (more than 3,000 animals from 290 species); open-air, naturalistic enclosures; captive breeding of endangered species; and attractive landscaping.

Popular attractions include the **Elephants of Asia** exhibit, reminiscent of the hills of Burma; and the **Fragile Forest**, showcasing various rainforest ecosystems. The zoo also has the world's largest captive **orangutan colony**. The little ones will be enthralled with **Children's World**, where they can pet animals, watch a sheep dog at work, and take a ride on a miniature train.

If your child fancies having a **Jungle Breakfast** among orangutans, book a place at the Jungle Flavours restaurant in advance (daily 9–10.30am; separate charge). Or feed some rare Hamadryas baboons when you hop on a buggy for the hour-long **Wild Discoverer Tour** (5 days advance book required; separate charge).

Animal shows go on several times a day at the open-air amphitheatre.

Tours

Ducktours

Tickets at Duck Tours Counter, Suntec City Mall Galleria, 3 Temasek Boulevard; tel: 6333 3825; www.ducktours.com.sg; daily 10am–6pm; entrance charge; MRT: City Hall, then shuttle bus to Suntec City; map p.136 C2

If you can't decide between a bus tour and a river cruise for the family, simply go with a Ducktour. Kids will love the one-hour ride on the Duck, a converted amphibious vehicle that first splashes into the Kallang Basin for a scenic cruise up to the Merlion at Marina Bay, and then goes ashore, waddling through the historical Civic District.

The same company also offers **Hippotours**, which are city sightseeing trips on open-top double-decker buses. You can hop on and off at designated stops along the way.

Churches, Mosques and Temples

Singapore has an enviable record of religious and ethnic harmony, although it was not one that was won lightly. The country was wrecked by two communal riots in the 1950s and 1960s, but for the most part today, its people are accepting of one another's faiths. Naturally then, there are plenty of places of worship, many of which have been declared national monuments for their architectural and historical value.

Abdul Gaffoor Mosque

41 Dunlop Street; tel: 6295 4209; Sat–Thur 9am–8pm, Fri 9am–12.30pm, 2.30pm–8pm; free; MRT: Little India; map p.133 C1

Built in 1859 and named after a lawyer's clerk, this Renaissance- and Arabian-style mosque is an oasis of calm in exuberant Little India. The prayer hall, decorated with Moorish arches, has a tableau tracing the origins of Islam.

Al Abrar Mosque

192 Telok Ayer Street; tel: 6220 6306; daily 11am–9pm; free; MRT: Tanjong Pagar; map p.139 C2

This mosque was built between 1850 and 1855 by the Muslim Chulia community from South India. Declared a national monument in 1974, it is a mansion compared to the earlier structure that sat here in the 1830s, which was a mere thatched building known as Kuchu Palli ('hut mosque').

Armenian Church

60 Hill Street; tel: 6334 0141; www.armeniansinasia.org; daily 9am–6pm; free; MRT: City Hall; map p.136 A2

Also called St Gregory the Illuminator, this exquisite church was built in 1835 and designed by colonial architect George Coleman. The oldest in Singapore, it houses a cemetery in its grounds, where the tombstones of some eminent names in Singapore's history lie. Among them are the Sarkies brothers who founded Raffles Hotel and Agnes Joaquim, after whom Singapore's national flower is named.

Agnes discovered a purple bloom, later named Vanda Miss Joaquim, behind her home in Tanjong Pagar in 1893.

Buddha Tooth Relic Temple and Museum

288 South Bridge Road; tel: 6220 0220; www.btrts.org.sg; daily 7am–7pm; free; MRT: Chinatown; map p.138 B3

Right in the heart of Chinatown lies this five-storey-high Buddhist shrine housing

Below: the graceful Armenian Church is a quiet sanctum in the bustling Civic District.

Left: worshippers at Sri Veeramakaliamman Temple *(see p.44).*

Archbishop of Singapore. It was gazetted as a national monument in 1973. Two colonial architects, Denis Lesley Sweeney and J. Turnbull Thomson, submitted designs for the cathedral in a competition. The former was eventually the victor, for his design, inspired by St Paul's in Covent Garden and St Martin-in-the-Fields in London, was less expensive than Thomson's.

Hajjah Fatimah Mosque

4001 Beach Road; tel: 6297 2774; daily 9am–9pm; free; MRT: Lavender; map p.137 D4

Built by a British architect in 1846, this mosque was named after a faithful Muslim woman who, after her husband's death, ran her shipping business so well that the proceeds enabled her to build the mosque on the site of their home. Its Gothic-style spire, which tilts at six degrees, has earned the mosque the nickname 'Leaning Tower of Singapore'.

Jamae Mosque

218 South Bridge Road; tel: 6221 4165; daily 10am–7pm; free; MRT: Chinatown; map p.138 C3

Sporting an eclectic mix of architectural styles, this mosque features pagoda-like minarets that are rare in mosque architecture, perhaps as a gesture of deference to the predominantly Chinese neighbourhood. It has a South Indian-style entrance gate and neoclassical-style prayer halls and shrine. The mosque was constructed in 1826 by Muslim Chulia immigrants who came from South India's Coromandel Coast.

Over 85 percent of Singapore residents say they have a faith: 43 percent are Buddhist, 15 percent are Muslim, 15 percent are Christian, 8 percent are Taoist and 4 percent are Hindu. Others profess to minority beliefs.

---

sacred objects dedicated to the Maitreya Buddha (Future Buddha). Its architecture, interiors and statuary are inspired by the styles of the Tang dynasty – a golden age for Buddhism in China.

Entering the 80-m- (262-ft-) high main hall, you will see an intricately carved 5-m (16-ft) wooden Maitreya Buddha image. A hundred other Buddha statues line both sides of the hall. The next floor is designated as an exhibition hall for religious artworks and a library of Buddhist texts. A permanent collection of cultural artefacts, some of which were purchased from Sotheby's and Christie's auctions, is kept in a climate-controlled hall on the third floor.

The temple's centrepiece is one of the Buddha's sacred teeth, an object dogged by much controversy; its authenticity has been doubted by Buddhism scholars and some members of the public. It is held on the fourth floor in a golden stupa and only taken out for viewing on Vesak Day and Chinese New Year. About 220kg (485lb) of the 420kg (925lb) of gold needed to construct the 3.5-tonne stupa was donated by devotees. Curtains obscuring the stupa from view are unveiled two times a day (9am and 3pm). On the roof, you can admire the blooms of the Dendrobium Buddha Tooth, an orchid hybrid specially named after the temple.

Cathedral of the Good Shepherd

Queen Street; tel: 6337 2036; Mon–Fri 7am–5.30pm, Sat 7am–7.30pm, Sun 7.30am–7pm; free; MRT: City Hall; map p.136 A2

Built in 1846 in the design of a crucifix, the cathedral is the oldest Roman Catholic church in Singapore and home to the present

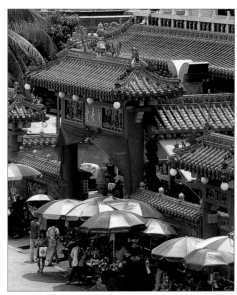

Above: Kwan Im Thong Hood Cho Temple.

Kong Meng San Phor Kark See Temple

88 Bright Hill Road; tel: 6849 5300; daily 8.30am–4pm; free; MRT: Bishan, then taxi or bus: 410

Built in 1980, Singapore's largest Buddhist temple is spread over 12 hectares (30 acres). Its **Hall of Great Compassion** houses a 9-m- (29.5-ft-) high marble Goddess of Mercy (Guan Yin), crafted in the Indian tradition with 1,000 arms and eyes. Also look out for the huge image of the Medicine Buddha, which sits beneath a golden stupa in the **Pagoda of 10,000 Buddhas**. **Vesak Day** celebrations are held here on a grand scale, sometimes stretching over three weeks.

SEE ALSO FESTIVALS AND EVENTS, P.57

Kwan Im Tong Hood Cho Temple

178 Waterloo Street; tel: 6337 3965; daily 6.15am–6.15pm; free; MRT: Bugis; map p.136 B3

Built in 1895 and refurbished in 1982, the temple is a highlight not for its architecture but rather for the glimpses of colourful local life it offers. Pensive supplicants inside the temple kneel before the Goddess of Mercy in prayer. Some shake canisters with numbered bamboo fortune sticks until one falls out, then consult with the fortune tellers who wait outside along with traditional medicine and flower sellers. From lottery numbers to prospects for offspring, the goddess tries to unravel everything about the future.

Some Chinese worshippers can also be seen offering incense sticks to Lord Krishna and other Hindu deities at the highly ornamented **Sri Krishnan Temple** next door to the Kwan Im Thong Hood Cho Temple – perhaps for double assurance.

Leong San See Temple

371 Race Course Road; tel: 6298 9371; daily 6am–6pm; free; MRT: Farrer Park; map p.133 D3

The ornately decorated Leong San See Temple (Dragon Mountain Temple) is dedicated to the Goddess of Mercy. Dating back to 1913, it also bears an image of Confucius at its altar and is hence popular with many parents who bring their children here to pray for success at examinations and filial piety. Note especially the dragon sculptures on top of its roofs. At the back is a courtyard with old ancestral tablets.

Lian Shan Shuang Lin Monastery

184E Jalan Toa Payoh; tel: 6259 6924; daily 8.30am–5pm; free; MRT: Potong Pasir

Its name means 'Twin Grove of the Lotus Mountain Temple'. Completed in 1912, the temple was modelled after Xi Chan Si, a well-known *cong lin* temple in Fuzhou. *Cong lin* means 'layers of forest' and Xi Chan Si is a monastery that was built according to an established layout that allows monks to move around in a set pattern to perform rituals. This enables them to find their way about in any *cong lin* temple they might be in, whatever its size.

Shuang Lin Monastery was the fulfilment of Low Kim Pong's (1838–1908) dream. Low was a successful trader and a leader of the local Hokkien community. The story goes that one day in 1898, he had a dream in which he saw a golden light shining from the west. He found out the next day that his son had the same dream. Taking it as an omen, father and son went to the harbour and waited. At sunset a boat sailed in from the west, carrying 12 Buddhist monks and nuns who were on their way back to China after six years of pilgrimage in India, Sri Lanka and Burma. Inspired, Low persuaded the group to stay and donated substantial funds to build Shuang Lin Monastery, which took over a decade to finish.

The **Main Hall** is noted for its decorative panels, wood-carvings and sculptures of deities. The temple underwent major restorations from 1991, with new structures built in traditional style. In 2002 the new seven-storey granite **Dragon Light Pagoda** – topped with a golden spire – was completed by craftsmen from China as a spectacular finale to the 11-year restoration programme that cost over S$40 million.

Malabar Muslim Jama-Ath Mosque

471 Victoria Street; tel: 6294 3862; daily 10am–noon and 2–4pm; free; MRT: Lavender; map p.133 E1

This beautiful mosque is covered in pretty blue mosaics and topped by a

Above: giant Buddha image at the Sakya Muni Buddha Gaya Temple.

golden dome. It harks back to the era Kampong Glam was founded. The mosaic tiles were only added after the mosque opened in 1963. This is the only mosque in Singapore built by Indian Muslims from the Malabar coastal region of Kerala.

St Andrew's Cathedral

11 St Andrew's Road; tel: 6337 6104; Mon–Sat 9am–5pm, guided tours Mon–Sat 10.30am–noon (except Wed) and 2.30pm–4pm (except Sat); free; MRT: City Hall; map p.136 B1

The grandest church in Singapore, St Andrew's Cathedral is, befittingly, a gazetted monument. It owes its smooth white surface to the curious plaster used by the Indian convict labourers who built it. Called Madras *chunam*, the plaster was made of egg white, eggshell, lime, sugar, coconut husk and water, and gave the building a smooth polished finish.

The original cathedral, designed in Palladian style by George Coleman, was twice struck by lightning and demolished in 1852. The present cathedral, in the style of an early Gothic abbey and designed by Ronald MacPherson, was conse-

crated in 1862. The gleaming white exterior contrasts with the dark pews inside, as sunlight gently filters through the stained-glass windows in the morning.

Sakya Muni Buddha Gaya Temple

366 Race Course Road; tel: 6294 0714; daily 8am–4.30pm; free; MRT: Farrer Park; map p.133 D3

Also known as the Temple of 1,000 Lights, this stunning temple has a 15-m- (49-ft-) high Buddha image that sits under a halo of lightbulbs, on a base depicting scenes from the life of the Buddha. Worshippers may illuminate the lights around the statue for a small donation or have their fortune told by spinning a wheel on the left of the prayer hall. Visitors are advised to dress conservatively.

Sri Mariamman Temple

244 South Bridge Road; tel: 6223 4064; daily 7am–noon and 6–9pm; free; MRT: Chinatown; map p.138 C3

This temple is synonymous with its tall *gopuram* (tower), adorned with colourful renditions of Hindu deities, at the entrance. Dedicated to the goddess Mariamman –

Below: at the Lian Shan Shuang Lin Temple.

43

who is known for curing serious illnesses – it is the oldest and most important Hindu shrine in Singapore. Here, devotees perform prayers amid gaudy statues and vivid ceiling frescoes. Built in 1827 by Naraina Pillai, the first recorded Indian immigrant to enter Singapore, it was a simple shed that eventually became the annual site of **Thimithi**, the Hindu fire-walking festival in October. In an elaborate ceremony that honours the goddess Draupathi, the faithful work themselves into a trance and walk over burning embers to fulfil their vows. Curiously, it is a ritual that also draws participation from a small number of Chinese devotees. The right to take photographs in the temple will cost a donation of S$3.
SEE ALSO FESTIVALS AND EVENTS, P.59

Sri Srinivasa Perumal Temple

397 Serangoon Road; tel: 6298 5771; daily 6.30am–noon and 6–9pm; free; MRT: Farrer Park; map p.133 D3

This temple's five-tier tower was a donation from P. Govindasamy Pillai, one of the earliest Indian immigrants who made good. He set up a chain of popular general-goods stores in Little India

and was known for his philanthropic work, a legacy continued by his sons today. The temple is at the centre of the Hindu trinity made up of Brahma the Creator, Vishnu the Preserver and Shiva the Destroyer. It is dedicated to Krishna, one of the incarnations of Vishnu. Perumal is another name for Krishna and statues of him – coloured blue to signify blue blood – are everywhere in the temple. The temple ceiling is dominated by a colourful circular pattern depicting the nine planets of the universe.

The annual **Thaipusam** procession sets off from here and makes its way to the Sri Thandayuthapani Temple on Tank Road (see below).
SEE ALSO FESTIVALS AND EVENTS, P.56

Sri Thendayuthapani Temple

15 Tank Road; tel: 6737 9393; daily 8am–noon and 5.30–8.30pm; free; MRT: Dhoby Ghaut; map p.135 E2

Better known to most Singaporean Hindus as the Chettiar Temple, this was built in 1859, by the Chettiars, an Indian caste of moneylenders. Take a good look at the 48 glass panels on the roof, designed to catch sun's rays. It is also here, during the annual

Thaipusam festival, that hundreds of pilgrims end their walk from the Sri Srinivasa Perumal Temple (see above) on Serangoon Road.
SEE ALSO FESTIVALS AND EVENTS, P.56

Sri Veeramakaliamman Temple

141 Serangoon Road; tel: 6295 4538; daily 5.30am–noon and 4–9pm; free; MRT: Little India; map p.133 C1

Dating to 1855 and built by indentured Bengali labourers, this temple is dedicated to the multi-armed goddess Kali, the manifestation of anger in the face of evil, who is both loved and feared. In one of her images at the temple, she is shown ripping a hapless victim apart. As consort to Shiva, the goddess is also known as Parvati in her benign form. The main shrine has a striking Kali statue, flanked by those of her sons Ganesh, the Elephant God, and Murugan, the Child God.

Tuesdays and Fridays are considered sacred days and are especially busy with devotees streaming in to pray and ask for blessings.

Sultan Mosque

3 Muscat Street; tel: 6293 4405; Sat–Thur 9am–noon, 2–4pm, Fri 2.30–4pm; free; MRT: Bugis; map p.136 C4

The largest mosque in Singapore, this dates back to 1924. Swan and Maclaren, the architectural firm responsible for the mosque, adopted the design of the Taj Mahal and combined it with Persian, Moorish, Turkish and classical themes. The muezzin calls the faithful to prayer five times a day; the women to their enclave upstairs, and the men to the main prayer hall. With its

Below: a temple musician at the Sri Srinivasa Perumal Temple.

Above: the Sultan Mosque is one of the most important places of worship for Muslims in Singapore.

During renovations of Thian Hock Keng in 1999, a rare silk scroll bearing the calligraphy of Qing-dynasty emperor Guang Xu (1871–1908) was found. The emperor inscribed four large characters, *bo jing nan ming* ('the wave is calm in the South Seas'), on the scroll and gifted it to the temple to mark the completion of its first major restoration in 1906. He also gave Yueh Hai Ching Temple a similar piece of calligraphy.

striking golden domes and soaring minarets, this is one of the loveliest places of Muslim worship in Singapore.

Telok Ayer Chinese Methodist Church

235 Telok Ayer Street; tel: 6324 4001; Mon–Fri 9am–5pm, Sat 9am–1pm; MRT: Tanjong Pagar; map p.139 C2

The building that houses the church today was built 1924–25 and gazetted as a national monument in 1989. Its unusual architecture is a blend of East and West – with a flat-roofed Chinese pavilion and a ground floor graced by European-style columns.

Thian Hock Keng Temple

158 Telok Ayer Street; tel: 6423 4616; daily 7.30am–5.30pm; MRT: Tanjong Pagar; map p.139 C2

Telok Ayer Street, which means 'Water Bay' in Malay, once stood on Singapore's shoreline. Today the reclaimed land is blocked from the sea by a wall of skyscrapers. It was here that seafarers and immigrants from the Fujian province in China set up a joss house in the 1820s in gratitude for their safe arrival in Singapore. The joss house eventually

became the Thian Hock Keng Temple, the Temple of Heavenly Happiness, dedicated to Ma Chu Po, by 1842. The Goddess of the Sea could reputedly calm rough waters and rescue those in danger of drowning.

Visually extravagant and built without the use of a single nail with imported materials from China and Europe, Thian Hock Keng is a must-see among Singapore's many Chinese temples. Dragons, venerated for protection on sea voyages, leap along the roof and curl around granite pillars. Incense wafts from giant brass urns in front of altars laden with offerings.

Yueh Hai Ching Temple

30B Phillip Street; tel: 6533 8537; daily 6am–6pm; free; MRT: Raffles Place; map p.139 D3

Built in the 1830s by the local Teochew community for the protection of traders travelling between Singapore and China, this temple combines the practice of Buddhism and Taoism. Its ornate roof depicts scenes from Chinese village life, including an opera stage and houses. Huge, distinctive incense coils are hung and burnt in the courtyard. There's also a large terracotta furnace in the courtyard, where paper money is burnt to assist the deceased in their journey to the netherworld.

Below: an image of Kali at the Sri Veeramakaliamman Temple.

Dance

Singapore's dance offerings are often based on cross-cultural exchanges of interpretations from the East and West, and dancers and choreographers tend to move between projects and ensembles. Increasingly, as the corp of local dancers mature, there is also a burgeoning of professional ensembles. One pivotal company is the Singapore Dance Theatre, hailed as an 'Asian Jewel'. Its repertoire ranges from *Sleeping Beauty* and *The Nutcracker* to contemporary ballet set to pop music. The venues for performances are also diverse, from the superb Esplanade Theatre to the lawn at the Fort Canning Park.

Companies

Arts Fission

01-07/09 and 03-03/04 ONE-TWO-SIX Cairnhill Arts Centre, 126 Cairnhill Road; tel: 6238 6469; www.artsfission.org
One of the most cutting-edge dance laboratories in Singapore, Arts Fission adopts a multidisciplinary approach and draws inspiration from cultural roots and heritage to create a new genre of contemporary Asian dance. Besides productions on stage, it has an affinity for site-specific performances.

ECNAD

04-06/07 Telok Ayer Performing Arts Centre, 182 Cecil Street; tel: 6226 6772; www.ecnad.org; MRT: Tanjong Pagar; map p.139 C2

Tickets to performing arts and sport events can be purchased in person or booked by phone or online (and paid for in the latter two cases by credit card) with **SISTIC** (tel: 6348 5555; www.sistic.com.sg) or **Tickets.com** (tel: 6296 2929; www.tdc.sg). Check websites for their ticketing outlets.

As suggested by its name, which is the word 'dance' spelt backwards, ECNAD set out in 1996 to turn the Singapore dance scene around. Its dance pieces combine movements and sounds with fantastical sets and costumes. Watching an ECNAD production is like taking in a surrealistic visual feast. Apart from its larger-scale productions, ECNAD also hosts open rehearsals and intimate performances in its studios.

Odyssey Dance Theatre

04-04/08/09 Telok Ayer Performing Arts Centre, 182 Cecil Street; tel: 6221 5516; www.odysseydancetheatre.com
This contemporary-dance company busies itself with three main performances a year and with showcases at international festivals. It also organises a biennial dance festival, Xposition 'O' *(see opposite)*.

Singapore Dance Theatre

2/F, Fort Canning Centre, Cox Terrace; tel: 6338 0611; www. singaporedancetheatre.com
The grande dame of the

Above: *Swan Lake* is one of the classic ballets performed by the Singapore Dance Theatre.

Singapore dance scene, the Singapore Dance Theatre (SDT) is a melting pot of dancers and choreographers from all over the world, who deliver modern dance interpretations and classical dance pieces such as *The Nutcracker* and *Giselle* with equal aplomb. It performs at the Esplanade Theatre and the Victoria Theatre, and features its outdoor dance showcase *Ballet Under the Stars* outside its studios on the lawn of the Fort Canning Park. SDT is also a regular at the Singapore Arts Festival.

Left: fluid movements in the Singapore Dance Theatre's performance of the contemporary work *Negro Y Blanco*.

Raffles Place; map p.139 D4
In 1905 this former town hall was converted into a 900-seat theatre, used by amateur English-drama troupes. Until the Esplanade was opened in 2002, Victoria Theatre was the most prestigious performance venue in Singapore for almost a century.

Festivals

Da:ns Festival
www.dansfestival.com
Organised by the Esplanade – Theatres on the Bay in October, this is probably the best dance-genre festival in Singapore. Past festivals featured performances by the Compañía de Danza Española Aída Gómez from Spain, the Eifman Ballet of St Petersburg as well as screenings of movies centred on dance.

Xposition 'O' Contemporary Dance Fiesta
www.xposition-o.com
This biennial festival organised by the Odyessey Dance Theatre has featured international dance companies from Finland, Hong Kong, Korea and other countries.

Ballet Under The Stars is possibly the most popular of Singapore's outdoor arts events. Held several times a year at Fort Canning Park, the event sees ballet buffs bringing out their picnic baskets and rugs for an evening of performances by the Singapore Dance Theatre under the stars. For schedules, see www.singaporedancetheatre.com.

Venues

Esplanade Theatres
Esplanade – Theatres on the Bay, 1 Esplanade Drive; tel: 6828 8222; www.esplanade.com; MRT: City Hall; map p.136 B1
The Esplanade is the city's premier performing arts centre, and its 2,000-seat Theatre has played host to numerous dance performances, including those of the Singapore Dance Theatre. Full-scale ballets have also been held here by internationally renowned groups, in addition to contemporary and avant-garde performances by companies like the Bill T. Jones/Arnie Zane Dance Company and Italy's Com-

pany Il Posto. Experimental dance presentations are also staged in the smaller, 220-seat **Theatre Studio**.
SEE ALSO ARCHITECTURE, P.27; MUSIC, P.90; THEATRE, P.121

University Cultural Centre
National University of Singapore, 50 Kent Ridge Crescent; tel: 6516 2492; www.nus.edu.sg; MRT: Clementi, then bus: 96
Used mostly by students, this has also hosted acclaimed international performers. It has a 1,700-seat concert hall and a 450-seat theatre.

Victoria Theatre
9 Empress Place; tel: 6338 8283; www.nac.gov.sg; MRT:

Below: the Victoria Theatre is still a sought-after dance venue.

Environment

The smallest country in Southeast Asia, Singapore has an area of just 699sq km. Yet this geographical blip has one of the highest road densities. With some 730,000 vehicles on the roads, equivalent to 220 cars per road-km, the island has a road density that is more than double the UK's. One would expect such a large car population and Singapore's urban sprawl to result in a polluted city, but dedicated measures have made this island one of the least polluted places in the world. These include keeping a tight rein on vehicular growth and efforts to promote recycling and green the cityscape.

Air Pollution

A tiny island filled with too many people with high disposable incomes faces a potential problem: too many cars choking the roads and causing air pollution. But while traffic in the rest of Asia crawls at a snail's pace during rush hour, in Singapore it cruises at a reasonable 60–70km/h (37–44 miles/h) on the expressways at peak times. Air quality is maintained at a good level. Despite having one of the highest car densities in the world, Singapore has found a solution to a problem that has stumped traffic authorities elsewhere, using a combination of regulation and technology.

VEHICULAR POPULATION CONTROL

To control the number of vehicles and minimise pollution, Singapore uses various measures. For starters, cars in Singapore are probably among the most expensive in the world. After a hefty 45 percent tax on car imports, a registration fee of 150 percent and an annual road tax pegged to the engine capacity of the car, a 1,600cc saloon can easily cost in excess of S$60,000. In addition, a potential vehicle owner needs to bid for a Certificate of Entitlement (COE) in order to be 'entitled' to a new vehicle. If successful, the vehicle entitlement is valid for only 10 years from the vehicle's date of registration. In 2007 the COE premiums ranged S$10,000–15,000, jacking up the eventual price of a 1,600cc saloon to about S$75,000.

ELECTRONIC ROAD PRICING

In 1999 the government struck another brainwave in the form of the Electronic Road Pricing (ERP) system. Overhead ERP gantries are strategically located in the Central Business District and along expressways. These deduct a fixed toll during peak hours from cash cards inserted in the special in-vehicle units (IU) installed in cars. Sensors on the gantries are linked to a central system

Above: an ERP gantry.

that logs all vehicles passing under them. Motorists without IUs or with insufficient cash on their cards will have their licence plates photographed. A few days later, summonses to pay fines arrive in the mail.

The ERP system has drawn a mixed response. Government coffers have swelled, but the scheme has also succeeded in reducing traffic during peak hours. Traffic during ERP operating hours has dropped by 15 percent.

OTHER MEASURES

While discouraging car ownership, the authorities have

Left: this developed city still enjoys blue skies and lush greenery.

plans for recycling efforts in Singapore, setting a recycling rate of 60 percent by 2012. Since 2001 recycling efforts have gone door-to-door. Residents living in flats are given specific bins and bags for the disposal of cans, paper, glass bottles and plastic containers. Another of NEA's efforts is a green pact supported by numerous companies that aims to systemically reduce packaging waste. Singapore produces about 1,200 tonnes of packaging waste a day; NEA hopes this five-year voluntary agreement will lower the stress on the country's landfills.

also poured in millions of dollars to facilitate a more efficient public transport system as an alternative to driving. In addition, car-sharing schemes also maximise vehicle use, while the Park-and-Ride Scheme, which allows drivers to park their cars near MRT stations and bus interchanges, encourages drivers to continue their journeys by MRT or bus.

Those who can't live without a car are persuaded to use smaller-capacity cars with lower road tax. Owners of hybrid vehicles and compressed natural gas (CNG) vehicles enjoy green-vehicle tax rebates.

Climate

To combat the urban heat, the city has a legion of green belts, such as parks nestled between skyscrapers. The National Parks Board spends millions every year to keep the city verdant, and a large part of its budget goes towards maintaining nature reserves in the suburbs as well.

Temperatures range between 24–33°C (75–91°F),

with humidity around 75 percent. Residents escape the heat by retreating into air-conditioned homes, shopping malls and offices. With indoor temperatures often set at 22°C (72°F) or lower, and cardigans and jackets permanent fixtures of office wardrobes, it has been said Singapore indulges in air-conditioning overkill. The demand for air conditioning in this tropical land is unlikely to diminish, and has thus led to a pressing need for more energy-efficient buildings.

Recycling

The National Environment Agency (NEA) has grand

Below: heed the sign.

Water

For years Singapore has depended on Malaysia for its water supply, but as its contracts are reaching an end and the threat of non-renewal looms, the island has looked into producing its own supply. NEWater – the brand name given to reclaimed water produced by the Public Utilities Board – is essentially treated sewage water. It is supplied to industries requiring high-purity water and is also blended with reservoir water before undergoing further treatment for human consumption.

The **NEWater Visitor Centre** offers tours of the NEWater treatment process, plus interactive games and multi-media shows (20 Koh Sek Lim Road; tel: 6546 7874 or 6593 1533; www.pub.gov.sg; Tue–Sun 9am–5.30pm; free; MRT: Tanah Merah, then bus 12, 24, 31, 38 or free shuttle service at specified times).

Essentials

Travelling in Singapore is a cinch. English is widely spoken, public transport is efficient, and streets and addresses are clearly marked. When you first arrive in Singapore, head to one of the Singapore Visitors Centres run by the tourism board to get maps, brochures and advice on things to do and see. In addition, this section offers the practical information you need to know to enjoy this city, from currency and entry regulations to telecommunications and advice on taxes and tipping. Also included are details on where to get medical help and assistance in emergencies.

Embassies

Australia
25 Napier Road; tel: 6836 4100
Canada
11-01 One George Street;
tel: 6854 5900
New Zealand
15-10 Ngee Ann City Tower A,
391A Orchard Road;
tel: 6235 9966
UK
100 Tanglin Road;
tel: 6424 4200
USA
27 Napier Road; tel: 6476 9100

Emergencies

Fire and ambulance: **995**
Police: **999**

Entry Requirements

Visa requirements vary from time to time, so check with a Singapore embassy or consulate. Most visitors are given a 30-day social visit pass on arrival. Renewals can be made at the **Immigration and**

Metric to Imperial Conversions
1 metre = 3.28 feet
1 kilometre = 0.62 mile
1 hectare = 2.47 acres
1 kilogram = 2.2 pounds

Checkpoints Authority
(10 Kallang Road; tel: 6391 6100;
www.ica.gov.sg).

Health

Singapore has no free medical care and medical evacuation is very expensive, so be sure you are covered by insurance. Most hotels have doctors on call.

HOSPITALS
Raffles Hospital
585 North Bridge Road;
tel: 6311 1111;
www.rafflesmedical.com
Singapore General Hospital
1 Hospital Drive; tel: 1800-223 3322; www.sgh.com.sg

PHARMACIES
Pharmacies, many with qualified pharmacists, are open 9am–9pm, but it is wise to travel with your own prescriptions and medication.

Internet

To get online, head to an Internet café; try **Chills Café** (01-07, Stamford House, 39 Stamford Road; tel: 6883 1016; www.chillscafe.com.sg; open daily 9am–midnight). **Wireless@SG**

is a scheme that provides free wireless connection at selected hot spots. You will need a mobile device with WiFi facility, and will need to register online with a service provider: **iCELL** (tel: 6309 4520; www.icellnetwork.com), **QMax** (tel: 6895 4833; www.qmax.com.sg) or **Singtel** (tel: 1688; www.singtel.com). Check the Infocomm Development Authority website (www.ida.gov.sg) for locations of hot spots.

Money

The Singapore dollar (S$ or SGD) is divided into 100 cents, with coins of 5, 10, 20, 50 cents and S$1. Bills in common circulation are S$2, S$5, S$10, S$20, S$50, S$100, S$500 and S$1,000.

ATMS
ATMs are found in banks, shopping malls and MRT stations; many feature the Cirrus and PLUS systems.

CREDIT CARDS
Major credit cards are widely accepted. Report lost or stolen cards immediately

Left: don't be deterred by the many do's and don'ts in Singapore; it's still a great city.

Scheme. The refund applies to purchases exceeding S$100. Show your passport to the retailer and fill out a voucher. Before departure, validate the voucher at the airport customs, then present it together with your items at the Global Refund Counter (tel: 6225 6238) or Premier Tax Free Scheme Counter (tel: 1800-829 3733).

Telephones

The country code for Singapore is 65; there are no area codes. To call overseas from Singapore, dial the access code 001, 013 or 019, followed by the relevant country code.

Only GSM mobile phones with roaming facility can hook up automatically to the local networks. All local mobile numbers begin with an '8' or '9'.

Some public phones can be used for international calls. Phone cards are available from post offices and convenience stores.

Tipping

Most hotel and restaurant bills come with a 10 percent service charge on top of the 7 percent GST. Tipping is optional, although appreciated.

Tourist Information

The **Singapore Tourism Board** (24-hour infoline: 1800-736 2000; www.visitsingapore.com) has visitors centres at the following locations: Orchard Road (opposite Somerset MRT); ION Orchard, Bugis Street; and the arrival halls and transit lounges of Changi Airport terminals 1, 2 and 3.

---

to the police (tel: 1800-353 0000 for locations) and to your card company.

American Express
Tel: 1800-737 8188
Diners Club
Tel: 6416 0800/0900
MasterCard
Tel: 800-110 0113
Visa
Tel: 800-448 1250

CURRENCY EXCHANGE

Money-changing services are available at the airport and in banks, hotels and shopping malls. Moneychangers give slightly better rates than banks; hotels give the worst.

TRAVELLERS' CHEQUES

These can be cashed at banks and are accepted at many establishments.

Postal Services

Postal services are provided by **Singapore Post** (tel: 1605). Branches include: **1 Killiney Road** (Mon–Sat 9am–9pm, Sun and public holidays 9am–4.30pm); **Changi Airport Terminal 2** (daily 8am–9.30pm).

You can also buy stamps and weigh letters

> Singapore is 8 hours ahead of GMT.

and small packages at self-service automated machines found in MRT stations.

Taxes

A Goods and Services Tax (GST) of 7 percent is charged on most purchases. This is refundable for purchases from shops participating in the **Global Refund Scheme** and the **Premier Tax Free**

Below: the Singapore Post is highly reliable.

Fashion

When it comes to fashion, Singaporeans are not an adventurous lot, tending to opt for comfort over style. Traipse the heartlands and you will see their denizens in their 'uniform' of T-shirt and shorts – or if they are feeling dressy that day, T-shirt and jeans. In the CBD, corporate types stride purposefully in plain pastel business shirts and trousers or skirts. But thankfully, changes are afoot: in the hipper districts of the city, trendy boutiques chalk up fashion credits for the rest of the island with threads designed by local style mavens and those inspired by the latest international fashion trends.

Local Designer Boutiques

With its small domestic market, Singapore's local fashion industry is miniscule compared to cities like Paris and Milan. The few local fashion designers who have found success have had to venture abroad. Singaporean names that have made it on the world fashion map include **Andrew Gn**, whose dazzling coats are much sought after in Europe and New York, and **Ashley Isham**, who first won attention at London Fashion Week in 2003. That said, there are also smaller labels that have found a following

of fans at home and in the Asian region.

Some local labels have chain stores, much like Topshop in London. These include **GG>5** and **M)phosis**, which are firm favourites of young women in search of funky wear for the office, and can be found in just about every mall. Their shoe equivalent, **Charles & Keith**, also available in most malls, offers myriad affordable styles.

Benno La Mode
04-06A and 04-07 The Heeren Shops, 260 Orchard Road; tel: 6732 2886; MRT: Somerset; map p.135 D4

Indonesian-born Benno Asmoro's slightly crazed, Victorian-inspired clothes are not for the faint-hearted. Sexy, flouncy tops and skirts are his signature.

Hansel
Felt, 01-02 Stamford House, 39 Stamford Road; tel: 6337 0992; www.ilovehansel.com; MRT: City Hall; map p.136 A2
'Quirky, intelligent and vibrant' best describes this kooky label by Central St Martin's alumnus Jo Soh. The label is a hit in Australia.

Nicholas
02-03 Stamford House, 39 Stamford Road; tel: 6339

The annual Singapore Fashion Festival is a glamorous turnout of the top and up-and-coming names from Singapore and around the world. The 2010 event featured runway shows of international designers like **Roberto Cavalli**, as well as top local labels like **alldressedup** and **Woods & Woods**, at its main tent showcase on Orchard Road. Fringe catwalk events are held in malls around the city.

Below: ritzy Orchard Road is the style capital of Singapore.

"Criss Cross Boy Loves Plain Jane"

"Abracadabra!"

"The 3 Flying Ducks"

"Nice Try!"

2006   2005   200

boutiques, which stock hard-to-find, cult labels from around the world. Here are some of their favourites.

Antipodean
27A Lorong Mambong, Holland Village; tel: 6463 7336; www.antipodeanshop.com; MRT: Buona Vista
Carries top designer names from Australia and New Zealand, including Akira Isogawa, Morrison, and the cult jewellery designer Elke Kramer.

The Asylum
22 Ann Siang Road; tel: 6324 8264; www.theasylum.com.sg; MRT: Tanjong Pagar; map p.138 C3
This graphic design firm-cum-boutique stocks funky accessories, experimental music, limited edition fashion products from cool local designers, design books and contemporary art.

Felt
01-18 Capitol Building, 11 Stamford Road; tel: 6837 3393; www.felt.com.sg; MRT: City Hall; map p.136 A2
Besides cult labels from Australia and New Zealand, including Lisa Ho, Tina Kalivas and Zambesi, Felt also carries Singaporean label Hansel (see opposite).

Front Row
02-08-09 Raffles Hotel Shopping Arcade, 328 North Bridge Road; tel: 6224 5501; www.frontrowsingapore.com; MRT: City Hall; map p.136 B2
Emerging Asian designers get their day in the sun at this achingly hip boutique. Labels like A.P.C, Flynow Leather, Nsha and Ek Thongprasert share shop space with chunky Dr. Martens and limited edition Jeremy Scott heels.

Many local labels go by the sizes 'small', 'medium' and 'large'. As a rough guideline, 'small' is equal to a US0–2/UK6–8; 'medium' is US4/UK10, and 'large' is equivalent to US8/UK12. The largest size is often 'extra large' (US10/UK14).

The hansel Art Series '06-0

0223; www.nicholasnic.com; MRT: City Hall; map p.136 A2
Nicholas offers three different collections – Gold, Black and Pink – each with its own character. Gold features romantic looks in ethereal fabrics like silk and cotton voile; Black is all edgy and androgynous; while Pink is targeted at the younger set with cutesy looks that incorporate ribbons and corsages. Designer Nic Wong has won myriad fashion awards in Singapore, including the Mercedes Benz Fashion Award in 2004.

Woods & Woods
Front Row, 02-08-09 Raffles Hotel Shopping Arcade, 328 North Bridge Road; tel: 6224 5501; www.woods-woods.com; MRT: City Hall; map p.136 B2

Award-winning designer Jonathan Seow regularly shows his collections at Berlin and Paris Fashion Weeks. His Woods & Woods label is all about the details – fine stitching and quality fabrics are fused with understated silhouettes and neutral colour tones.

Boutiques
Beyond cookie cutter mall boutiques, Singapore's fashionistas have come to love their multi-brand

Asian sizing is small, to say the least. Many Westerners lament the fact that it is hard to find clothes that fit them in Singapore. For larger sizes, or simply clothes that fall longer, check out international chain stores like Country Road, Mango, Zara and Topshop.

White Room
37 Haji Lane; tel: 6297 1280; www.atwhiteroom.com; MRT: Bugis; map p.137 C3
Find local maverick labels Fru Fru & Tiger Lily, Fantastik Antik and Stray at this quirky shop where goods are displayed under a massive table.

Custom Classics
CYC Shanghai Shirt Co
02-21 Raffles Hotel Shopping Arcade, 328 North Bridge Road; tel: 6336 3556; www.cyc customshop.com; MRT: City Hall; map p.136 B2
This stalwart bespoke tailor offers great value for money,

with its finely crafted shirts designed for both men and women. You can customise yours according to fabric, colour and shape, all the details down to the buttons and monograms.
Feng
120 Sophia Road; tel: 6334 9752; MRT: Dhoby Ghaut; map p.136 A4
'Feng' is translated as 'sew' in Mandarin, a very apt name for a seamstress' shop that can help realise any pattern you bring in. In-the-know locals come here to have their evening gowns and cheongsams made.
PIMABS
32B Boat Quay; tel: 6538 6466; www.pimabs.com; MRT: Raffles Place or Clarke Quay; map p.139 D4
Helmed by local fashion designer Leslie Chia, Pimab's specialises in bespoke tailoring services for men at reasonable prices.

Above: vintage remains very popular in Singapore.

Cheap Chic
77th Street
03-105/106 Far East L3, 14 Scotts Road; tel: 6732 1707; www.77thstreet.com; MRT: Orchard; map p.134 B1
This streetwear pioneer is a favourite with younger people for its affordable togs. You'll find t-shirts, low-slung jeans, sexy tops, backpacks and just about every accessory you can think of. Other locations in malls throughout the city.

Flesh Imp
03-27/28 Wisma Atria, 435
Orchard Road; tel: 6238 6738;
www.fleshimp.com; MRT:
Orchard; map p.134 C4
Hot both in the club and
fashion scenes, this mid-
priced streetwear label has
seen collaborations with
American graffiti artists. It is
particularly popular with DJs.

Fourskin
03-349/354 Marina Square, 6
Raffles Boulevard; tel: 6333 1878;
MRT: City Hall; map p.136 C1
Hip t-shirts with fantastic
graffiti prints are this local
label's signature. You'll also
find trendy flip-flops, bags
and other accessories.

Odette
02-29 Change Alley, 30 Raffles
Place, Chevron House; tel: 6438
8380; www.odette.com.sg; MRT:
Raffles Place; map p.139 D3
A collection of pretty
dresses designed by local
label Swirl. There are incred-
ibly feminine pieces for any
occasion for the girly girl

Above: stylish shoppers perusing Singapore's boutiques.

here, many of which are
made with vintage fabrics
and in very small quantities.

Shoes and Accessories

Charles & Keith
B1-18/19 Wisma Atria, 435
Orchard Road, tel: 6238 3312;
www.charleskeith.com; MRT:
Orchard; map p.134 C4
The dizzying variety of shoes,
bags and accessories is
enough to send any
footwear-addicted woman
into a frenzy. Shoe addicts
are known to cart home
shoes by the boxes, aided, of
course, by prices that go
easy on the pocket.

LeftFoot
02-07A Orchard Cineleisure,
8 Grange Road; tel: 6736 3227;
www.leftfoot.com.sg;
MRT: Somerset; map p.135 C3
Open till late at weekends,
this stocks streetwear train-
ers and limited editions from
brands like A Bathing Ape,
Vans and Visvim.

On Pedder
02-12P/Q Tower B, Ngee Ann
City, 391 Orchard Road;
tel: 6835 1307; MRT: Orchard;
map p.134 C4

This boutique stocks the
hottest looks of the season
from both the world's most
coveted names and more
obscure designers. There's a
range of lovely jewellery,
handbags and of course,
shoes that keep the chichi
crowd coming back for
more. For cheaper options,
its sister label Pedder Red is
found one level down.

TANG + Co
02-12 Paragon, 290 Orchard
Road; tel: 6737 8281;
www.tangs.com;
MRT: Orchard; map p.134 C4
The shoe department at
TANGS department store
has proved so popular over
the years that it has evolved
into a boutique of its own.
Career women come here
for affordable, stylish and
mid-range designer shoes
and handbags.

Vintage

The Attic Lifestyle Store
04-146A Far East Plaza,
14 Scotts Road; tel: 6732 3459;
MRT: Orchard; map p.134 B1
Packed to the rafters with
vintage clothes, costume
jewellery, 1970s lamps and all
sorts of old-school knick-
knacks, it truly is a treasure
hunt in this crammed space.

Left: Front Row is a hot
boutique on Ann Siang Hill
(see p.53).

55

Festivals and Events

With its multiracial character, it's no surprise Singapore is a constant hive of activity, celebrating one cultural festival after another. Almost every month of the year, its streets, temples and ethnic enclaves come alive with a motley assortment of religious and cultural celebrations. A boom in world-class venues and a growing population of fun-seeking city-dwellers have led to a significant increase in contemporary events, from the Singapore Biennale to the New Year Countdown Party.

Public Holidays

New Year's Day	1 Jan
Labour Day	1 May
National Day	9 Aug
Christmas Day	25 Dec
Variable dates	
Chinese New Year	Jan/Feb
Good Friday	Mar/Apr
Vesak Day	May
Deepavali	Oct/Nov
Hari Raya Puasa	
Hari Raya Haji	

Festivals and Events

JANUARY TO MARCH
Chinese New Year

Chinese New Year falls on the first day of the lunar calendar, usually between mid January and mid February. Chinese custom decrees that the previous year's debts be paid, the home cleaned and new clothing purchased. It is also a time for reaffirming ties at the family reunion dinner which takes place on the eve. The 15-day festival, beginning with a two-day holiday, is commemorated by feasting and the giving of *hong bao*, red packets of 'lucky money'.

On the days leading up to Chinese New Year, Chinatown streets are lit and packed with people jostling for festive goods. Dragon and lion dancers throng the streets, making plenty of noise to keep the mythical monsters associated with the New Year at bay. The area then mostly empties out for the first few days of the New Year.

A riverside carnival called **River Hongbao** usually takes place at the Marina Bay Promenade with all sorts of entertainment and food stalls.

The celebrations end with the **Chingay** parade, an exuberant procession held on the Sunday following the New Year. There are lavish floats, stilt walkers, martial arts performances and more.

Thaipusam

This Hindu festival is observed between January and February, in the Tamil month of Thai. Devotees honour Lord Muruga, god of bravery, power and virtue, by performing feats of mind over spirit. The festival begins at dawn at the Sri

Srinivasa Perumal Temple in Serangoon Road. Here, devotees who have entered a trance have their bodies pierced with metal hooks or spikes attached to a *kavadi*, a cage-like steel contraption that is carried on their shoulders. The procession makes its way to the Sri Thandayuthapani Temple on Tank Road.

Right: the Chinese New Year bazaar in Chinatown.

Left: a Hindu devotee carries a *kavadi* as an act of penance during Thaipusam.

of Asian and Western performing arts. Past performers have included the Washington Ballet and the London Philharmonic Orchestra, and also more cutting-edge ventures like a Lithuanian adaptation of Shakespeare's *Othello*. The festival also features an eclectic fringe segment and workshops by visiting companies.

Dragon Boat Festival

Every fifth Chinese lunar month (usually May or June) colourful boats with prows carved to represent dragons and birds crest the waves of Marina Bay, propelled by dozens of pairs of strong arms. The Dragon Boat Race is an international-class event that draws teams from Australia, Europe and the US, among others. The festival honours a Chinese patriot, Qu Yuan, who drowned himself in 278 BC to protest against the corruption in the imperial court. Fishermen tried to rescue him but failed. Small packages of rice were then thrown into the water to

For the most current list of events and celebrations, check the Singapore Tourism Board website at www.visit singapore.com or go to any of its Visitors Centres. *The Straits Times* and tourist magazines like *I-S, Changi Express* and *Time Out Singapore* also provide details.

As part of the celebrations, caged birds are released and free meals are distributed to the poor. On the eve of Vesak, monks at the Kong Meng San Phor Kark See Monastery lead devotees through a 'three-step-one-bow' ritual around the temple grounds. This is believed to purify negative actions of the past and is an act of homage to Buddha.

Singapore Arts Festival

This annual event in June showcases a bonanza

APRIL TO JUNE
Singapore International Film Festival

SEE ALSO FILM, P.60

World Gourmet Summit

A two-week-long event with workshops and seminars on fine food and wines. Singapore's best chefs and restaurants are feted with awards while guest chefs from around the world play host at selected restaurants with special menus.

Vesak Day

Usually celebrated in May, this is the most important event in the Buddhist calendar, honouring Buddha's birth, death and enlightenment. Temple celebrations begin at dawn with a candlelight procession.

Below: fireworks explode in New Years' celebration, watched by Singapore's icon, the Merlion.

distract fishes from his body. Drums and gongs were sounded to frighten away predators and villagers decorated their boats with dragon heads and tails with the same purpose in mind. Today several varieties of these rice dumplings are available throughout the year.

The Great Singapore Sale

Held islandwide from end May to early July, the Great Singapore Sale indulges those with a passion for shopping – with goods at shopping malls all over slashed down to bargain prices.

JULY TO SEPTEMBER
Singapore Food Festival

The island celebrates another favourite pastime – eating – with a month-long food fiesta in July. Various food-tasting events and unique dining experiences that cover a gamut of cuisines are held.

National Day

Until 2012, the parade, which marks the anniversary of the island's independence in 1965, is being held at the newly built Marina Bay Floating Stadium until the new Sports Hub at Kallang is built. The pomp and pageantry culminates in a stunning firework display.

>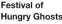
> The **Formula 1 Singapore Grand Prix** made its debut in September 2008. The annual night race promises dramatic twists and turns on 5.05km (3.15 miles) of public roads in the Marina Bay area. See www.singaporegp.sg for details.

Festival of Hungry Ghosts

Traditional Chinese believe the gates of hell are opened throughout the seventh lunar month, usually August/September, to allow ghosts to wander the earth. To appease the spirits, joss sticks and paper money are burnt and feasts whipped up as offerings. After the ghosts have had their fill, the food is eaten by the celebrants. Neighbourhood banquets, which include Chinese opera performances or *getai* (mini pop concerts), are held, climaxing in a lively auction.

Monkey God's Birthday

The Monkey God is a character from the Chinese classic *Journey to the West*, celebrated for protecting his master, a monk of the Tang dynasty dispatched to India to collect Buddhist sutras. During this festival in September, acrobats perform at various temples.

Above: Chinese opera is often performed as entertainment to appease spirits during the Festival of Hungry Ghosts.

Singapore Grand Prix

In September 2008, the world's first F1 night race was held in Marina Bay and it has become a highly anticipated annual event since. The Singapore Grand Prix runs counter-clockwise, which makes it only one of three circuits in the world to do so. Held over one weekend in September, the organisers spare no expense in drawing the crowds with events like F1 Rocks, which featured big names like Beyonce, Black Eye Peas, No Doubt and ZZ Top in 2009.

OCTOBER TO DECEMBER
Mid Autumn Festival

On the 15th day of the eighth lunar month, usually in October, the Chinese commemorate the 14th-century revolution that overthrew the Mongol dynasty in China. Mooncakes – rich pastries filled with lotus-seed or red-bean paste and salted egg yolks – are eaten. The cakes, as the legend goes, were used by rebel forces to smuggle messages about the revolution to the people,

Below: 'sale' is a word that sends Singaporeans into a buying frenzy.

while lanterns were used to signal the start of the civilian uprising. Today the festival is marked by an impressive display of lanterns at the Chinese Garden in Jurong.

Navaratri

Meaning 'nine nights' in Tamil, Navaratri pays homage to the three consorts of the Hindu gods with nine days of traditional Indian music and dance at Hindu temples. The festival concludes with a procession. It is also an opportunity to experience Indian arts; performances are held at the Sri Thendayuthapani and other Hindu temples.

Thimithi Festival

Thimithi is a breathtaking firewalking ceremony in October at the Sri Mariamman Temple on South Bridge Road. Male devotees sprint barefoot across glowing charcoals without any apparent injury to their feet, in honour of Draupathi, a legendary heroine deified by South Indian Tamils. On the eve of the festival, a magnificent silver chariot honouring Draupathi makes its way to the Sri Mariamman Temple from the Sri Srinivasa Temple in Little India.

Pilgrimage to Kusu Island

During this month-long festival falling between the first and 15th day of the ninth Chinese lunar month (usually October/November), Taoists

Above: firewalkers prepare for their walk across hot charcoals at the Sri Mariamman Temple in Chinatown during Thimithi Festival.

and Muslims take the ferry to Kusu Island to make offerings and pray at the Tua Pek Kong Temple and at the Malay shrine. The legend behind the pilgrimage tells of a turtle (*kusu*) that turned itself into an island in order to save two shipwrecked sailors.

Deepavali

Also known as the Festival of Lights, to symbolise the conquest of good over evil, this is the most important festival in the Hindu calendar. Usually occurring in October or November, it is celebrated by the traditional lighting of oil lamps at home and in Little India, which is turned into a fairyland of twinkling lights. Prayers are recited in temples and statues of deities carried around the grounds.

Christmas

A sizeable percentage of the population is Christian but almost everyone, regardless of religion, gets into the spirit and exchanges gifts come Christmas time. A yuletide light-up transforms Orchard Road into a riot of lights and glitzy displays. As with all things Singaporean, Christmas here is celebrated with a difference – just tuck into a tandoori turkey and you'll see!

VARIABLE DATES
Hari Raya Puasa

This Muslim celebration falls on the first day of the 10th Muslim month; the date varies from year to year. During Ramadan, the month preceding Hari Raya Puasa, all able Muslims observe a strict fast from sunrise to sunset so that they are better able to commiserate with the less fortunate. On Hari Raya Puasa, Muslims ask for forgiveness from family members, make new resolutions and feast on traditional food. The other Muslim festival celebrated with a holiday is **Hari Raya Haji**, which marks the sacrifices made by Muslims who undertake the pilgrimage to Mecca.

Below: malls dress up in dazzling lights for Christmas.

Billed as an international event with an Asian flavour, the **Singapore Biennale**, held from September to November every two years, is the island's largest contemporary visual arts event. Exhibitions featuring some of the world's leading-edge artists are held in various venues across the city.

59

Film

Singaporeans love going to the movies – which explains the glut of cineplexes across the island. They love a good Hollywood blockbuster, so much so that some movies open here even before they do in the US. When it comes to Singapore-produced movies, the output has been slim, with about half a dozen Singaporean feature films made each year. Admittedly, there are some duds that feature wooden acting and overused clichés, but for the most part, Singaporean films are slowly but steadily winning critical and commercial success, both at home and abroad.

Singapore's Film Industry

Singapore had its golden age of cinema in the 1950s and 1960s when it was home to two powerhouse movie studios, Cathay and Shaw Brothers. Movies then were mainly made in Bahasa Malayu and exported to the region.

Following Singapore's separation from Malaysia in 1965, the film industry moved to Kuala Lumpur. Over the next few decades, Singapore served more as an exotic location for foreign films, including Noel Coward's *Pretty Polly* (1967) and Paul Theroux's *Saint Jack* (1979).

The 1990s saw a revival for the film industry. Director Eric Khoo's *12 Storeys* (1997) was the first Singaporean film shown at the Cannes Film Festival. In 1998 Glen Goei's *Forever Fever*, a *Saturday Night Fever*-inspired tale, was picked up by Miramax and released in the US as *That's the Way I Like It*. But it was local TV comic-turned-film-maker Jack Neo's *Money No Enough* (1998) that really warmed Singaporeans to local filmmaking efforts. Pro-

The **Singapore International Film Festival** in April presents a varied diet of arthouse films from various countries. Local films are also screened. Fringe events include retrospectives, tributes, seminars and film-appreciation workshops.

duced for less than S$1 million, the film raked in S$5.8 million, making it the most commercially successful Singaporean film to date.

Milestone Films

12 Storeys (1997), directed by Eric Khoo
Its indulgently lengthy frames capture the lives of lonely residents in a block of flats. The only Singaporean film to date to be selected for the *Un Certain Regard* section at Cannes, in 1997.

15 (2002), directed by Royston Tan
This film about restless Chinese teenagers who turn to gangs was heavily censored on release (references to gangs are considered risky in Singapore). It's available uncut on DVD only in the UK and US.

881 (2007), directed by Royston Tan
Tan achieved commercial success with this film about the trials and tribulations of two friends who pursue their dream of becoming *getai* (concerts held during the Festival of Hungry Ghosts) singers.

Be With Me (2005), directed by Eric Khoo
Inspired by the life story of Theresa Chan, an elderly woman who has been deaf and blind since she was a teenager, this film is made up of three poignant stories interwoven around the desire for love and companionship. It was the opening film for the Directors' Fortnight programme at Cannes in 2005.

Money No Enough (1998), directed by TL Tay
This film is very telling of Singaporean heartlanders' taste for local movies. They loved this wacky story of working-class Chinese Singaporeans striving to make a quick buck in a ruthless society.

My Magic (2008), directed by Eric Khoo
After the screening of *My Magic* at the 61st Cannes Film

Left: Royston Tan's *881* was a commercial hit.

The Alliance Française's Cine Club screens French films regularly at the AF Theatre for members and non-members.

The Arts House
1 Old Parliament Lane; tel: 6332 6900; www.theartshouse.com. sg; MRT: City Hall; map p.139 D4
Its theatre screens foreign-language and local films.

Cinema Europa
2–3F VivoCity, 1 HarbourFront Walk; tel: 1900-912 1234; www. gv.com.sg; MRT: HarbourFront
Part of the Golden Village VivoCity cineplex, this screens foreign-language arthouse flicks throughout the year.

Cinematheque
National Museum of Singapore, 93 Stamford Road; tel: 6332 3659; www.nationalmuseum.sg; MRT: City Hall or Dhoby Ghaut; map p.136 A2
The home of the museum's film programme, which is inclined towards historical and significant Singapore-produced films, in addition to foreign-language classics.

The Picturehouse
5–6/F, Cathay Cineplex, 2 Handy Road; tel: 6235 1155; www.the picturehouse.com.sg; MRT: Dhoby Ghaut; map p.136 A3
The first dedicated arthouse cinema in Singapore, a venue for international film festivals.

Festival, a 15-minute plus standing ovation ensued. The film – a mostly Tamil drama about an alcoholic magician struggling to repair his relationship with his young son – was Singapore's first contender for the Palme d'Or, the festival's top prize. Its lead, first-time actor Bosco Francis, won Best Male Actor at the Asian First Film Festival.

Perth (2004), directed by Djinn
Lim Kay Tong plays a taxi driver, who, like some Singaporeans, aspires to save enough money to retire in Perth, Australia. He takes on a job ferrying prostitutes to their clients, becomes obsessed with one, and finds himself in a bloody mess.

Spread over five floors of an old shophouse, the **Screening Room** (12 Ann Siang Road; tel: 6221 1694; www.screen ingroom.com.sg; map p.138 C3) is an entertainment hub boasting a cushy loft theatre which regularly screens arthouse films that would otherwise be bypassed in Singapore.

Singapore Dreaming, (2006), directed by Colin Goh and Woo Yen Yen
A cogent portrayal of the local obsession with what are known locally as the 5Cs: cash, credit card, car, condo and country club. The story revolves around the members of an extended family who try to win over their parents' favour and hard-earned cash.

Singapore GaGa (2005), directed by Tan Pin Pin
In this acclaimed documentary, the director explores what it means to be Singaporean through the aural landscape created by ordinary people.

Cinemas
Cineplexes mostly screen commercial movies and are found in almost every mall. Listed below are screens that are more likely to show arthouse films that have toured the festival circuit. Listings for film screening times are available in daily papers.

Alliance Française de Singapour
1 Sarkies Road; tel: 6737 8422; www.alliancefrancaise.org.sg; MRT: Newton

Below: Eric Khoo's *Be With Me* is inspired by Theresa Chan's life story.

Food and Drink

There are few places in the world where life revolves around food like it does in Singapore. Singaporeans talk about food all the time, displaying remarkable critical abilities in all matters gastronomic. They can debate on where to get the freshest seafood, the spiciest chilli sauce, the best chicken rice or satay for hours on end and preferably over a meal. Whether served on polystyrene plates in a rough-and-ready food centre or on bone china in a chi-chi restaurant, food is a major focus in Singapore. There are few cuisines that are not represented in Singapore, so much so that the choice is wonderfully daunting.

Cultural and Culinary Diversity

Singapore's extraordinary cultural diversity has given it an explosion of flavours – Chinese, Malay, Indian – and the hybrid Peranakan cuisine that is entirely its own.

PERANAKAN CUISINE

Peranakans are descendants of early immigrants from China who settled in Penang, Melaka and Singapore and married local Malay women. The product of this union is the unique Peranakan culture and a cuisine that imaginatively blends Chinese ingredients with Malay spices and herbs.

Central to the cuisine is *rempah*, a mixture of spices and herbs such as chillies, shallots, lemon grass, candlenuts, turmeric and *belacan* (shrimp paste), ground by hand in a pestle and mortar. It is this nose-tickling mixture that imparts a distinctive flavour and aroma to Peranakan cuisine.

Although best eaten in a Peranakan home, the food can be enjoyed in a small number of restaurants. Look out for dishes like *otak otak*, a blend of fish, coconut milk, chilli paste, galangal and herbs wrapped in banana leaf. Another is *ayam buah keluak*, which combines chicken with Indonesian black nuts to produce a rich gravy. Be sure to leave room for the desserts, which are colourful cakes and sticky sweet delicacies usually with coconut milk as the main ingredient.

CHINESE CUISINE

While there are unique Singapore-inspired Chinese dishes like chilli or pepper crabs, the large Chinese population here generally ensures the authenticity of the cuisine. The meal is usually eaten in the traditional style – by helping oneself with chopsticks to a selection of dishes shared by all diners.

The adaptation to regional and climatic demands, as well as foreign influence, has led to a great variety of cuisines from all over China. In Singapore you don't just say you'll eat Chinese; it will be Sichuan, Cantonese, Teochew or any of a dozen distinct types of food from China's various regions.

Below: a favourite get-together for Chinese families is a dim sum brunch at a Chinese restaurant or teahouse.

Left: South Indian fare features fiery-hot dishes.

generally mild, although anything prefixed by the word *masala* is likely to be spicy. The so-called 'banana leaf' restaurants in Little India are well known for their spicy fare served on banana leaves.

Indian Muslim food is very popular in Singapore. One speciality is *murtabak*, which is a fluffy pan-fried bread stuffed with minced lamb or chicken. When the bread is served plain, it is called *prata*. Another is *nasi briyani*, a fragrant rice dish redolent of saffron and cooked with seasoned mutton or chicken.

MALAY CUISINE

Malay food in Singapore is an amalgam of traditional dishes from Peninsular Malaysia with strong influences from the Indonesian islands of Sumatra and Java. Rice is the staple that counterbalances the spiciness of the food. Malay dishes are flavoured with a wide array of spices and herbs such as lemon grass, kaffir lime leaves, galangal, tamarind, turmeric, cumin and garlic. Coconut milk is used in gravies, cakes, desserts and drinks. Another vital ingredient is *belacan*, a pungent dried

Below: satay is a signature of Malay cuisine.

shrimp paste often combined with pounded fresh chillies to make *sambal belacan*.

Nasi padang, originally from the Padang area in West Sumatra, with a variety of spicy meat, chicken and vegetable dishes served with rice, is a perennial favourite. Another well-loved snack is satay, small bamboo skewers of marinated beef, mutton or chicken that are grilled over charcoals and served with sliced onion, cucumber, rice cakes and peanut sauce.

INDIAN CUISINE

Indian food, characterised by the complex use of spices, is not always spicy. Northern Indian cuisine is more aromatic than spicy, its rich flavour resulting from the use of spices tempered by yoghurt. The tandoor or clay oven is used for baking leavened *roti* (bread) or naan, and to produce delicious marinated fish or chicken dishes.

Fiery curries are a speciality of southern Indian cuisine, and coconut milk is often used in the gravy instead of yoghurt. *Korma* dishes are

SEAFOOD

Next to Peranakan food, seafood-based cuisine is perhaps the closest there is to a home-grown culinary art. Asian spices combined with Chinese cooking methods create dishes like chilli or pepper crabs, steamed prawns and crispy fried baby squid. Singaporeans adore seafood and will happily make the pilgrimage to the East Coast to find the best seafood restaurants.

Singapore Signatures

A visit to Singapore would not be complete if you did not try these signature dishes. The best versions are usually found in hawker centres.

If you don't fancy local fare, take your pick from the large number of French, Italian, Mediterranean and Greek or Thai, Japanese, Korean and Vietnamese restaurants. Some of the best chefs in the world have been drawn to these shores and set up restaurants here.
(See Restaurants, p.102–13)

Chilli Crabs

Singaporeans will tell you this dish is best made with meaty Sri Lankan crabs. The thick, tangy and spicy gravy is mopped up with fried or steamed buns.

Fish-head Curry

This speciality is unique to the Singaporean Indian community, although many Chinese restaurants are also drawing crowds for their versions. Massive heads of fish are stewed in a spicy gravy, which also holds vegetables like aubergines and okra.

Hainanese Chicken Rice

Chicken is poached in hot stock and then blanched in cold water, rendering it succulent and juicy. The chicken pieces are then served with rice that has been steamed with ginger, garlic and chicken stock, and a vinegary chilli sauce.

Laksa

Rice noodles are bathed in curried coconut gravy that is spiced with herbs and laced with fish cake, cockles, prawns and bean sprouts. The famous Katong laksa can now be found in franchises all across the island.

Sambal Stingray

Thin slabs of stingray (skate) are grilled and served on a banana leaf with a rich layer of chilli jam (sambal) made with chillies and garlic.

Drinks and Desserts

Teh halia, or ginger tea, a staple of Indian drink vendors, is a strong contender to the lattes of Starbucks. So are *kopi tarik* and *teh tarik*, 'pulled coffee' and 'pulled tea' that is poured from cup to pitcher and back again to ensure the ingredients are well mixed.

In hawker centres and food courts, try freshly squeezed fruit juice, cold soya bean milk or sugar-cane juice with a wedge of lemon. The local beer is Tiger, a refreshing pilsner-style beer.

Local desserts to try include *cendol*, which is shaved ice and green jelly strips in coconut milk, and *ice kacang* (or *ais kacang*), shaved ice with red beans, jelly cubes, evaporated milk and coloured syrups.

Hawker Centres

The hawker centre offers multi-ethnic Singapore food at its best. Whether it is a simple dish of noodles for S$3 or a S$20 three-course meal of barbecued fish, chilli prawns and stir-fried vegetables with rice, the cost is a fraction of what you would pay for a similar meal in a restaurant. Low prices aside, the experience is unique, and an enjoyable thing to remember from your stay in this food-crazy city.

Changi Village Food Centre

Block 2 Changi Village Road; daily 7.30am–late; bus: 2, 29, 59 or 109

It's most famous for *nasi lemak*, a coconut-milk-based rice dish with fried chicken, *ikan bilis* (whitebait) and egg; the longest queues are at stall 57. Also check out Charlie's Snack Bar (stall 8) for cheap fish and chips and over 50 varieties of beer.

Chinatown Complex Food Centre

335 Smith Street, Chinatown Complex; daily early morning–late; MRT: Chinatown; map p.138 B3

The stalls here offer a mind-boggling array of Chinese favourites, from *wonton* noodles to roast meats. The basement fresh-produce market is also worth exploring. There's live fish, poultry, flowers and all manner of Asian vegetables.

East Coast Lagoon Food Village

1220 East Coast Parkway, next to car park E2; daily 11am–late; MRT: Bedok, then bus: 401; bus: 31, 36, 43 or 196

Where else can you have some of the best local food in a lovely Indonesian-style structure and just a stone's throw from the sea? Try the curry puffs (stall 28), barbecued-pork noodles (stall 45)

Below: freshly baked buns.

Here's how you order a meal at a hawker centre. If there's a group of you, have one person sit at a table to reserve the seats. The others, having noted the table number, should order their food and tell the hawkers where they are seated at, unless the hawker stall is a self-service operation. If you are on your own, you may have to share a table with strangers if the hawker centre is crowded.

Above: hotels serve local hawker food too.

Above: numerous hawker stalls serving a wide variety of local fare are housed in the Lau Pa Sat Festival Market.

and vermicelli with satay sauce (stall 17). Haron's (stall 55) has the best satay. Best visited at night when all the stalls are open.

Lau Pa Sat Festival Market
Corner of Boon Tat Street and Robinson Road; daily noon–10pm; tel: 6220 2138; www.laupasat.biz; MRT: Raffles Place; map p.139 D2
This Victorian octagonal-shaped structure, whose Hokkien name translates into 'old market', was built in Glasgow and shipped in 1894 to Singapore and reassembled on the waterfront. Formerly a fresh-produce market, it now has some 60 food stalls selling a variety of hawker fare. It underwent a $4 million makeover in 1996. In the evenings, the adjacent **Boon Tat Street** is closed to traffic and transformed into an alfresco dining area with satay hawkers.

Makansutra Gluttons Bay
01-15 Esplanade Mall, 8 Raffles Avenue; www.makansutra.com; Mon–Thur 5pm–2am, Fri–Sat 5pm–3am, Sun 4pm–1am; MRT: City Hall; map p.136 B1
The people behind Singapore's hawker-food bible *Makansutra* have gathered up to 10 of the best

hawker stalls in Singapore together in this unbeatable waterfront location.

Newton Food Centre
Newton Circus, 500 Clemenceau Avenue; daily noon–1am; MRT: Newton; map p.132 A2
The prices at this noisy and packed hawker centre are higher than at other food centres, but it is still a great place to order barbecued seafood and Hokkien fried noodles.

Tekka Centre
665 Buffalo Road; daily 7am–10pm; MRT: Little India; map p.132 C1
Stalls selling Malay, Chinese and Indian food draw sizeable crowds here for breakfast. Tekka also has a fresh-produce market with an amazing array of fresh produce seldom found elsewhere in Singapore. Upstairs are clothing, brassware and antiques shops.

Cookery Schools

at-sunrice
Fort Canning Centre, Fort Canning Park, Canning Rise; tel: 6336 3307; www.at-sunrice.com; MRT: City Hall or Dhoby Ghaut; map p.136 A2
This culinary centre offers cooking demonstrations, tasting classes and hands-

on cooking classes on Asian cuisine. Some of their short courses include 'Techniques of Healthy Cooking and Nutrition', 'Soups, Stocks and Sauces' and 'Singapore Cuisine'.

Coriander Leaf Cooking Studio
3A Merchant Court, 01-12 Clarke Quay, River Valley Road; tel: 6732 3354; www.coriander leaf.com; MRT: Clarke Quay; map p.135 E1
This culinary school emphasises home cooking. Its half-day courses are held in a studio and highlight the best of South Asian, Southeast Asian, Middle Eastern and fusion cooking. Coriander Leaf also runs an excellent fusion restaurant. SEE RESTAURANTS, P.102

Shermay's Cooking School
01-76 Chip Bee Gardens, Block 43 Jalan Merah Saga; tel: 6479 8442; www.shermay.com; MRT: Buona Vista
Cookbook author Shermay Lee teaches Peranakan cuisine based on her grandmother's traditional recipes. There are also other classes on French and Chinese cuisine and European and local pastries to suit both novice and advanced chefs.

65

Gay and Lesbian

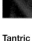

Singapore has a thriving gay and lesbian community, despite the fact that homosexual sex is outlawed. The government has in recent years become more accepting of homosexuality, and has openly acknowledged that the civil service does not discriminate against the hiring of gays. In general, though, Singapore society is still fairly conservative; public displays of gay affection are likely to draw stares. But that's as much response as you'll get, as Singaporeans do not usually react aggressively to homosexuality. There are a good number of gay and lesbian bars, mostly located in the Tanjong Pagar area.

Gay Bars and Clubs

BackStage Bar
13A Trengganu Street; tel: 6227 1712; www.backstagebar.moonfruit.com; Sun–Thur 7pm–2am, Fri–Sat 7pm–3am; MRT: Chinatown; map p.138 B3
The posters of Broadway musicals set this venue's stall out. There are several floors in this place, so feel free to wander around. Watch an old movie on a sofa or pose at the bar. The booze here is very cheap, so guests are often very happy.

Play
21 Tanjong Pagar Road; tel: 6227 7400; www.playclub.com.sg; Wed–Fri 9pm–3pm, Sat 9pm–4am, MRT: Chinatown; map p.138 B2
The dance floor here is always packed, with some shirtless eye candy to sweeten the deal too. Hot local DJs play to a mixed crowd of gay men, lesbians and their straight friends.

Taboo
65/67 Neil Road; tel: 6225 6256; www.taboo.sg; Wed–Thur 8pm–2am, Fri 10pm–3am, Sat 10pm–4am; MRT: Outram Park or Tanjong Pagar; map p.138 B2
One of the longest-surviving gay clubs in Singapore, Taboo is spread over three floors and boasts a happy hour that lasts till midnight. On the first level, a DJ spins pop remixes and guests chill out at the long bar. On the second floor, there are comfy sofas and a heaving dance crowd. The attic is a decidedly cosier place, where groups of people sit around and chat over drinks. There are special events aplenty here, such as Bodwatch (a swimsuit show) and Handbag Night every second Saturday of the month (expect handbag tunes and diva music).

In 2001 Singapore hosted its first national gay party on Sentosa that was such a hit, it evolved into a three-day annual event. Gay men from all over Asia flew into Singapore to partake of the revelry, so much so that the government soon put an end to it by withdrawing the organisers' permit.

Tantric
78 Neil Road; tel: 6423 9232; www.backstagebar.moonfruit.com; Sat 8–4pm; MRT: Outram Park or Tanjong Pagar; map p.138 B2
It is hard to miss Tantric, thanks to the flashy rainbow flag at its front. Like its sister bar BackStage, it has an alfresco area and a small interior. The vibe here tends to be a bit sleazy – the expat men draw plenty of local fans and the prices for drinks are suitably stiff. Most people come here for a few chasers before heading to Taboo.

Lesbian Bars and Clubs

The Empire
4/F, 114 Neil Road; tel: 6536 0456; Mon–Thur 8pm–1am, Fri–Sat 8pm–3am; MRT: Outram Park or Tanjong Pagar; map p.138 B2
It is women only at this relaxed rooftop bar, which offers a fantastic view of the surrounding area. There's a pool table and an extensive menu of martinis. At weekends the tables make

Left: homosexuality is still a sensitive issue in Singapore.

Girl parties are held regularly in Singapore. These include the very popular Herstory bashes that include 'pageants' like Butch Hunt and Femme Quest, as well as 'Herstory Idol', where winners are decided by lesbian voters. Check out www.herstory.ws and www.twoqueensparty.me for event listings.

way for a dance floor where the ladies let rip.

Cows & Coolies
30 Mosque Street; tel: 6221 1239; Mon–Thur 5pm–1am, Fri–Sat 5pm–2am;
MRT: Chinatown; map p.138 C3
This is where Mandarin-speaking ladies hang out and sing Chinese pop hits or play pool.

Crocodile Rock
05-29 Far East Plaza, 14 Scotts Road; tel: 6738 0535; Tue–Wed 7.30pm–midnight, Thur 7.30pm–1am, Fri–Sat 7.30pm–3am; MRT: Orchard; map p.134 B1
This lesbian pub has been in business for 15 years and counts a couple of men as part of their regular clientele. Like most lesbian crowds in Singapore, the guests here love a good karaoke session too.

Websites

Various websites offer excellent social networking for gay and lesbians in the Asian region. Check out www.fridae.com and www.trevvy.com for the latest happenings and to see what's getting the community hot under the collar.

Given Singapore's strict rules against homosexual activity, it is no wonder that groups like **People Like Us** (www.plu.sg) are constantly campaigning for legislative changes.

For more information, you can also head down to **Pelangi Pride Centre** (www.pelangipridecentre.org), which has a good library and archive.

Right: despite the restrictions, Singapore still has a vibrant gay party scene.

History

1365

The Javanese *Nagarakretagama* records a settlement called Temasek – the old name that used to refer to Singapore.

1390S

Temasek is settled by a scion of the Srivijaya empire, Parameswara (also known as Iskandar Shah).

14–15TH CENTURIES

Siam (Thailand), followed by Java's Majapahit empire, seizes Temasek. Temasek exists as a vassal of the Malay kingdom of Melaka and is governed by a *temenggong* (chief) from Johor.

17TH CENTURY

Singapore is forgotten and left to the Orang Laut (sea nomads).

1819

Sir Thomas Stamford Raffles, representing the British East India Company, arrives in Singapore. The *temenggong* and Sultan Hussein allow Raffles to open a trading post in Singapore in exchange for money.

1824

The British agree to withdraw from Indonesia, in return for Dutch recognition of British rights over Singapore. Singapore is ceded to the British.

1826

The trading stations in Penang, Melaka and Singapore are named the Straits Settlements, under the administration of the East India Company.

1867

The Straits Settlements become a Crown Colony controlled by the Colonial Offiice in London.

1911

The population of Singapore grows to 250,000 and the census records 48 races, speaking 54 languages, on the island.

1920S

The Great Depression's effects are felt in Singapore as prices of commodities, such as rubber, collapse.

1942

The Japanese occupy Singapore for 3½ years. It is renamed Syonan, the 'Light of the South'.

1945

Japanese rule end in August, with the landing of Allied troops.

1946

The British declare Singapore a Crown Colony.

1948

The British allow limited elections to the Legislative Council. A state of emergency is declared following the Malayan Communist Party's uprising against imperialism.

1951

Three Legislative Council elections. Singapore is formally proclaimed a city with a royal charter.

1955

Rendel Commission granted by the British leads to elections; David Marshall becomes the chief minister.

1956

PAP Central Executive Committee elections, in which the Communists decline to run, are held. Chinese students riot; PAP leaders are arrested.

1958

A constitutional agreement for partial independence for Singapore is signed in London.

1959

The People's Action Party (PAP) wins 43 out of 51 seats in the fiirst elections. Lee Kuan Yew becomes the fiirst prime minister.

1963

Singapore joins the Federation of Malaysia, made up of Malaya, Sabah (North Borneo) and Sarawak.

1964

PAP wins only one seat in the Malaysian general elections. Communal riots ensue.

1965

Singapore leaves the Malaysian federation, becoming an independent nation. The country joins the Commonwealth and the United Nations.

1967

Singapore, Malaysia, Thailand, Indonesia and the Philippines form the Association of Southeast Asian Nations (ASEAN).

1968

PAP sweeps the fiirst parliamentary general elections, winning all 58 seats.

1978

The British Far East Command ceases.

1981

In a by-election, J.B. Jeyaretnam of the Workers' Party wins the fiirst seat to be held by a member of an opposition party.

1987

The US$5 billion Mass Rapid Transit (MRT) system opens.

1990

Goh Chok Tong becomes prime minister. The amended constitution provides for an elected president.

1991

PAP's share of votes in the general elections falls to 59.7 percent, the lowest since it has been in power.

1996

Singapore is no longer regarded as a developing nation by the OECD.

1998

Singapore's economy is affected by the economic crisis in Southeast Asia.

1999

President Ong Teng Cheong steps down. S.R. Nathan is elected as the president.

2000

Economic growth hits 10.1 percent.

2001

Goh Chok Tong leads PAP to win 75.3 percent of votes in the general elections. Unemployment reaches 4.7 percent, a 15-year high.

2002

An Al-Qaeda-linked terrorist plot to bomb the US embassy is uncovered. The S$600 million Esplanade – Theatres on the Bay opens.

2003

Outbreak of Severe Acute Respiratory Syndrome (SARS) in April is quickly controlled. The North-East MRT line opens.

2004

Prime Minister Lee Hsien Loong takes offiice. The economy shows positive signs of recovery.

2005

Plans to build two 'integrated resorts', mega entertainment and leisure complexes, in Marina Bay and Sentosa are afoot.

2006

PAP wins 66.6 percent of votes in the general elections, sweeping all but two seats.

2007

Singapore acquires rights to host a leg of the Formula 1 World Championships.

2008

The 165-metre-high Singapore Flyer is launched, making it the world's tallest Giant Observation Wheel.

2009

Singapore hosts the Asia-Pacifiic Economic Cooperation (APEC) meetings for the fiirst time.

Hotels

There are myriad grades of hotels in Singapore to suit all budgets. Be it luxury accommodation from internationally renowned brand names, funky boutique outfits that appeal to the trendy jetsetter, or budget digs and backpacker hostels, visitors are – to put it mildly – spoiled for choice. Most visitors prefer to stay in the city, around the Civic District and Orchard Road, where the more expensive hotels are clustered. But if you want to avoid the crowds and stiff prices, head to Little India or Chinatown for cheaper-but-cheerful options. Here are our favourite places to lay your hat.

Singapore River

The Fullerton

1 Fullerton Square; tel: 6733 8388; www.fullertonhotel.com; $$$$; MRT: Raffles Place; map p.139 D4

Business travellers will appreciate its proximity to the financial district. Its contemporary art deco interior is filled with Philippe Starck fittings, and there are excellent restaurants and the trendy Post Bar on site. One Fullerton across the road entices with more waterfront wining and dining options.
SEE ALSO ARCHITECTURE, P.28

Gallery

1 Nanson Road; tel: 6849 8686; www.galleryhotel.com.sg; $$$; MRT: Clarke Quay, then taxi; map p.135 D1

With its postmodernist architecture and compact rooms and suites artfully decorated by young artists, this is definitely a hotel for design-conscious visitors. Many rooms overlook the Singapore River. Complimentary Internet access is provided in every room.

Grand Copthorne Waterfront

392 Havelock Road; tel: 6733 0880; www.millenniumhotels.com.sg; $$$; MRT: Clarke Quay or Tiong Bahru, then taxi; map p.135 C1

This may be a modern business hotel but it is also ideal for partiers as it is situated right next door to one of Singapore's best dance clubs, Zouk. Rooms are all equipped with broadband Internet access.

Marina Bay

Conrad Centennial

2 Temasek Boulevard; tel: 6334 8888; www.conradhotels.com; $$$$; MRT: City Hall; map p.136 C2

Stylish, modern business hotel adjacent to Suntec City and Marina Square, making it a great location for shopping. It has large rooms, marble-clad bathrooms and an outdoor swimming pool with a bar.

Below: the rooms at the Gallery are decorated by young artists.

> Price categories are for a double room without breakfast and taxes:
> $$$$ = over S$300
> $$$= S$200–300
> $$= S$100–200
> $= under S$100

Left: funky furnishings in the New Majestic's lobby *(see p.73).*

and modern architecture. It is located just across sights like the Armenian Church and Fort Canning Park. Also well known for its Spa Park Asia.

Hangout@Mt Emily
10A Upper Wilkie Road; tel: 6438 5588; www.hangout hotels.com; $; MRT: Dhoby Ghaut; map p.136 A4
Funky budget-class hotel. Clean and comfortable but no frills. You sleep in Zonk Out rooms, meet fellow travellers in the Veg Out lounge, eat at the Pig Out café, and exercise at the Work Out room.

Hotel Grand Pacific
101 Victoria Street; tel: 6336 0811; www.allsonhotels.com; $$; MRT: City Hall; map p.136 B3
This good-value hotel is close to the museum district. The guest rooms are designed with a contemporary skew. Facilities include an outdoor swimming pool and work-out room.

Hotel Rendezvous
9 Bras Basah Road; tel: 6336 0220; www.rendezvoushotels. com: $$$; MRT: Dhoby Ghaut; map p.136 A3
Modern-style hotel located close to the Singapore Art Museum. Its **Rendezvous restaurant** is known for *nasi padang* (Indonesian-style rice and curries), and the Palong lobby bar is ideal for relaxing after a day of sightseeing.
SEE ALSO RESTAURANTS, P.104

Raffles
1 Beach Road; tel: 6337 1886; www.raffles.com; $$$$; MRT: City Hall; map p.136 B2
The city's most famous (and most expensive) luxury hotel, beautifully restored to its former grandeur. A total of 14 restaurants and bars, offering everything from fine-dining

---

www.yoursingapore.com is set up by the Singapore Tourism Board as a hotel directory and search facility. www.stayinsingapore.com is the Singapore Hotel Association's website.

Mandarin Oriental
5 Raffles Avenue; tel: 6338 0066; www.mandarinoriental.com; $$$$; MRT: City Hall; map p.136 C1
Formerly known as the Oriental, this offers rooms with excellent views of the surrounding bay area on the higher floors. Located opposite Suntec City and next to Marina Square shopping mall. Several restaurants serving American, Chinese, Italian and Japanese cuisines.

Pan Pacific
7 Raffles Boulevard; tel: 6336 8111; www.singapore.pan pacific.com; $$$$; MRT: City Hall; map p.136 C1
This John Portman-designed five-star hotel boasts a lofty 35-storey atrium and comfortable, good-sized rooms. Good restaurants, a bakery and lounge bar.

Ritz-Carlton Millenia
7 Raffles Avenue; tel: 6337 8888; www.ritzcarlton.com; $$$$; MRT: City Hall; map p.137 C1
With an impressive contemporary art collection and Singapore's largest guest rooms, plus stunning bathrooms with views to match. Restaurants serve Western, Cantonese and seafood cuisines. The bar with a riveting glass sculpture as its talking point is perfect for after-dinner drinks.

The Civic District

Carlton
76 Bras Basah Road; tel: 6338 8333; www.carlton.com.sg; $$$; MRT: City Hall; map p.136 B2
In the heart of the museum district and near the Chijmes entertainment hub. Premier rooms in the Annex Wing offer marble bathrooms and flat-screen TVs.

Grand Park City Hall
10 Coleman Street; tel: 6336 3456; www.parkhotelgroup. com; $$–$$$; MRT: City Hall; map p.136 A2
This business hotel is a combination of both traditional

71

Above: top-notch service at Raffles.

Continental to innovative fusion. Expect old-world atmosphere and charm.
SEE ALSO MONUMENTS, P.80; SHOPPING, P.116

Strand
25 Bencoolen Street; tel: 6338 1866; www.strandhotel.com.sg; $; MRT: Bugis or Dhoby Ghaut; map p.136 A3
Clean and comfortable and one of the better budget hotels around. Close to the museum district and Chijmes, and within walking distance of Orchard Road. Its café on the ground level is great for coffee and sandwiches.

Swissôtel The Stamford
2 Stamford Road; tel: 6338 8585; www.swissotel-the stamford.com; $$$$;
MRT: City Hall; map p.136 B2
Formerly the world's tallest hotel until it was supplanted

in mid 1999, this hotel is practically part of the large shopping complex Raffles City. Business travellers are well catered to with its business and convention centres. Several restaurants and bars, including the excellent **Equinox** complex, plus a luxurious spa and well-equipped fitness centre.
SEE ALSO RESTAURANTS, P.104

Chinatown and the CBD

Amara
165 Tanjong Pagar Road; tel: 6879 2555; www.amara hotels.com; $$$; MRT: Tanjong Pagar; map p.138 B1
Chic hotel with a spa, fitness centre, swimming pool and tennis courts. Dining options include its award-winning Thai restaurant **Thanying**, as well as a Chinese restaurant and coffee shop.
SEE ALSO RESTAURANTS, P.106

Berjaya
83 Duxton Road; tel: 6227 7678; www.berjayaresorts.com; $$; MRT: Tanjong Pagar; map p.138 B2
A boutique property occupying a row of restored shophouses. Rooms are smallish, but the Garden Suites have their own little courtyard.

Furama City Centre
60 Eu Tong Sen Street; tel: 6533 3888; www.furama.com/ citycentre; $$; MRT: Chinatown; map p.138 C4
After a S$22 million renovation to woo business travellers, the rooms are now comfortable and cosy. Good location for shopping and nightlife as it is near Boat Quay and Clarke Quay.

Hotel 1929
50 Keong Saik Road; tel: 6347 1929; www.hotel1929.com; $$; MRT: Outram Park; map p.138 B3
Ultra-hip boutique hotel in the heart of Chinatown that has made headlines in numerous design magazines. Highlights here include a rooftop jacuzzi, the well-known contemporary European restaurant **Ember**, and retro vintage furniture in the pretty, although small, rooms.
SEE ALSO RESTAURANTS, P.106

Link
50 Tiong Bahru Road; tel: 6622 8585; www.linkhotel.com.sg; $$; MRT: Tiong Bahru or Outram Park, then taxi
Luxury meets the heartlands in this boutique hotel converted from two blocks of apartments. Inside it is all plush and contemporary Asian design; outside is an experience all unto itself – at its doorstep are a popular hawker centre and an old-world bird arena where elderly folk make a sport of coaxing their birds to break into song.

M Hotel
81 Anson Road; tel: 6224 1133; www.mhotel.com.sg; $$$; MRT: Tanjong Pagar; map p.138 C1
Excellent location in the financial district for business travellers. It offers wireless Internet access throughout the hotel and top-notch business facilities, including fully furnished and serviced offices. Rooms have harbour or city views.

If yours is the child that gets nothing but the best, consider luxury hotel rooms specially created for children. The Four Seasons Singapore and Swissôtel The Stamford offer fully furnished children's rooms complete with plush toys, mini bathrobes, slippers, cutlery and other child-friendly accessories.

Above: Hotel 1929 has cosy, stylish rooms.

New Majestic
31–37 Bukit Pasoh Road; tel: 6511 4700; www.newmajestic hotel.com; $$$; MRT: Outram Park; map p.138 B2
So cool it almost hurts. Different themed rooms with unique murals are a draw, as is the small swimming pool with portholes at the bottom, which look down to the lauded modern Cantonese restaurant **Majestic**.
SEE ALSO RESTAURANTS, P.105

Royal Peacock
55 Keong Saik Road; tel: 6223 3522; www.royalpeacockhotel. com; $$; MRT: Outram Park; map p.138 B2
Baroque-style décor and jewel-toned colours in this boutique hotel. Rooms have plush purple carpeting, red walls and wooden sleigh beds.

Scarlet
33 Erskine Road; tel: 6511 3333; www.thescarlethotel.com; $$; MRT: Tanjong Pagar or Chinatown; map p.138 C3
Sexy, gothic and like a deep, dark boudoir, this Baroque-inspired boutique hotel

Price categories are for a double room without breakfast and taxes:
$$$$ = over S$300
$$$ = S$200–300
$$ = S$100–200
$ = under S$100

attracts media and design types who come here to drink at the rooftop bar and sup at the acclaimed restaurant. The rooms are small and there's a tiny jacuzzi and gym.

Orchard Road

Four Seasons
190 Orchard Boulevard; tel: 6734 1110; www.fourseasons. com/singapore; $$$$; MRT: Orchard; map p.134 B4
A statement in understated elegance, this hotel is located just behind Orchard Road. Luxurious interiors, large plush rooms and expensive artworks belie its rather plain façade. Restaurants serve contemporary fare and refined Cantonese cuisine, plus a cosy alfresco bar with views of Orchard Road. Its air-conditioned tennis courts are a dream in humid Singapore.

Goodwood Park Hotel
22 Scotts Road; tel: 6737 7411; www.goodwoodparkhotel.com. sg; $$$; MRT: Orchard
Charming historical building dating back to 1900 that used to serve as a social club for the German community. Its suites open out to the swimming pool. Five acclaimed eateries, including a grill, Chinese restaurant and coffee lounge for local high tea.
SEE ALSO MONUMENTS, P.80

Grand Hyatt
10 Scotts Road; tel: 6738 1234; www.singapore.grand.hyatt.com; $$$$; MRT: Orchard; map p.134 B1
Minimalist, almost stark décor, comfortable rooms and excellent service. Its eateries – including the stylish **mezza9** with an elegant **martini bar**, and Straits Kitchen serving local fare – are very popular. Its free-form pool with lush gardens is a haven in this busy neck of the woods.
SEE ALSO NIGHTLIFE, P.96; RESTAURANTS, P.107

Mandarin Orchard
333 Orchard Road; tel: 6737 4411; www.meritus-hotels.com; $$$$; MRT: Orchard or Somerset; map p.135 C4
Serious shoppers would do well to stay here as all the major malls and boutiques are within walking distance. Its **Chatterbox** coffee house is noted for its rendition of a Singaporean favourite: Hainanese chicken rice.
SEE ALSO RESTAURANTS, P.108

Marriott
320 Orchard Road; tel: 6735 5800; www.marriott.com; $$$$; MRT: Orchard; map p.134 C4
The pagoda-roofed landmark is perfect for shoppers and partiers. Its Crossroads

Below: the New Majestic's pool has portholes that overlook the Majestic restaurant.

73

Above: drinks in the lounge at the Royal Plaza on Scotts.

alfresco café is the place to watch the world pass by, while the TANGS department store is just next door.

Orchard
442 Orchard Road; tel: 6734 7766; www.orchardhotel.com.sg; $$$; MRT: Orchard; map p.134 B1

Deluxe rooms in the Orchard and Claymore wings have been recently refurbished. The lobby coffee shop serves both buffet and à la carte meals; Hua Ting restaurant is one of the best in town for Cantonese cuisine and dim sum.

The Regent
1 Cuscaden Road; tel: 6733 8888; www.regenthotels.com; $$$$; MRT: Orchard; map p.134 A1

Large, well-appointed rooms and excellent service expected of the Regent

Price categories are for a double room without breakfast and taxes:
$$$$ = over S$300
$$$ = S$200–300
$$ = S$100–200
$ = under S$100

brand. Café with both Western and Asian dishes and Cantonese restaurant serving good dim sum. The Orchard MRT station is a 10-minute walk away.

RELC International
30 Orange Grove Road; tel: 6885 7888; www.relcih.com.sg; $$; MRT: Orchard; map p.134 A2

The humble neighbour to the upscale Shangri-La, this still manages to impress. Rooms are spacious with balconies and business travellers will appreciate its well-equipped conference rooms.

Royal Plaza on Scotts
25 Scotts Road; tel: 6737 7966; www.royalplaza.com.sg; $$$; MRT: Orchard; map p.134 B1

Owned by the Sultan of Brunei, this business hotel has an excellent location for shoppers. Perks include a complimentary mini-bar in all rooms and proximity to the adjacent DFS Galleria mall.

Shangri-La
22 Orange Grove Road; tel: 6737 3644; www.shangri-la.com; $$$$; MRT: Orchard; map p.134 A2

Its three towers are set amid luxuriant gardens. The plush Valley Wing is where visiting heads of state and other VIPs have stayed. There are superb Cantonese and classy Californian eateries, an excellent Japanese restaurant and a 24-hour coffee shop. Orchard MRT station is a good 15-minute walk away, though.

YMCA International House
1 Orchard Road; tel: 6336 6000; www.ymcaih.com.sg; $$; MRT: Dhoby Ghaut; map p.136 A3

Situated at the top end of Orchard Road, this has a rooftop swimming pool, fitness centre and cybercafé. Choose from guest rooms with attached bathrooms or four-person dormitories.

Little India

Albert Court Village
180 Albert Street; tel: 6339 3939; www.albertcourt.com.sg; $$; MRT: Little India; map p.136 A4

A boutique hotel adjacent to the Little India district. The interior décor exudes nostalgic charm, furnished with Peranakan teak carvings and old brassware. The comforts, however, are thoroughly modern. No pool.

Parkroyal on Kitchener Road
181 Kitchener Road; tel: 6428 3000; www.parkroyalhotels.com; $$$; MRT: Farrer Park; map p.133 D2

This newly refurbished hotel, formerly the New Park, caters to corporate travellers with the usual business mod cons. But leisure travellers will not be

If you find yourself at the airport but with no place to spend the night in Singapore, head to the Singapore Hotel Association counters at Terminals 1 and 2, where staff at their four counters can help. Two of those counters are open 24 hours.

disappointed with its spacious rooms and great location close to Serangoon Road.

Perak

12 Perak Road, tel: 6299 7733; www.peraklodge.com; $; MRT: Little India; map p.133 C1

This occupies a restored shophouse. Lovely atmosphere with friendly staff, plus a courtyard with a fish pond. All rooms come with electronic room safes and breakfast.

Sentosa

Amara Sanctuary Resort Sentosa

1 Larkhill Road; tel: 6825 3888; www.amarasanctuary.com; $$$$; MRT: HarbourFront, then resort shuttle bus from VivoCity

A brand-new resort nestled on a hillside, this is surrounded by 3.5 hectares (8.6 acres) of gardens and natural tropical rainforest. Design-wise it is an exotic blend of colonial architecture and modern concepts. The beautiful guest rooms, suites and villas provide plush comfort and state-of-the-art facilities.

Capella

1 The Knolls, Sentosa; tel: 6377 8888; www.capellasingapore.com; MRT: HarbourFront, then resort shuttle bus from VivoCity

Built to complement the new integrated resort nearby, this temple of luxury boasts the biggest designer names from architect Lord Norman Foster to fashion designer Peter Som in its 'company of creators'. Play on the championship golf course that's just a stone's throw away, or sink into the sumptuous guest rooms and villas that overlook the South China Sea.

The Sentosa

2 Bukit Manis Road; tel: 6275 0331; www.thesentosa.com; $$$; MRT: HarbourFront, then resort shuttle bus from VivoCity

This resort-style hotel on a forested hill is so stunning, you

might be tempted to park yourself here and not venture into the city. Features hotel-style rooms and suites and villas with private pools. **The Cliff** serves superb seafood, and the sea-facing bar is perfect for sunset cocktails. Be sure to book a massage at its **Spa Botanica**.

SEE ALSO PAMPERING, P.99; RESTAURANTS, P.110

Shangri-La's Rasa Sentosa Resort

101 Siloso Road; tel: 6275 0100; www.shangri-la.com; $$$; MRT: HarbourFront, then resort shuttle bus from HarbourFront Centre

Singapore's only beachfront hotel overlooks the South China Sea. It serves a fine buffet breakfast and has good restaurants. Not the most convenient place to stay at, but it offers plenty of recreational activities, from sailing to cycling. Ideal for families. Currently undergoing renovations; the hotel is scheduled to reopen in 2011.

The East Coast

Changi Village

1 Netheravon Road; tel: 6379 7111; www.changivillage.com.sg; $$; MRT: Tanah Merah; bus 2 or 9

A multimillion-dollar renovation has transformed this former transit hotel into a chic resort. Free shuttle service from the airport to the city. Changi Beach and Changi Village nearby are great places to chill out at.

Grand Mercure Roxy

50 East Coast Road; tel: 6344 8000; www.mercure.com; $$; bus 16, 31, 135 or 196

Value-for-money four-star hotel with the Parkway Parade Shopping Centre just opposite. It is also a short walk to the East Coast beach. Spacious rooms with a contemporary look, café and Chinese restaurant. No MRT station nearby, but buses across the street service the city.

Below: the lobby at the Amara Sanctuary Sentosa Resort.

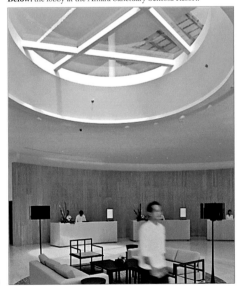

Literature

Singapore's literature is published in its four main languages: English, Chinese, Malay and Tamil. Most of the country's literary works portray and explore various aspects of Singapore society. Given the small domestic market, it cannot be said that local literature has a huge following. Yet that doesn't mean that Singaporean's aren't voracious readers. On any given day, the major bookshops like Borders and Kinokuniya see a healthy crowd. Like their outlook in life, Singaporeans' tastes in books are international; weekly bestseller lists include books by authors like Dan Brown and Mitch Albom.

Poets and Authors

Many recognise Singapore's first-generation writers as those who emerged with the country's independence in 1965. Names like Edwin Thumboo, Arthur Yap, Goh Poh Seng, Lee Tzu Pheng and Chandran Nair published mainly poetry in English. Today's Singaporean poets are a new generation under the age of 40, including Alvin Pang, Cyril Wong, Felix Cheong and Alfian Sa'at. They have published works both in Singapore and internationally.

Short stories are often the choice for local fiction writers. Goh Poh Seng's *If We Dream Too Long* (1972) is widely recognised as the first true Singaporean novel. Catherine Lim, Singapore's most widely read author – due in no small part to her first two books of short stories, *Little Ironies: Stories of Singapore* (1978) and *Or Else, the Lightning God and Other Stories* (1980), being GCSE set texts.

Over the last few years, the leading non-fiction author has been Singapore's former Prime Minister Lee Kwan Yew.

Considered the founder of modern Singapore, Lee has written two books, which sold out within days of release.

Another Singaporean non-fiction best-seller was 2009's *Men In White*, written by Sonny Yap, Leong Weng Kam and Richard Lim, all senior staffers of the main local newspaper *The Straits Times*.

Further Reading

GENERAL

The Air-Conditioned Nation: Essays on the Politics of Comfort and Control, by Cherian George (Landmark, 2000). Insights into what makes Singapore tick.

Complete Notes from Singapore: The Omnibus Edition, by Neil Humphreys (Marshall Cavendish Editions, 2007). A British humourist writes on Singapore's idiosyncracies.

From Third World To First: The Singapore Story: 1965–2000, by Lee Kuan Yew (HarperCollins, 2000). The man responsible for Singapore's transformation tells his story.

Singapore The Encyclopedia, by various authors (Editions Didier Millet, 2006).

Writing under the pseudonym James Lee, Australian-born Jim Aitchinson publishes more than a dozen books a year for his series *Mr Midnight*. This Asian series of horror and suspense stories for children is a runaway hit, with over 40 volumes already in print since 1998. His readers are invited to send in story ideas, which he then adapts into his books.

Everything you've always wanted to know about Singapore is in here.

FICTION AND POETRY

Foreign Bodies, by Hwee Hwee Tan (Michael Joseph, 1997). Asiaweek hailed it one of the 'Best Books of 1999', while a local reviewer called it 'fascinatingly shallow'.

One Fierce Hour, by Alfian Sa'at (Landmark, 1998). Highly charged poems about life in Singapore by this acclaimed poet and playwright.

Raffles Place Ragtime, by Philip Jeyaretnam (Times Books International, 1988). About love and ambition in Singapore.

BESTSELLER

Left: browsing in Kinokuniya.

The Shrimp People, by Rex Shelley (Times Books International, 1991). An evocative tale on Singapore's Eurasians that won the National Book Prize.

Bookstores

25 Degrees Celcius
25 Keong Saik Road; tel: 6327 8389; www.25degreec.com; Mon–Sat 11am–7pm; MRT: Outram Park; map p.138 B2
A bookstore-cum-café that specialises in cook books.

Books Actually/ Polymath & Crust
86 Club Street; tel: 6222 9195; www.booksactually.com; Mon–Sat 11am–9pm, Sun noon–6pm; MRT: Chinatown; p.138 C3
Now spanning three levels, Books Actually and its sister Polymath & Crust stock lesser-known works and titles from small foreign presses.

Books Kinokuniya
03-09/15 Ngee Ann City; tel: 6737 5021; www.kinokuniya. com.sg; Sun–Fri 10am– 9.30pm, Sat 10am–10pm; MRT: Orchard; map p.134 C4
This huge store has just about every English-language title imaginable. Also has books in Chinese, French and German.

Borders
1/F, Wheelock Place, 501 Orchard Road; tel: 6235 7146; www. borders.com.sg; Sun–Thur 9am–11pm, Fri–Sat 9am–midnight; MRT: Orchard; map p.134 B4
This American chain outlet is popular and always packed.

Earshot
1/F, The Arts House, 1 Old Parliament Lane; tel: 6334 0130; www.earshot.com.sg; daily 11am–10pm; MRT: Raffles Place; map p.139 D4
This bookshop-music store-café carries many local works.

Harris Book Company
04-25/26/27/28 313@Somerset,

Below: Wheelock Place is home to Borders bookstore.

313 Orchard Road; tel: 6514 6755; www.harrisbook.com; daily 10.30am–10.30pm; MRT: Somerset; map p.135 D3
Excellent English-language bookstore with a good collection of periodicals.

MPH
B1-24/25/26 Raffles City Shopping Centre, 252 North Bridge Road; tel: 6336 4232; www.mph. com.sg; daily 10am–10pm; MRT: City Hall; map p.136 B2
The flagship store of a reliable and trusted English-language bookstore chain.

Select Books
03-15 Tanglin Shopping Centre, 19 Tanglin Road; tel: 6732 1515; www.selectbooks.com.sg; Mon–Sat 9.30am–6.30pm, Sun and public hols 10am–4pm; MRT: Orchard; bus: 7, 106, 111 or 123; map p.134 A1
The specialist in books on Southeast Asia.

Sunny Bookstore
03-58/59 Far East Plaza, 14 Scotts Road; tel: 6733 1583; Mon–Thur 10.30am–8pm, Fri–Sat 10.30am–9pm, Sun 11.30am–7pm; MRT: Orchard; map p.134 B1
Filled with brand-new and secondhand titles from every literary genre.

Times Bookstore
04-18 Plaza Singapura, 68 Orchard Road; tel: 6837 0552; www.timesbookstores.com.sg; Sun–Thur 10.30am–9.30pm, Fri–Sat 10.30am–10pm; MRT: Dhoby Ghaut; map p.135 E3
This household name has a wide selection of paperbacks and magazines.

Woods in the Books
58 Club Street; tel: 6222 9980; www.woodsinthebooks.sg; Mon–Sat 11am–9pm, Sun noon–6pm; MRT: Chinatown; map p.138 C3
This quiet bookstore specialises in picture books for children and adults.

Monuments

B y international standards, Singapore's monuments are small and can barely boast grandeur along the lines of, say, the Eiffel Tower in Paris or the Statue of Liberty in New York City. But what Singapore's monuments lack in size, they make up for with charm and character. From the grande dames of hotels, the Raffles and Goodwood Park, to the quaint Cavenagh Bridge, to the Gothic-style convent now reinvented as the nightlife hub Chijmes, each has a unique story to tell. Let these eclectic structures lead you through the city's history, culture and development.

Anderson Bridge

Singapore River; MRT: Raffles Place; map p.139 D4

Anderson Bridge was built in 1910 when it became apparent that the adjacent Cavenagh Bridge could not cope with increasing traffic. It was named after Sir John Anderson, governor of the Straits Settlement. During the Japanese Occupation (1942–5), the severed heads of criminals were hung on the bridge as a warning to discourage people from breaking the law.

Cavenagh Bridge

Singapore River; MRT: Raffles Place; map p.139 D4

Cavenagh Bridge is the oldest suspension bridge in Singapore. It was constructed in Scotland and assembled here by Indian convict labourers in 1869. The bridge was named in honour of Major General Cavenagh, the last India-appointed governor. Originally planned as a drawbridge, it was found upon completion to be suitable only as a fixed structure. It is now a pedestrian bridge.

Chijmes

30 Victoria Street; tel: 6337 7810; www.chijmes.com.sg; MRT: City Hall; map p.136 B2

This neo-Gothic-style former Convent of the Holy Infant Jesus (CHIJ) school building was painstakingly restored with the help of conservationist Didier Reppelin. The name Chijmes (pronounced 'chimes') was adopted to incorporate the initials of the convent, church and school that had stood here since its founding in 1854. The convent also ran an orphanage; its **Gate of Hope** was where babies would be left by their unmarried mothers.

Chijmes is today a collection of restaurants, pubs and handicraft shops. Don't miss the Belgian-crafted stained-glass windows in the chapel, which is now renamed **Chijmes Hall** and a venue for concerts and weddings. The **Fountain Court**, flanked by pubs and restaurants with alfresco dining areas, reverberates with life when there are free outdoor concerts. Alfresco dining in its softly lit courtyard is a delight.

Below: the Gothic-inspired Chijmes is a nightlife destination.

Left: the water of the Fountain of Wealth is said to bring good luck to whoever touches it.

built in gratitude for a donation 'towards the cost of the Singapore Water Works' given in 1857 by the trader and public benefactor Tan Kim Seng (1805–64). This Victorian cast-iron fountain has been part of Singapore's urban landscape since 19 May 1882. During Tan's lifetime, one of the major problems of the town was its inadequate water supply. Tan donated a generous sum of $13,000 to support the construction of a system to provide piped water to the town. The ambitious plans were only approved after his death in 1864.

Esplanade Park

Along Connaught Drive; free; MRT: City Hall; map p.136 B1
The Esplanade Park and the tree-lined **Queen Elizabeth Walk** was formerly a seafront promenade where Europeans spent their leisure time strolling or playing cricket during colonial times.

At the park's southern end is the **Lim Bo Seng Memorial**, with its four bronze lions. It is dedicated to local hero and martyr Lim Bo Seng (1909–44), an active member of an underground resistance movement against the Japanese in World War II.

Further along is the **Cenotaph**, built to remember the soldiers who died fighting in the two World Wars. Standing at nearly 20m (66ft) tall, it is made from smooth granite, and the words 'Our Glorious Dead' are engraved on its surface. The structure was erected in memory of 124 British men who gave their lives in World War I. Their names are cast on a metal plate that sits before the foundation stone laid by Sir Lawrence Guillemard, governor of the Straits Settlement, on 15 November 1920. After World War II, more inscriptions were made on the reverse side of the stone.

At the park's northern end is the **Tan Kim Seng Fountain**, commissioned by the Municipal Council and

Below: the Cenotaph honours the heroes of World War II.

Fountain of Wealth

Suntec City Mall, 3 Temasek Boulevard; tel: 6295 2888; free; MRT: City Hall; map p.136 C2
The water of the gigantic Fountain of Wealth in the centre of Suntec City supposedly brings good fortune to those who touch it. So some visitors actually buy test tubes of the lucky water to take home. Others perform a special ritual to harness the forces of the excellent *feng shui* that surrounds both the Fountain and Suntec City.

The massive bronze structure, which covers 1,683sq m (18,115sq ft), is listed in the Guinness World Records as

The entire Suntec City development is inspired by *feng shui* principles. Based on the human hand, it has four 45-storey towers representing the four fingers while a shorter 18-storey tower is the thumb. The fountain, with its water symbolising wealth, is held in the palm of the hand.

the world's largest and was inspired by the Hindu mandala. The fountain is switched on daily 9am–10pm. There is also a free nightly laser show at 8pm and 9pm.

Goodwood Park Hotel

22 Scotts Road; tel: 6737 7411; www.goodwoodparkhotel.com; MRT: Orchard

This castle-like hotel, built in 1900 as the Teutonia Club for German residents in Singapore. Designed by colonial architect R.A.J. Bidwell, it has an interesting history. During World War II, the Japanese used the building as a military headquarters, and in 1945, the British turned its premises into a war crimes court. It is now a luxury hotel.

SEE HOTELS, P.73

Istana

Orchard Road; www.istana.gov. sg; MRT: Dhoby Ghaut; map p.132 A1

The Istana is the official residence of Singapore's president. The palace and its sprawling gardens are strictly off-limits to the public, except on National Day and

certain public holidays when the gates are thrown open to curious sightseers.

The Istana was completed in 1869 by the colonial engineer J.F.A. McNair and served as the residence of the British governor until the island became self-governing in 1959. Facing the Istana squarely is the **Istana Park**, dominated by an imposing steel sculpture that is flanked by gardens of heliconia and lotus-filled ponds. The café is a pleasant stop for a drink.

Merlion Park

By the Esplanade Bridge, next to One Fullerton; free; MRT: Raffles Place; map p.139 E4

The Merlion Park is the home of the Merlion statue, the city's tourism mascot inspired by the creature Prince Sang Nila Utama saw when he arrived in Singapore (then known as Temasek) in the 13th century. Believing it to be a *singa* (lion), he renamed the island Singapura, meaning 'Lion City'. Once located at the original Merlion Park by the Esplanade Bridge, the Merlion became a popular

tourist attraction for visitors. Today the Merlion is found just 120m (394ft) away from its original site, adjacent to One Fullerton. Built from cement fondue by the late Singaporean craftsman Lim Nang Seng, the Merlion statue measures 8.6m (28ft) high and weighs 70 tonnes.

Parliament House

1 Parliament Place; tel: 6332 6677; www.parliament.gov.sg; tours by appointment only; MRT: City Hall or Clarke Quay; map p.139 D4

The new Parliament House was completed in 1999, right next door to the old Parliament House, which is now the arts hub called **The Arts House**. The new building is five times larger than the old one, and retains the colonial architectural style to preserve a sense of history. Porcelain dating back to the Ming and Yuan dynasties was found on the site during construction and is now displayed in the new complex.

SEE ALSO FILM, P.61; THEATRE, P.121

Raffles Hotel

1 Beach Road; tel: 6337 1886; www.raffles.com; MRT: City Hall; map p.136 B2

Nearly all visitors to Singapore end up at the Raffles at

> Travelling scribes who have laid their hats at the Raffles include Somerset Maugham and Rudyard Kipling, who described it as a place 'where food is as excellent as the rooms are bad. Let the traveller take note. Feed at Raffles and sleep at the Hotel de l'Europe'. The latter was demolished in 1934 to make way for the Supreme Court building. The Raffles has since earned itself a stellar reputation.

Below: the Goodwood Park Hotel is styled after a Bavarian castle.

Above: the Raffles Hotel's genteel courtyard.

spot on 29 January 1819. To mark this momentous event, a white marble statue of him was erected on what is now the northern bank of the Singapore River. This white stone statue, circa 1972, is a replica cast from the original bronze statue created in 1887. The bronze statue was relocated outside the Victoria Concert Hall in 1919 to mark the 100th anniversary of Singapore's founding.

one point or another, usually to try the world-famous Singapore Sling in the **Long Bar** (invented here in 1915) or to walk through the lush gardens. Enter via its cast-iron porticoed entrance on Beach Road – the hotel originally faced the beach before it was reclaimed – which leads into the lobby with marbled floors embellished with plush Persian carpets. Opened in 1887 by the Sarkies Brothers, this 'Grand Old Lady of the East' has seen its fair share of kings and queens, presidents and prime ministers, movie actors and lions of literature,

as well as ordinary people attracted to this icon of tropical elegance and style.

The Raffles' history is a chequered one. It was briefly used by the Japanese forces in World War II when it was renamed Syonan Ryokan (Light of the South Hotel). In the early 1990s the hotel underwent a major facelift that involved years of tracking down original plans and finding skilled craftsmen to repair and re-create the original fittings. The result is a resounding success and the Raffles can once again take her place among the great hotels of the world.

The hotel also houses a **shopping arcade**, the **Jubilee Hall** theatre and the **Raffles Hotel Museum** (daily 10am–7pm; free), a repository of Raffles memorabilia, some of which were found during renovation work.
SEE ALSO HOTELS, P.71; SHOPPING, P.116; THEATRE, P.121

Raffles' Landing Site

Northern bank of the Singapore River; free; MRT: Raffles Place; map p.139 D4
The founder of modern Singapore, Sir Thomas Stamford Raffles, is said to have landed on this very

War Memorial Park

Beach Road; free; MRT: City Hall; map p.136 B2
The War Memorial Park is dedicated the thousands of civilians who suffered and died in Singapore in World War II. Popularly known as the 'Chopsticks Monument', the memorial consists of four interlinked tapering columns representing each of the four main ethnic groups. Beneath the 61-m columns are urns containing the remains of some of those who died.

Below: the War Memorial honours civilians who died in World War II.

Watch the ceremony of the changing of the sentry guards that takes place on the first Sunday of every month at 6pm at the Istana's gates. But forget about getting a glimpse of the palace building from the gates. The grounds are massive and all you will see is an endless expanse of green. Interestingly, Singapore's current president, S.R. Nathan, prefers to live in his own humbler abode in eastern Singapore. He uses the Istana for receiving foreign dignitaries and for hosting state functions.

81

Museums and Galleries

For a small country, Singapore has a disproportionally large number of museums and galleries; visitors will be spoilt for choice. There are history museums that capture and catalogue the stories of the early days of the island and Southeast Asia through artefacts and war relics; art and design museums and commercial galleries that showcase cutting-edge creativity; and idiosyncratic repositories that display the quirky and niche tastes of the people, such as the Mint Museum of Toys.

Art Retreat

10 Ubi Crescent, Lobby C, 01-45/46/47 Ubi Techpark; tel: 6749 0880; www.artretreat museum.com; free; Tue–Sat 11am–6pm, guided tours by appointment; MRT: Eunos or Paya Lebar; bus: 63

This private museum could well be the best-kept secret of Singapore's art scene, and is well worth an excursion to the suburbs. One of its two galleries hosts exhibitions of works selected from its solid collection of Southeast Asian art by renowned artists such as Affandi, S. Sudjojono, Lee Man Fong and Chen Wen Hsi,

and paintings by European masters like Russel Flint, Edvard Munch and Karel Appel. The other gallery is solely dedicated to the brilliance of the much-admired Chinese master Wu Guanzhong. Other than the permanent collection, the main gallery also features temporary exhibitions from other collections.

Asian Civilisations Museum

1 Empress Place; tel: 6332 2982; www.acm.org.sg; Mon 1–7pm, Tue–Thur & Sat–Sun 9am–7pm, Fri 9am–9pm;

entrance charge; MRT: Raffles Place; map p.139 D4

From prehistoric agricultural tools to fabric displays and bronze artefacts, the exhibits in the 11 galleries at this museum reveal the cultural and historical diversity of West, South and Southeast Asia, as well as China. In the **China Gallery**, learn about the Middle Kingdom from the displays – the Chinese deities and fragile Dehua porcelain are the highlights, while the **West Asia Gallery** impresses with Qur'an-inspired calligraphic art. The **South Asia galleries** hold religious statuary and architectural motifs of the Indian subcontinent.

Even visitors who are not history buffs will find the

The former artefacts wing og the Asian Civilisations Museum at 39 Armenian Street reopened in April 2008 as a **Peranakan museum**. It showcases the hybrid culture that has evolved through intermarriage between Chinese men and Malay women from the 17th century onwards.

Below: a recreated Chinese scholar's studio, with a 19th-century wooden couch bed from Fujian, at the Asian Civilisations Museum.

Left: Gallery 2.1 at the Singapore Art Museum.

and Museum, formerly located at Changi Prison, moved to this new site in 2001. The museum focuses on the memories and lives of both POWs and civilian internees who survived the Japanese Occupation (1942–5) with a collection of wartime memorabilia, including drawings by W.R.M. Haxworth and photographs by George Aspinall, which were taken and developed under great danger.

Particularly compelling are the **Changi Murals**. Painted by British POW Stanley Warren, the five murals, each with a Biblical significance, are replicas of the restored originals at Changi Prison. The chapel, a symbolic replica of the one at Changi Prison, is housed in the courtyard. There are also videos and rare books depicting life during the war years.

snazzy interactive zones and videos highly entertaining. To fully appreciate the museum, take the free one-hour guided tour (Mon 2pm, Tue–Fri 11am and 2pm, Sat–Sun 11am, 2pm and 3pm; not available end Dec–early Jan).

Baba House

157 Neil Road; tel: 6227 5731; www.nus.edu.sg/museum/baba; guided tours by appointment; entrance charge; MRT: Outram Park; map p.138 A2
Opened in 2008, this treasury of Peranakan history and material culture is nestled among a cluster of conservation terrace houses. The three-storey building it is housed in was built in the 1860s and is perhaps the last Peranakan house still owned by its original owners. Its opulent interior bears intricately carved wooden windows, doors, timber brackets and partition screens. The exhibition space hosts heritage art shows and yearly Peranakan festivals. The museum even has a live-in *bibik* (Peranakan colloquialism for matron) housekeeper and tour guide.

Battle Box

Fort Canning Park, 2 Cox Terrace; tel: 6333 0510; www.legendsfortcanning.com/fortcanning/battlebox.htm; daily 10am–6pm; entrance charge; MRT: City Hall or Dhoby Ghaut; map p.135 E2
This bomb-proof bunker with 22 rooms and corridors 9m (29.5ft) underground was where Lieutenant-General Percival decided to surrender to the Japanese on 15 February 1942. The bunker is equipped with wax robots and film projections to re-create the events leading to Singapore's fall. An exhibition inside the tunnels details the desperate battle against the Japanese. The bunker leads to the former Far East Command Building, now The Legends country club.

Changi Chapel and Museum

1000 Upper Changi Road North; tel: 6214 2451; www.changimuseum.com; daily 9.30am–5pm; free; MRT: Tanah Merah, then bus: 2 or MRT: Tampines, then bus: 29
The historic Changi Chapel

Chinatown Heritage Centre

48 Pagoda Street; tel: tel: 6338 6877; www.chinatownheritagecentre.sg; daily 9am–8pm; entrance charge; MRT: Chinatown; map p.138 C3
The Chinatown Heritage Centre was opened in 2002

Below: notes left in remembrance of POWs at the Changi Museum.

to give Chinatown a sense of history. Occupying three restored shophouses on Pagoda Street, the museum showcases the lifestyles, traditions and rituals of the people who lived and worked there in 15 galleries. The dark and cramped living quarters of early Chinatown are realistically re-created using authentic furniture, utensils and other paraphernalia.

Above: antique fire engine at the Civil Defence Heritage Gallery.

Civil Defence Heritage Gallery

Central Fire Station, 62 Hill Street; tel: 6332 2996; www.scdf.gov.sg; Tue–Sun 10am–5pm; free; MRT: Clarke Quay or City Hall; map p.136 A1

Housed in Singapore's oldest fire station, the Civil Defence Heritage Gallery traces Singapore's civil defence development from the 1900s. The museum has displays of antique fire engines and interactive stations depicting what fire fighters and rescuers undergo in a rescue operation. Register for a guided tour and you'll get to climb up the hose tower, the lookout point for fire fighters in the early days.

SEE ALSO ARCHITECTURE, P.26

Fort Siloso

33 Allanbrooke Road, Sentosa; tel: 1800-736 8672; www. sentosa.com.sg; daily 10am– 6pm; entrance charge; MRT: HarbourFront, then Sentosa Express from VivoCity

Singapore's only preserved coastal fort on Sentosa's western tip is another of the island's must-see sights. At Fort Siloso the British built numerous guns and tunnels for the defence of Singapore, which proved to be ineffective in World War II as the Japanese invaded from the Malay peninsula and not from the sea.

The interactive displays along the underground passages, the cannons and guns, and the video games tell the fort's history from its construction through to its fall in World War II. Also here are the **Surrender Chambers**, which bring to life Singapore's formal surrender to the Japanese in 1942 with a mix of gripping audio-visual footage, artefacts and realistic wax figurines.

Fuk Tak Chi Museum

43 Pekin Street; tel: 6532 7868; daily 10am–10pm; free; MRT: Raffles Place; map p.139 C3

Dating from 1824, this is Singapore's oldest temple, set up by the Hakkas and Cantonese. The museum has a collection of 200 artefacts, including a Chinese gold belt, abacus board and a rental expiry notice from early Chinatown residents.

Hua Song Museum

Haw Par Villa, 262 Pasir Panjang Road; tel: 6733 0077; www.huasong.org; Tue–Sun 9am–6pm; entrance charge; MRT: Buona Vista, then bus: 200 or MRT: HarbourFront, then bus: 10, 30 or 143

Hua Song means 'in praise of the Chinese community'. This museum located within Haw Par Villa is dedicated to the dreams, sacrifices and achievements of Chinese migrants who ventured overseas to seek their fortunes. Highlights include **The Survivors**, a tribute to Chinese women who were integral to the development of overseas Chinese communities. **En En's Kitchen** is a replica of a traditional Chinese kitchen, while in the **Grand Food Hall**, various types of Chinese food are showcased. All its galleries chart the history of the Chinese diaspora.

Images of Singapore

40 Imbiah Road, Sentosa; tel: 1800-736 8672; www. sentosa.com.sg; daily 9am–7pm; entrance charge; MRT: HarbourFront, then Sentosa Express from VivoCity

A museum that explores four experiences – Four Winds of Singapore, Celebration City, Singapore Adventure and Singapore Celebrates – Images of Singapore. These take you through Singapore's history and give a sneak preview of the country's rich cultural diversity through multimedia shows and walk-through settings.

Istana Kampong Gelam/ Malay Heritage Centre

85 Sultan Gate; tel: 6391 0450; www.malayheritage.org.sg; Istana compound daily 8am–9pm, Malay Heritage Centre Mon 1–6pm, Tue–Sun 10am–6pm; entrance charge; MRT: Bugis; map p.137 C4

The old royal palace of Istana Kampong Gelam was built in the early 1840s by Sultan Ali Iskandar Shah on the site of his father Sultan Hussein's original wooden construction. Erected on stilts, the original building was styled after a Malay palace with a verandah on the upper floor. Restored in 2004, the palace has been converted into a Malay Heritage Centre with nine galleries chronicling Malay history and culture. Exhibits include artefacts unearthed during restoration, such as earthen pots and rifles belonging to World War II Malay soldiers.

There are daily cultural programmes at the centre as well as guided tours (prebooking is required).

Labrador Park

Labrador Villa Road, off Pasir Panjang Road; tel: 1800-471 7300; www.nparks.gov.sg; 24 hours (park is lit 7am–mid-night); free; MRT: HarbourFront, then bus: 408 (Sat, Sun and public holidays 11am–9pm); bus: 10, 30, 51, 143 or 176

Labrador Park houses World War II gun batteries, along with bunkers and other relics that have been restored. Storyboards posted in the 17-ha park explain the development of the battery and its fortification. The Bunker Path winds around underground chambers, gun emplacements, an 1892 ammunition storeroom, a six-pounder quick-fire gun and remains of an old fort wall. In addition, an aerial staircase built into the edge of the secondary forest offers a panoramic view of the sea.

The **Labrador Park Secret Tunnel** guided tours of war tunnels are available (daily from 10am to 7pm; tel: 6339 6833).

Malay Village

39 Geylang Serai, Opposite Paya Lebar MRT station; tel: 6748 4700; daily 10am–10pm; free except museums; MRT: Paya Lebar

The village brings together various aspects of Malay art, music, history and food in a setting comprising traditional *bumbung panjang* (long roof)

> Labrador Park is also a gazetted nature reserve. Of interest to nature lovers is its rich variety of flora and fauna, including the white-crested laughing thrush, the yellow-vented bulbul and the regal white-bellied sea eagle.

or *rumah Melayu* (Malay house) architecture – wooden and thatched-roof buildings with high-pitched roofs and steep, slightly flared sides.

The village houses a rather banal **Cultural Museum** with a display of traditional daggers, musical instruments, typical Malay household items and an elaborate bridal chamber. The other equally ho-hum attraction, **Kampung Days**, is a re-creation of a typical Malay village in the 1950–60s.

Mint Museum of Toys

26 Seah Street; tel: 6339 0660; www.emint.com; daily 9.30am–6.30pm; entrance charge; MRT: City Hall; map p.136 B2

A treasure trove of toys put together by a private collector, this is a definite draw for both adults and kids. Rare collections of Popeye the Sailor, Felix the Cat and superheroes from Batman to Superman are lovingly kept in this museum across the street from the Raffles Hotel. The museum is owned by Chang Yang Fa, who started collecting the toys when he was six years old. He has accumulated some 50,000 pieces, estimated to be worth S$5 million, from auctions and curio shops around the world.

National Museum of Singapore

93 Stamford Road; tel: 6332 3659; www.nationalmuseum.sg; Singapore History Gallery daily 10am–6pm, Singapore Living galleries daily 10am–8pm;

Below: wax figures and British-built artillery at Fort Siloso.

entrance charge; MRT: Dhoby Ghaut or City Hall; map p.136 A2

Billing itself as 'Singapore's oldest museum with the youngest and most innovative soul', the National Museum reopened in late 2006 after a three-year, S$132 million facelift, its Neo-Palladian and Renaissance architectural elements restored and its approaches to chronicling Singapore's history reinvigorated.

Stories of Singapore's history are told in the **Singapore History Gallery**; look out for the 11 national treasures, ranging from the Singapore Stone, a rock with inscriptions dating back to the 10th century, to 14th-century Majapahit gold ornaments excavated from Fort Canning Hill. The **Singapore Living Galleries** celebrate the creativity of Singaporeans through the themes of food, fashion, film and photography. Past temporary exhibitions (separate charge) have included Greek masterpieces from the Louvre and paintings commissioned by the British Resident William Farquhar that record the flora and fauna of the region.

The museum also has an line-up of performing and visual arts programmes, as well as audio guides to help you discover its wonderful architectural details, including the 15-m- (49-ft-) high glass rotunda that illuminates like a lantern at night, with images that depict scenes from Singapore's history.

NUS Museums

National University of Singapore, 50 Kent Ridge Crescent; tel: 6516 8817; www.nus.edu. sg/museum; Tue–Sat 10am–7.30pm, Sun 10am–6pm; free; MRT: Clementi, then bus: 96

The NUS Museums feature three well-curated galleries. The impressive **Lee Kong Chian Art Museum**, named after the first Chancellor of the former University of Singapore, is noted for its collection of Chinese art spanning some 7,000 years of civilisation and culture. There are close to 4,000 pieces of artwork, which include paintings and calligraphic works as well as ceramics, bronzes and sculptures. The **South and Southeast Asian Gallery** mirrors classical traditions as well as modern trends and

comprises ceramics, textiles, sculpture and paintings. Be sure to stop at the **Ng Eng Teng Gallery**, which houses the sculptures of the late Ng Eng Teng, who was known for his whimsical renditions of the human form.

Raffles Museum of Biodiversity Research

64 Science Drive 2, Block S6, 03-01, National University of Singapore; tel: 6516 5082; rmbr.nus.edu.sg; Mon–Fri 9am–5pm; free; MRT: Buona Vista, then bus: 95

Although primarily a research facility, the Raffles Museum also has a public gallery where you can view exhibits from the oldest and largest collection of Southeast Asian plant, animal and fungi specimens, some dating as far back as the 19th century. Some of these flora and fauna are extinct while others are still thriving in Singapore. Specimens of animals that no longer exist include the 19th-century leathery turtle from Siglap, the Changi dugong and the banded-leaf monkey.

red dot design museum

28 Maxwell Road; tel: 6327 8027; www.red-dot.sg; Mon, Tue and Fri 11am–6pm, Sat, Sun and public holidays 11am–8pm; entrance charge; MRT: Tanjong Pagar; map p.138 C2

Located in the historical red dot Traffic building, this museum is the only one of its kind in Singapore and the second red dot design museum in the world (the first is in Germany), run by the German body that presents the prestigious red dot design award. Its stark, industrial-looking interior is a fittingly cool background to the interactive installations and exhibits of the slickest, most acclaimed products from around the world.

Below: the Fashion Gallery at the National Museum presents fresh perspectives on Singapore fashion.

Above: the red dot design museum is housed in the traffic-stopping-red red dot Traffic building.

On the first weekend of the month, the red dot design museum hosts MAAD, a weekend market that boasts original works by Singaporean designers. The market is curated by a committee of established artists and designers so only the most original and creative works are presented. Check www.maad.sg for details.
(See also Shopping, p.116)

Reflections at Bukit Chandu

31-K Pepys Road; tel: 6375 2510; www.s1942.org.sg; Tue–Sun 9am–5pm; entrance charge; MRT: HarbourFront, then bus: 10, 30 or 143

This World War II site is dedicated to the heroes of the Malay Regiment, made up of the British, Australian and Malay soldiers, who fought 13,000 Japanese soldiers at the Battle of Pasir Panjang in 1942. Five galleries showcase artefacts and multimedia interactive shows and provide rich insight into the war, while the *Sounds of Battle* video in the theatre practically transports you onto the battlefield with realistic sound effects of machine-gun firing and human cries.

Royal Selangor Pewter Centre

01-01 3A, River Valley Road, Clarke Quay; tel: 6268 9600; www.royalselangor. com.sg; daily 9am–9pm; entrance charge; MRT: Clarke Quay; map p.135 E1

Get an introduction to pewter, an alloy made of copper, antimony and tin, by taking a tour of the collection of 75 pewter-

ware pieces here. If what you see, from tobacco boxes to pewter-making tools, suitably impresses, take the School of Hard Knocks course to fashion your own pewter souvenir (separate charge).

Sculpture Square

155 Middle Road; tel: 6333 1055; www.sculpturesq.com.sg; Mon–Sat 11am–6pm; free; MRT: Bugis; map p.136 B3

The building was constructed in 1870 as a church and then a girls' school. Its chapel, with arch windows and circular vents, is one of the few

Gothic-style buildings still standing in Singapore. It is now the pillar-free Chapel Gallery with a dramatic 9-m- (29.5-ft-) high ceiling.

Sculpture Square is the only space in Singapore solely devoted to contemporary three-dimensional art, with an active schedule of exhibitions all year round. Its shaded courtyard and cool garden are good spots to take a breather from the city.

Singapore Art Museum

71 Bras Basah Road; tel: 6332 3222; www.singart.com; Mon–Sun 10am–7pm, Fri 10am–9pm; entrance charge; MRT: Dhoby Ghaut or City Hall; map p.136 A3

Institutional and private collectors in Singapore avidly

Below: Ng Eng Teng Gallery exhibits at the NUS Museums.

Plan well and you could enjoy some museum visits free of charge or at a big discount. The Asian Civilisations Museum offers a 50 percent discount on admission every Friday 7–9pm. The National Museum has free admission to the Singapore Living galleries daily 6–8pm, while the Singapore Art Museum charges no admission 6–9pm on Friday. Check www.nhb.gov.sg for more details.

amass art from the region, and the Singapore Art Museum is one of them. This powerhouse of 20th-century Southeast Asian art showcases an excellent sampling of works by the region's leading names, such as Affandi, Hendra Gunawan and Georgette Chen. It also ranks among the finest contemporary art museums in the region; past temporary exhibitions have included works from the Guggenheim Museum in New York and the Louvre in Paris.

The museum is housed in a colonial-era structure built in the early 1800s, which was formerly occupied by St Joseph's Institution, a school set up by missionaries. Even if not for the artworks, the museum is worth visiting just to see the splendidly restored chapel and the school hall, now called the Glass Hall. The latter features a colourful glass sculpture by American artist Dale Chihuly.

Singapore City Gallery

45 Maxwell Road, URA Centre; tel: 6321 8321; www.ura.gov.sg/gallery; Mon–Sat 9am–5pm; free; MRT: Chinatown or Tanjong Pagar; map p.138 C2
If you've wondered about what makes this city tick, then a trip to this gallery to understand the city planners'

work is in order. Its highlight is an enormous scaled and detailed 11x11-m (36x36-ft) architectural model of Singapore's central area. Spread over two storeys are the rest of the gallery's 50 exhibits, including a multimedia exhibit that charts Singapore's architectural development over the past 180 years. You can also survey the vision the planners have for this island in the 21st century.

Singapore Philatelic Museum

23B Coleman Street; tel: 6337 3888; www.spm.org.sg; Mon 1–7pm, Tue–Sun 9am–7pm; entrance charge; MRT: Clarke Quay or City Hall; map p.136 A2
This museum is housed in the former Anglo Chinese School, which was restored in 1995. Although small, the interactive museum has regular thematic exhibitions inspired by stamps, first-day covers and postcards. Peruse Singapore's early stamps and stamp archival materials such as artworks and proofs.

Singapore Tyler Print Institute

41 Robertson Quay; tel: 6336 3663; www.stpi.com.sg; Tue–Sat 10am–6pm; free;

MRT: Clarke Quay, then taxi; bus: 32, 54, 64, 123, 143, 139, 186 or 195; map p.135 D1
Housed in a restored 19th-century warehouse, this is dedicated to printmaking, papermaking and paper-based art. STPI collaborates with leading and emerging artists from around the world to explore new techniques and aesthetics of printmaking and to create works on paper. Artists who have worked and presented at the gallery include Donald Sultan (US), Zhu Wei (China), Liu Kuo-Sung (Taiwan), as well as local Chinese ink painter Chua Ek Kay, watercolourist Ong Kim Seng and photographer Russell Wong.

Sun Yat Sen Nanyang Memorial Hall

12 Tai Gin Road; tel: 6256 7377; www.wanqingyuan.com.sg; Tue–Sun 9am–5pm; entrance charge; MRT: Novena, then bus: 21 or 131
In 1906 Dr Sun Yat Sen, the leader of China's nationalist movement, arrived in Singapore to rally support for his cause among the overseas Chinese in Nanyang (meaning 'Southern Seas' in Chinese and referring to Southeast Asia). He was

Below: the Singapore Art Museum.

Right: the seated statue of Dr Sun Yat Sen in front of the Sun Yat Sen Memorial Hall.

given a villa for his use, where he plotted the overthrow of the Qing dynasty. The bungalow later became known as the Sun Yat Sen Villa. It was the headquarters of the Singapore branch of the Kuomintang.

This two-storey Victorian-style bungalow, built in 1900, is now the Sun Yat Sen Nanyang Memorial Hall. Architecturally it represents a prevalent type of residence that existed in Singapore in the 19th century. A statue of Dr Sun sits just in front of the building in the garden.

Six exhibition halls spread over two storeys feature exhibits such as a set of life-sized wax figures showing Dr Sun holding a secret meeting at the villa. Dr Sun's revolutionary activities in Southeast Asia are also told through some 400 photographs.

Art Galleries

Art-2 Gallery
01-03 MICA Building, 140 Hill Street; tel: 6338 8713; www.art2.com.sg; Mon–Sat 11am–7pm; MRT: Clarke Quay or City Hall; map p.136 A1
This focuses on sculptures, ceramics, paintings and prints from Singapore and around the region.

Artfolio
02-25 Raffles Hotel Shopping Arcade, 328 North Bridge Road; tel: 6334 4677; www.artfolio.com.sg; Mon–Sat 11am–7pm, Sun noon–5pm; MRT: City Hall; map p.136 B2
Contemporary Asian paintings and sculptures, including those by prominent Malaysian-born Eng Tay and Singaporean artists Thomas Yeo and Tan Chin Chin.

Art Forum
82 Cairnhill Road; tel: 6737 3448; www.artforum.com.sg; Mon–Sat 10am–6pm; MRT: Newton
Well-established gallery in an old-style shophouse, with a focus on contemporary Southeast Asian art.

Art Seasons Gallery
5 Gemmill Lane; tel: 6221 1800; http://artseasons.museum; Mon–Fri 11am–8pm, Sat noon–6pm; MRT: Chinatown; map p.139 C3
Concentrates on contemporary talents from China.

Fill Your Walls
04-02, 21 Tanjong Pagar Road; tel: 6222 1667; www.fill-your-walls.com; Mon–Sun 10am–10pm; MRT: Tanjong Pagar or Outram Park; map p.138 B2
Serves as a platform for emerging local artists to create, display and market their works.

HeinArt Gallery
02-67 Chinatown Point, 133 New Bridge Road; tel: 6535 5692; www.heinartgallery.com; Tue–Sun noon–7pm; MRT: Chinatown; map p.138 C3
A strong supporter of Singaporean artists, this is excellent for local landscape and still-life paintings.

Night and Day
139 A/C Selegie Road; tel: 6884 5523; www.nightandday.sg; By appointment only; MRT: Dhoby Ghaut; map p. 136 A4
When Night and Day first

started in 2007, artists and patrons were invited to 'vandalise' the walls with graffiti. It was founded as a platform for local artists to showcase their talent. There is also a chill-out bar on the second floor.

Opera Gallery
03-05 ION Orchard, 2 Orchard Turn; tel: 6735 2618; www.operagallery.com; Mon–Fri 11am–8pm, Sat–Sun 10am–8pm; MRT: Orchard; map p.134 C4
Arguably the best gallery in Singapore to view paintings by 19th-century European masters.

Post-Museum
107-109 Rowell Road; tel: 6396 3598; www.post-museum.org; Tue–Fri 6pm–10pm, Sat–Sun noon–10pm; MRT: Little India; map p.133 D2
Independent of the government, it seeks to promote contemporary art and provide a space for art lovers to come together. Classes are also conducted here, ranging from sign language to art history.

Soobin Art International
04-90/95 Ubi Techpark Lobby E, 10 Ubi Crescent; tel: 6837 2777; www.soobinart.com.sg; Mon–Sat 11am–6pm; MRT: Paya Lebar then taxi; map 136 A1
Soobin is especially strong in contemporary Chinese works. Artists who have shown here previously include Shen Xiaotong and Yue Minjun.

Music

With its small domestic market and local musicians competing with international acts from the US and the UK, Singapore does not have a big contemporary music scene, although indie bands such as Electrico and The Observatory are quietly thriving. Classical music, introduced by Europeans in the 19th century, has managed to gain a healthy following over the years, while the island's jazz scene is enlivened by first-rate jazz bars graced by visiting international musicians. Meanwhile, annual music festivals like WOMAD and Mosaic have become destination events.

Classical and Opera

The **Singapore Symphony Orchestra** (SSO), the country's first professional orchestra, was formed in 1979. Its repertoire tends to be mainstream, with most concerts comprising standard works. But the works of many Asian composers have also been given a fair share of airing, and naturally, local musicians and the works of Singaporean composers feature prominently in its seasons too.

SSO performs over 50 symphonic concerts a year, both in Singapore and around the world, and also has free outdoor concerts in parks such as the Singapore Botanic Gardens.

Aiming to break new ground by extending classical music to a wider audience is the **T'ang Quartet**. Not your usual classical musicians, these four lads are hip and adventurous when it comes to programming, including contemporary and Asian works as well as chamber favourites in their repertoire. The quartet has performed in community events and schools besides formal concert halls, and has been lauded internationally. *The Boston Globe* called it 'astounding' and *The Times* praised its 'enthusiasm, energy and commitment'.

Opera was largely performed by visiting international companies until 1991, when the **Singapore Lyric Opera**

was formed. It performs one to two works per year.

Classical Venues

Esplanade Concert Hall
Esplanade – Theatres on the Bay, 1 Esplanade Drive; tel: 6828 8377; www.esplanade.com; MRT: City Hall; map p.136 B1
This 1,600-seat hall offers exceptional acoustics. SSO plays its regular season here.
SEE ALSO ARCHITECTURE, P.27; DANCE, P.47; THEATRE, P.121

Shaw Foundation Symphony Stage
Singapore Botanic Gardens, 1 Cluny Road; tel: 6471 7138; www.sbg.org.sg; MRT: Orchard, then taxi; bus: 7, 105, 123 or 174
This floating amphitheatre on Symphony Lake offers open-air concerts of various genres, from jazz and Latin to classical and pop. The audience sit by the water's edge.

Singapore Conference Hall
7 Shenton Way; tel: 6557 4019; www.sch.org.sg; MRT: Tanjong Pagar; map p.139 C1
This mainly hosts concerts by Singapore's only professional Chinese orchestra, the Singapore Chinese Orchestra.

Below: the T'ang Quartet is breaking new ground.

Left: a WOMAD performance by Madosini and Patrick Duff.

various locations around the city. Here at the Esplanade outlet, Paul Ponnudorai, hailed by *Time* magazine as 'quite possibly the greatest musical interpreter of our time', performs at weekends. At the Boat Quay outlet (tel: 6538 3029), packed to the rafters every day, the band Chroma-Zone performs Thursday to Saturday. Sunday sees fantastic jam sessions.

Jazz@Southbridge
01-10/12 Esplanade Mall, Raffles Avenue; tel: 6338 0789; www.southbridgejazz.com.sg; Mon–Fri 5pm–late, Sat–Sun noon–late, shows Tue–Sun 10pm; MRT: City Hall; map p.136 B1
One of the best jazz venues to listen to international and local performers showcasing a range of styles.

Music Stores

HMV
04-23/24 313@Somerset, 313 Orchard Road; tel: 6733 1822; www.hmvgroup.com; MRT: Somerset; map p.135 D3
The largest music shop in Singapore stocks just about every genre of music. (Also at B1-47 CityLink Mall; tel: 6238 7218.)

Straits Records
22 Bali Lane; mobile tel: 9835 3211; MRT: Bugis; map p.136 C3
Local music gets great support here. There is also a good collection of indie, hip hop and other alternative genres.

That CD Shop
01-01/03, 02-10/15 Pacific Plaza, 9 Scotts Road; tel: 6238 7254; MRT: Orchard; map p.134 B1
Jazz, lounge and chill-out tunes get plenty of airplay here. (Also at B1-87 Rafflles City; tel: 6336 5885 and 01-17/20 Tanglin Mall; tel: 6732 2568.)

WOMAD (www.womad singapore.com) is held in August at the Fort Canning Park, with world-music artists from all over the globe here for a weekend-long programme. **Baybeats** (www.baybeats.com.sg) is an indie rock event at the Esplanade Theatres in July. **Mosaic** (www.mosaicmusic festival.com) in March is literally a mosaic of different genres, from jazz to soul, performed by Singaporean and international acts at the Esplanade.

Above: the HMV music store at CityLink Mall.

Victoria Concert Hall
11 Empress Place; tel: 6338 4401; www.vch.org.sg; MRT: Raffles Place or City Hall; map p.139 D4
This hall, built in the 1800s, now hosts SSO'S chamber concerts and performances by other music groups.

Contemporary Venues

SEE NIGHTLIFE, P.97

Jazz Venues

Crazy Elephant
01-04 3E River Valley Road, Clarke Quay; tel: 6337 7859; www.crazyelephant.com;

Sun–Thur 5pm–2am, Fri–Sat 5pm–3am, shows Sun 10pm; MRT: Clarke Quay; map p.135 E1
Its blues-crazy patrons include big names like Deep Purple and Robbie Williams. Good Question plays on Monday, Latitude One plays on Thursday, while Seth and the Blues Machine takes centrestage the rest of the week. Sundays are for free jam sessions.

Harry's@The Esplanade
01-05/07 Esplanade Mall, 8 Raffles Avenue; tel: 6344 0132; www.harrys.com.sg; Sun–Thur 5pm–1am, Fri–Sat 5pm–2am; MRT: City Hall; map p.136 B1
The Harry's chain of bars has

Nightlife

In the last few years, Singapore's nightlife scene has undergone a remarkable transformation. No longer bland and boring, as was once the common description, it is now hip and happening, with bar-top dancing famously legalised and smoking no longer allowed in more than a few venues. Whether it is a night of pub-crawling or one of non-stop dancing, the options are plentiful. There are chill-out bars set in balmy alfresco locales, chic lounges for design-conscious partiers, bars and pubs with world-class bands performing nightly, and dance clubs that have been called some of the best in the world.

Bars and Pubs

Archipelago Craft Beer Hub
79 Circular Road, Boat Quay; tel: 6327 8408; www.archipelago brewery.com; Mon–Thur 2pm–1am, Fri 2pm–3am, Sat 3pm–3am, Sun 3pm–1am; MRT: Raffles Place; map p.139 C4
Archipelago was Singapore's first commercial brewery in 1931. It makes its comeback more than 70 years later with this beer bar, offering hand-crafted ales with Asian flavours (think palm sugar and coconut milk, tamarind and lemongrass).

Bacchus Boathouse
03-01 Fullerton Waterboat House, 3 Fullerton Road; tel: 6538 9038; www.bacchusboathouse.com; Mon–Fri noon–1.30pm, 6pm–10pm, Fri–Sat 6pm–2am; MRT: Raffles Place; map p.139 D4
Sitting on the rooftop of a former lighthouse right next to the Fullerton Hotel, this wine bar boasts a comprehensive list of Old and New World wines. The views from the open-air deck, over Marina Bay, are stunning too.

Balaclava
01-01B Suntec City, 1 Raffles Boulevard; tel: 6339 1600; www.imaginings.com.sg; Mon–Thur 3pm–1am, Fri 3pm–2am, Sat 6pm–2am; MRT: City Hall; map p.136 C2
Filled with suits – mainly lawyers and bankers from the nearby offices – it is always packed to the brim on Friday nights and during happy hour (3–8pm) on weekdays. Live acoustic sets provide entertainment.

Barfly
02-02 The Cannery, Block C Clarke Quay, River Valley Road;

Left: crowds pack the bar at trendy KPO *(see p.94).*

Night spots are scattered all over the island, but there are a few key areas where you could spend an entire night hopping from one venue to another. Along the Singapore River, there are bars and pubs at **Boat Quay** and more fashionable options at **Clarke Quay**. **Mohammad Sultan Road** and **Robertson Quay** have plenty of watering holes and some clubs. **Orchard Road** is rife with classy hotel bars, while **Emerald Hill** offers charming pubs that draw creative types. In **Rochester Park** and **Tanglin Village** are trendy alfresco bars and clubs in colonial-era bungalows.

tel: 6887 3733; www.barfly.com.sg; Tue–Thur 6.30pm–2am, Fri–Sat 6.30pm–4am; MRT: Clarke Quay; map p.135 E1
Named after the 1980s film by Charles Bukowski, Barfly was created by Raymond Visan, who was behind the famous Buddha Bar in Paris. Guests can dine on Asian fusion cuisine and then linger on plush banquettes late into the night in this part supperclub, part bar.

Bar Opiume
1 Empress Place; tel: 6339 2876; www.indochine.com.sg; Mon–Thur 5pm–2am, Fri–Sat

5pm–3am, Sun 5pm–1am; MRT: Raffles Place; map p.139 D4
Located at the Asian Civilisations Museum, Bar Opiume draws a hip crowd with its spacious interior and huge terrace. Ideal for taking in the shimmering CBD skyline and watching the river boats go by.

Brewerkz Restaurant and Microbrewery
01-06 Riverside Point, 30 Merchant Road; tel: 6438 7438; www.brewerkz.com; Mon–Thur noon–midnight, Fri–Sat noon–1am, Sun 11am–midnight; MRT: Clarke Quay; map p.138 C4
Handcrafted beer fresh from its onsite microbrewery and hearty American cuisine in an industrial-like setting. A brewmaster creates seven varieties of beer, including the bestselling India Pale Ale. Try the mussels with beer sauce.

Left: sample a wide choice of ales at Archipelago Craft Beer Hub *(far left)* or enjoy a drink atop Mount Faber at the Jewel Box *(near left, see p.94).*

Café Samar
27 Bali Lane; tel: 6398 0530; daily 10am–6pm; MRT: Bugis; map p.136 C3
This café does not serve alcohol, but it's worth checking out for its Arabic charms. Low-slung lamps, Persian carpets and reclining chairs all add to the ambience. Serves a Middle Eastern menu.
SEE ALSO RESTAURANTS, P.110

Coffee Bar K
01-76 UE Square, 205 River Valley Road; tel: 6720 5040; www.coffeebark.co.jp; Sun–Fri 6pm–3am, Sat 6pm–4am; MRT: Clarke Quay; bus: 32, 54, 143 or 195; map p.135 E1
Well-trained Japanese bartenders artfully present large drinks that are slightly expensive but too gorgeous to resist. Its extensive whisky list is also a huge draw.

Hacienda
13A Dempsey Road, Tanglin Village; tel: 6476 2922; www.hacienda.com.sg; Sun–Thur 5pm–1am, Fri–Sat 5pm–2am; MRT: Orchard or

Boozing in Singapore is expensive. Expect to pay S$10 and upwards for a pint of beer, S$12 for a shot of house spirits, S$15–20 for premium beer brands, and about $100 for a bottle of champagne. All bills are tagged with a 10 percent service charge and 7 percent tax. Tipping is not necessary, but, of course, always welcome.

Commonwealth, then taxi; bus: 7, 105, 123 or 174
A delightful villa setting to chill out in. Relax on the open-air deck or in a leafy courtyard while you sip a watermelon martini.

Ice Cold Beer
9 Emerald Hill Road; tel: 6735 9929; www.emeraldhillgroup.com; Sun–Thur 5pm–2am, Fri–Sat noon–3am; MRT: Somerset; map p.135 D4
The name says it all – this is the place to savour a variety of ice-cold beers. Their jumbo-sized hot dogs are the perfect accompaniment.

The Jewel Box
109 Mount Faber Road; tel: 6377 9688; www.mountfaber.com.sg; daily 11.30am–2pm, Sun–Wed 6pm–1am, Thur–Sat 6pm–2am, last order for dinner at 10.15pm; MRT: HarbourFront
Getting to this well-illuminated glass box atop Mount Faber by cable car is a pleasure in itself. The alfresco **Altivo** and the **Glass Bar** both have fantastic views of the harbour and the city.

Kazbar
01-03 Capital Square 3, 25 Church Street; tel: 6438 2975; www.kazbar.com; Mon–Fri noon–1am, Sat 5.30pm–1am; MRT: Raffles Place; map p.139 C3
Popular with oil traders and advertising types, this stylish lounge is decked in Middle Eastern style with cosy alcoves and a tented divan. Knock back a Kazbar Special cocktail and dine on authentic Moroccan cuisine.

KPO
1 Killiney Road; tel: 6733 3648; www.imaginings.com.sg; Mon–Sat 9.30am–1am, Sun 10.30am–11pm; MRT: Somerset; map p.135 D3
So named because it sits on the junctions of Killiney, Penang and Orchard roads. It is also housed in the premises of the Killiney post office. Its glass walls and steel architecture draw sophisticated yuppies. This two-storey bar feels like a modern home and boasts a balcony where one can watch the traffic go by with a cold drink in hand.

Loof
03-07 Odeon Towers Extension Rooftop, 331 North Bridge Road; tel: 6338 8035; www.loof.com.sg; Sun–Thur 5pm–1.30am, Fri–Sat 5pm–3am; MRT: City Hall; map p.136 B2
This playful rooftop bar attracts a laid-back crowd. Chill on leather loungers and pray for rain. When it pours, drinks are two for the price of one. Who needs happy hour?

Molly Malone's
56 Circular Road, Boat Quay; tel: 6536 2029; www.mollymalone.com; Mon–Tue 11am–1am, Wed–Thur & Sat 11am–2am, Fri 11am–3am, Sun 11am–midnight; MRT: Raffles Place; map p.139 C4
Like a scene straight out of Dublin, this offers Guinness and Kilkenny on tap, as well as decent pub grub and foot-stomping Irish music.

One Rochester
1 Rochester Park, off Buona Vista Road; tel: 6773 0070; www.onerochester.com; Sun–Thur 6pm–1am, Fri–Sat 6pm–2am, Sun 10am–3pm (brunch); MRT: Buona Vista
Set in a black-and-white colonial-era bungalow, this has four rooms with individual themes: a living room, play room, library and bar. The action happens mainly outside on the deck. Choose from over 200 bottles of wine, a list of sakes, martinis and lovely bar food.

Oosh
22 Dempsey Road, Tanglin Village; tel: 6475 0002;

Right: a slice of the Middle East at Kazbar.

www.oosh.com.sg; Mon–Thur noon–1am, Fri–Sat noon–2am, Sun noon–11pm; MRT: Orchard, then taxi; bus: 7, 105, 123 or 174

Singapore's largest alfresco bar and restaurant has five areas to eat, drink and relax in. Everything, from the premium booze and cigars to the designer furniture and landscaped gardens, is top-notch.

The Wine Company @ Dempsey

Block 14D Dempsey Road, Tan-glin Village; tel: 6479 9341; www.thewinecompany.com.sg; Mon–Thur 3pm–midnight, Fri 3pm–1am, Sat noon–1am, Sun noon–11pm; MRT: Orchard, then taxi; bus: 7, 105, 123 or 174

Hidden away in an old army barracks, this has a wonder-fully cosy courtyard where guests can eat and drink under the stars. Excellent South African wines.

Clubs

Attica/Attica Too

01-03 Clarke Quay, 3A River Valley Road; tel: 6333 9973; www.attica.com.sg; Attica: Sun–Tue 5pm–2am, Thur 5pm–3am, Wed, Fri, Sat 5pm–4am; Attica Too: Fri–Sat 11pm–6am; MRT: Clarke Quay; map p.135 E1

The cool and gorgeous congregate at Attica's lush, open courtyard with a fountain to groove to Latin, jazz and funk. At Attica Too upstairs, the sound is more Euro-trashy, with a crowd to match.

Butter Factory

02-02/03/04 One Fullerton, 1 Fullerton Road; tel: 6333 8243; www.thebutterfactory.com; Wed 10pm–3am, Thur 9pm–2am, Fri–Sat 10pm–4am; MRT: Raffles Place; map p.135 D1

With a swimming pool for a dance floor, complete with

Above: Café del Mar heats up Sentosa's nightlife.

life buoys and ladders. Expect to see celebs, models and other beautiful people among the civilian jeans-and-tee clubbers.

Café del Mar

40 Siloso Beach Walk, Sentosa; tel: 6235 1296; www.cafedelmar. com.sg; Sun–Thur 11am–11pm, Fri–Sat 11am–2am; MRT: Har-bourFront, then Sentosa Express from VivoCity

Lots of ladies slithering in skimpy bikinis to chill-out

Singaporeans love happy hour (usually 5–9pm) when establishments offer drinks at deep discounts. But if you want truly cheap beer, head to a hawker centre or *kopitiam* (basic coffee shop), where you can drink local and imported beers and ales for a song.

tunes or preening on lounge beds. Romp in the jacuzzi, sunken pools and cabanas or shimmy in the tiny dance club. Best of all are the sunsets seen from the popular deck.

St James Power Station

3 Sentosa Gateway; tel: 6270 7676; www.stjamespower station.com; opening hours vary for different venues; MRT: HarbourFront

There are nine venues in this huge former power station. The main space is the **Powerhouse**, a hip dance club, while **Movida** features a Paraguayan band that plays Afro-Cuban music, and the **Bellini Room** serves jazz and martinis. The **Gallery Bar** has a bird's-eye view of the other outlets.

Above: the Post Bar is popular with Raffles Place suits.

www.e-clubbing.com offers news, reviews and forums on some of the best clubs in Singapore. www.mumtazz.com is the top site for the latest information on Singapore's nightlife.

Zirca Mega Club
The Cannery, Clarke Quay, 3C River Valley Road; tel: 6235 2292; www.zirca.sg; Wed–Sat and eve of hols 10pm–late; map p.135 E1
Three clubs under one roof, each with its own entrance and exit. Zirca is a dance club with performances by aerialists and fire-twirlers, Rebel Boutique Club is a hip-hop arena while Yello Jello Retro Bar is a retro-themed disco room. Fabulous Sundays see a happy crowd of men.

Zouk/Velvet Underground
Jiak Kim Street; tel: 6738 2988; www.zoukclub.com.sg; Wed and Fri–Sat 10pm–late (Zouk), Tue–Sat 9pm–late (Velvet Underground); MRT: Clarke Quay, then taxi; bus: 16 or 195; map p.135 C1
One of Singapore's most enduring clubs with regular appearances by guest celebrity DJs. Its brand of trance and techno is always a hit with the younger crowd, while the adjoining **Velvet Underground** caters to a more mature audience. It is widely regarded as one of the best dance clubs in the world.

Hotel Bars
eM by the River
01-05 The Gallery Hotel, 1 Nanson Road; tel: 6836 9691; www.em-n-em.com; Mon–Thur 9am–2am, Fri 9am–3am, Sat 11am–3am, Sun 8am–2am; MRT: Clarke Quay, then taxi; bus: 51, 64, 123 or 186; map p.135 D1
Sharing is the buzzword at this chic bar where beers, cocktails and shooters arrive by the bottle, accompanied

by small glasses. Food is available late into the evening.

The Living Room
Marriott Hotel, 320 Orchard Road; tel: 6831 4506; www.bar noneasia.com; daily 4pm–6am; MRT: Orchard; map p.134 C4
Complete with paintings, chandeliers and a faux fireplace, this 'modern Victorian' living room is great for chilling out to lounge music on weekdays. It is extremely popular at weekends because it stays open till 6am.

Martini Bar
Grand Hyatt, 10 Scotts Road; tel: 6738 1234; www.singapore. grand.hyatt.com; daily 11am–2am; MRT: Orchard; map p.134 B1
Located in the **mezza9** restaurant, this glass-walled space is great for pre- or post-prandial drinks. There are over 30 martinis, which guests can enjoy on a sumptuous sofa or at the bar overlooking Scotts Road.
SEE ALSO RESTAURANTS, P.107

New Asia Bar
71/F, Swissôtel The Stamford, 2 Stamford Road; tel: 6837 3322; www.equinoxcomplex. com; Sun–Tue 3pm–1am, Wed–Thur 3pm–2am, Fri–Sat 3pm–3am; MRT: City Hall; map p.136 B2
Drink with the city spread out before you. Located on the 71st floor of the Swissôtel, this draws affluent locals, expats and business travellers with its spectacular views and happy-hour prices. On

Left: cocktails at the New Asia Bar.

Right: live music at Timbre.

Right: Singapore is shaking off its staid image and boasts some great dance clubs.

weekdays the crowd tends to disappear by the end of happy hour (10pm), while at weekends, the vibe is clubby with some action on the small dance floor.

Post Bar

The Fullerton Hotel, 1 Fullerton Square; tel: 6877 8135; www.fullertonhotel.com; Mon–Fri noon–2am, Sat 5pm–2am, Sun 3pm–2am; MRT: Raffles Place; map p.139 D4

Famous for the city's best caipirinha, this is all trendy chic with its high ceilings and beige décor. A sophisticated crowd plies the room, where drinks are pricey and the dress code is elegant.

Live Music

The Arena

01-08 Clarke Quay, 3B River Valley Road; tel: 6338 3158; www.thearenalive.com.sg; Tue–Sat 10pm–4am; MRT: Clarke Quay; map p.135 E1

This keeps the music fresh by changing its headline live act every two months. Bands from the US, UK, Australia and Asia perform anything from retro-pop to rock to soul.

Timbre Music Bistro

Garden, The Substation, 45 Armenian Street; tel: 6338 8030; www.timbre.com.sg; daily 6pm–late; MRT: City Hall; map p.136 A2

An atmospheric nook set in the garden of The Substation arts centre, overhung with trees. This is one of the best places to hear local musicians, who take to the stage nightly. The food and drinks aren't half bad either. So popular is this original Timbre that there are now four more Singapore outlets, including Timbre Mobile which changes its location every four months.

Wala Wala Café Bar

31 Lorong Mambong, Holland Village; tel: 6462 4288; www.imaginings.com.sg; Mon–Thur 4pm–1am, Fri 4pm–2am, Sat 3pm–2am, Sun 3pm–1am; MRT: Buona Vista

Renowned name in Singapore for live music. This laid-back café bar has local rock, pop-rock and acoustic bands and musicians playing nightly.

Pampering

It is sometimes said that Singaporeans are not the most stylish bunch. Say what you like about their sartorial sense, but when it comes to looking good, Singaporeans are big spenders. There are hardly any home-grown beauty and skincare brands; imported labels dominate the beauty counters in department stores. Beauty salons and slimming centres are around every corner, as are all manner of spas – big, boutique, luxury, budget, traditional, modern, Javanese, Thai – you name it, this city probably has it. Aesthetic and medical spas are also popular, especially in this age of non-invasive cosmetic surgery.

Spas

Amrita Spa & Wellness
Swissôtel Merchant Court, 20 Merchant Road; tel: 6239 1780; www.amritaspa.com; daily 10am–10pm; MRT: Clarke Quay; map p.138 C4
With eight spacious treatment rooms, a fitness centre, a manicure and pedicure station, a landscaped garden and a freeform pool. The menu is extensive; when in doubt, simply go for one of its signature Spa Ritual packages.

Aramsa Garden Spa
Bishan Park II, 1382 Ang Mo Kio Avenue 1; tel: 6456 6556; www.aramsaspas.com; Mon–Fri 10am–10pm, Sat–Sun 9am–10pm; MRT: Ang Mo Kio, then taxi or bus: 133, 136 or 262, or MRT: Bishan, then bus: 410
This is the only spa that's set amid the lush greenery of a park. Its individual spa suites are beautifully appointed and some even have sunken bathtubs in private gardens. Try the two-and-a-half-hour Botanical Energy Package that includes a floral exfoliation, re-mineralising mud therapy and shiatsu focus massage.

Benjaphan Thai Herbal Spa
03-02 King's Arcade, 559 Bukit Timah Road; tel: 6469 7622; www.benjaphan.com; Wed–Mon 11am–10pm; MRT: Newton, then taxi; bus: 74, 170, 171 or 174
If you are after an authentic yoga-style Thai massage (ask for the Royal Thai Massage), this is the only place in Singapore to come for it. Relax in the airy treatment rooms and let the therapist work her magic by climbing all over your body atop oversized massage beds. It will be a deep-tissue massage you won't soon forget.

St Gregory
5/F, Marina Mandarin, 6 Raffles Boulevard; tel: 6845 1161; www.stgregoryspa.com; daily 10am–10pm; MRT: City Hall; map p.136 B1
The only spa in Singapore to be awarded Leading Spa status by Leading Hotels of the World. It also houses the sole mineral-water swimming pool in the country. Try the Traditional Chinese Tui Na Massage.

Below: meditating in the Spa Botanica's labyrinth.

Left: water therapy – enjoy a relaxing outdoor rainforest shower at the Aramsa Spa.

www.hollywoodsecrets.com.sg; daily 9am–9pm; public holidays 11am–8pm; MRT: Somerset; map p.135 C4

This chain of one-stop beauty centres offers everything under one roof – manicures, pedicures, hair services, facial treatments and photography. The service is always good.

Pacific Specialist Practice

20-01 The Paragon, 290 Orchard Road; tel: 6887 1288; www.pachealthholdings.com/psp; call for appointment; MRT: Orchard; map p.135 C4

The who's who of Singapore's society come here for their non-invasive aesthetic treatments. There's everything from mesotherapy to obstetrics and gynaecology services. And if you are shy about the fact that you are getting 'work done', discreet alcoves in the waiting room ensure you won't be easily spotted.

SK-II Boutique Spa by Senze Salus

31 Scotts Road; tel: 6836 9168; www.senzesalus.com; Mon–Fri 10am–9pm, Sat–Sun 10am–7pm; MRT: Newton

The SK-II brand of skincare from Japan enjoys a huge following in Singapore. This spin-off face spa utilises the powers of its product range in pampering facials set in an elegant black-and-white colonial-era house. Many women emerge from here swearing the results are immediately evident.

Although known for spices and saris, Little India is also a beauty hub with boutiques offering everything from henna tattoos to Ayurvedic massage to the ancient beauty art of threading.

Late-night spas are starting to gain ground in Singapore. **Spa Lifestyle Inc** (www.wonngs.com), tucked away in the trendy Siglap neighbourhood stays open until 2am. **Aramsa – The Garden Spa** *(see left)* set in an idyllic park in Bishan opens until midnight on Fridays and Saturdays.

Spa Botanica

The Sentosa, 2 Bukit Manis Road, Sentosa; tel: 6371 1318; www.spabotanica.com; daily 10am–10pm; MRT: HarbourFront, then The Sentosa shuttle bus from VivoCity

Hidden away from the rigours of everyday life, Spa Botanica offers back-to-nature luxury, surrounded by verdant greenery. There are private Balinese-style pavilions, a mud pool and a labyrinth where you can literally get lost in thought. Choose from a large menu of treatments including Tibetan oil and clay massages and aromatherapy facials.

Spa Sauvignon

71 Bussorah Street; tel: 6296 0980; www.spasauvignon.com.sg; Mon–Fri 10am–10pm, Sat– Sun 10am–8pm, public holidays 10am–6pm; MRT: Bugis; map p.137 C3

As its name suggests, this spa harnesses the benefits of antioxidants in wine in all its signature treatments. When you are done with your treatment, sip a few glasses of wine before you head outside, into the thick of charming Arab Street.

Beauty

Hollywood Secrets
03-17 Mandarin Gallery, 333A Orchard Road; tel: 6734 6038;

Below: the float pool with waterfalls at the Spa Botanica.

Parks and Gardens

For an urban jungle, Singapore has plenty of green space – excellent respites from the assaults of city life. Then again, Singapore isn't called the Garden City for nothing. Seeing one park a day during your visit could be a nice way to unwind after a day of indulging in the trappings of the city. Larger parks like Fort Canning and the Botanic Gardens can be explored over an entire morning, while smaller ones like the Mandai Orchid Garden can be tail-end stops to stock up on exotic souvenirs.

Chinese Garden

1 Chinese Garden Road; tel: 6261 3632; main garden daily 6am–11pm, free; Bonsai Garden and Garden of Abundance daily 9am–6pm, entrance charge; MRT: Chinese Garden

This is a collection of theme gardens in the style of the Summer Palace in Beijing. The lovely twin pagodas afford nice views of the lake. Another attraction here is the Garden of Abundance, a Suzhou-style *penjing* (bonsai) garden with more than 1,000 bonsai, including a pair of 200-year-old *Podocarpus* trees shaped like lions. A good time to visit the garden is September/October, when it is lit at night by pretty lanterns for the **Mid Autumn Festival** celebrations.
SEE ALSO FESTIVALS AND EVENTS, P.58

> The **Japanese Garden** (Seiwaen), joined to the Chinese Garden by a bridge, is a picture of tranquillity with its Zen rock gardens, stone lanterns, ponds and shrubs.

Fort Canning Park

Canning Rise; tel: 6332 1302; www.nparks.gov.sg; free; MRT: City Hall or Dhoby Ghaut; map p.136 A2

Once known as Bukit Larangan (Forbidden Hill), this was the site of grand palaces, protected by high walls and swamps. Raffles built his residence here in 1822 and renamed it Government Hill. He chose the location for its good vantage to watch enemy movements at sea. It was later renamed Fort Canning after Viceroy Canning of India. In 1860 the British built a fort on the hill.

This lovely oasis is today a historical park with well-marked trails. Its two Gothic-style gates lead to the old cemetery used from 1823 to 1867, which was exhumed in 1970. Its tombstones, now embedded in its boundary walls, contain many well-known names, including colonial architect George Coleman. The park also holds an older tomb said to contain the remains of Iskandar Shah, the last ruler of pre-colonial Singapore. This

Above: remains of the old gates at Fort Canning Park.

has been consecrated as a Muslim *keramat* (shrine).

Midway up the park is the **Battle Box**, an underground bunker used in World War II. The whitewashed **Fort Canning Centre** houses the studios of the Singapore Dance Theatre and the culinary school **at-sunrice**. The green in front is a popular venue for open-air performances and music festivals like WOMAD.
SEE ALSO DANCE, P.47; FOOD AND DRINK, P.65; MUSEUMS AND GALLERIES, P.83; MUSIC, P.91

Kranji Commonwealth War Cemetary

9 Woodlands Road; tel: 6269 6158; daily 7am–6pm; free; MRT: Kranji

This peaceful park honours

Left: the floating Shaw Foundation Symphony Stage in the Botanic Gardens.

Singapore's oldest park set up in 1859, this renowned living museum of tropical plants is home to over 2,000 species of trees and shrubs, which have been integrated into the beautiful 52-hectare (129-acre) landscape. This is one of the two primary forests left in the city – Bukit Timah Nature Reserve *(see p.128)* is the other.

The main **Tanglin Core** features a lake with swans and turtles, an 1860s bandstand and bronze sculptures by Sydney Harpley. The **Central Core** has the **National Orchid Garden** (daily 8.30am–7pm; entrance charge) with over 1,000 orchid species, and the **Palm Valley** with the **Symphony Lake**, where regular concerts are held. The **Bukit Timah Core** is home to the Eco Lake and spice gardens. Parents will welcome the newest attraction in the park, the **Jacob Ballas Children's Garden**.

The open-air café **Les Amis** is a lovely spot for breakfast, and the restaurants, **Halia** and **Au Jardin**, are among the best in Singapore. SEE ALSO CHILDREN, P.37; MUSIC, P.90; RESTAURANTS, P.107

the men from Britain, Australia, Canada, India, Malaya, New Zealand and other commonwealth countries who died in World War II. Marked graves of 4,000 servicemen stand in neat rows. Another 24,000 names of soldiers who died but whose bodies were never recovered are inscribed on 12 columns.

Mandai Orchid Garden

200 Mandai Lake Road; tel: 6269 1036; www.mandai.com. sg; Mon 8am–6pm, Tue–Sun 8am–7pm; entrance charge; MRT: Ang Mo Kio, then bus: 138 or MRT: Choa Chu Kang, then bus: 927

Set on a hillside, this lush garden has a fine display of colourful orchids. Visitors can make their selections to take away, boxed for their flights.

Padang

In front of City Hall, across St Andrew's Road; free; MRT: City Hall; map p.136 B1

This well-manicured lawn was the focal point of the colonials. It was where flannelled cricketers played and where the British took a turn in the cool

of the evening in their horse-drawn carriages, exchanging gossip at the so-called Scandal Point. After the Japanese captured Singapore in 1942, European civilians were rounded up on the Padang and marched to Changi Prison. Now the Padang serves as the venue of myriad events, from the National Day Parade to rugby matches.

Singapore Botanic Gardens

1 Cluny Road; tel: 6471 7361; www.sbg.org.sg; daily 5am–midnight; free; MRT: Orchard, then taxi; bus: 7, 105, 123 or 174

Below: the Aranda Noorah Alsagoff vandaceous hybrid at the Mandai Orchid Garden.

Restaurants

What can be said about Singaporeans and eating that hasn't already been said? With the kind of gastronomic culture this island enjoys, it is no surprise that there are restaurants around every corner, each as lauded as the other. This section gives a round-up of the many eateries in the city, offering names that consistently serve great food at various price points. Included are some of the best fine-dining restaurants in Singapore's hotels, acclaimed culinary addresses helmed by innovative restaurateurs and chefs, and decades-old family eateries beloved by Singaporeans.

Singapore River

AUSTRALIAN

The Moomba
52 Circular Road; tel: 6438 0141; www.themoomba.com; Mon–Fri 11am–2.30pm, Mon–Sat 6.30–10pm; $$$ (set lunch) $$$$ (à la carte); MRT: Raffles Place; map p.139 C4

Over 90 percent of the produce the city's first Australian restaurant uses is imported from Australia. Excellent contemporary Australian cuisine and an extensive selection of boutique Australian wines.

FRENCH

Le Saint Julien
02-01 The Fullerton Waterboat House, 3 Fullerton Road; tel: 6534 5947; www.julienbompard.com; Mon–Fri noon–2pm and 6.30–10pm, Sat 6.30–10pm; $$$ (set lunch) $$$$ (à la carte); MRT: Raffles Place; map p.139 D4

Julien Bompard's resume includes Michelin-starred restaurants and Gaddi's at The Peninsula Hong Kong. Now the commander of his own place, Bompard does what he does best: classical French cuisine complemented by a fine wine list.

Saint Pierre
01-01 Central Mall, 3 Magazine Road; tel: 6438 0887; www.saint pierre.com.sg; Mon–Fri noon–3pm (last order 2pm), Mon–Sat 7pm–midnight (last order 9.30pm); $$–$$$ (set lunch) $$$$ (à la carte); MRT: Clarke Quay; map p.138 B4

Belgian chef-owner Emmanuel Stroobant whips up what is widely regarded as some of the best foie gras dishes in this smart, award-winning modern French restaurant. The pan-fried version with caramelised green apple and old port sauce is simply divine.

FUSION

Coriander Leaf
02-03 Block 3A Merchant's Court, River Valley Road; tel: 6732 3354; www.corianderleaf.com; Mon–Fri noon–2pm and 6.30–10pm, Sat 6.30–10.30pm; MRT: Clarke Quay; map p.135 E1

Below: chinoiserie-chic at Peach Blossoms.

> Prices for a three-course dinner per person without drinks and taxes:
> $$$$= S$45 and above
> $$$= S$30–$45
> $$= S$20–$30
> $= under S$20

Left: dine amid the lush greenery of the Botanic Gardens at Au Jardin.

menu reads like a poetic work of art, the décor is sexy, and the modern Chinese cuisine is simply splendid.

Peach Blossoms
5/F, Marina Mandarin, 6 Raffles Boulevard; tel: 6845 1111; www.marina-mandarin.com.sg; daily noon–2.30pm and 6.30–10.30pm; $$$$; MRT: City Hall; map p.136 C1
Wonderful Cantonese cuisine. The business crowd likes the dim sum lunch, and families flock here for the weekend buffets, where over 90 dishes such as braised superior shark's fin and Peking duck are served.

INDIAN
Rang Mahal
3/F, Pan Pacific Hotel, 7 Raffles Boulevard; tel: 6333 1788; www.rangmahal.com.sg; Mon–Fri, Sun noon–2.30pm, daily 6.30–10.30pm; $$$ (buffet lunch) $$$$ (à la carte); MRT: City Hall; map p.136 C1
Dine on classical northern, southern and coastal Indian specialities in a chic, modern

Below: savoury bouchees at Rang Mahal.

The brilliant pan-Asian and Mediterranean menu is given a terrific Western spin. Try the mezze platter and the spice-rubbed rack of lamb. This runs cookery classes as well.
SEE ALSO FOOD AND DRINK, P.65

INDIAN
Kinara
57 Boat Quay; tel: 6533 0412; www.thekinaragroup.com; daily noon–2.30pm and 6–11pm; $$; MRT: Raffles Place; map p.139 D4
Warm, friendly staff serve hearty North Indian cuisine in a beautiful space decorated with antique furniture from Rajasthan. The roasted leg of lamb, marinated for over 24 hours, is a must-try.

MODERN EUROPEAN
Pierside Kitchen & Bar
01-01 One Fullerton; tel: 6438 0400; www.marmaladegroup.com; daily 11.30am–3pm, Mon–Fri 5–11pm, Sat–Sun 5pm–midnight; $$$ (set lunch) $$$$ (à la carte); MRT: Raffles Place; map p.139 D4
By day stylish and by night intimate and relaxed, this serves a modern European menu alongside great views

of the Marina Bay. Must-haves are chef Robin Ho's oven-roasted miso cod and Valrhona choc fondant.

Marina Bay

AMERICAN
Morton's of Chicago
4/F, Mandarin Oriental, 5 Raffles Avenue; tel: 6339 3740; www.mortons.com; Mon–Sat 5.30–11pm, Sun 5–10pm; $$$$; MRT: City Hall; map p.136 C1
The dark-wood interiors, attentive waiters, 24-ounce Porterhouse and premium wine list are all part of the Morton experience. Start with a martini at the bar, with filet mignon steak sandwiches.

CHINESE
My Humble House
02-27/29 Esplanade Mall, 8 Raffles Avenue; tel: 6423 1881; www.tunglok.com; daily noon–3pm and 6.30–10.30pm; $$$ (set lunch) $$$$ (à la carte); MRT: City Hall; map p.136 B1
When the creative director is an artist-turned-restaurateur, you can only expect a restaurant so sensuous, even the sautéed spinach dish is named *Night is in the Air*. The

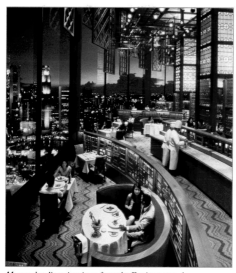

Above: dazzling city views from the Equinox complex.

interior. Whether it's a new twist to a traditional dish (tandoori salmon) or a classic favourite (*murg hazari*, or stuffed chicken), you can be assured of a memorable meal. The lunch buffet is fantastic value for money.

JAPANESE
Keyaki
4/F, Pan Pacific Hotel, 7 Raffles Boulevard; tel: 6826 8240; www.singapore.panpacific.com; daily noon–2.30pm, 6.30–9.30pm; $$$$ (set lunch) $$$$ (à la carte); MRT: City Hall; map p.136 C1
To get to the restaurant, you stroll past a Zen garden and fish pond before smiling, soft-spoken waitresses greet you at the entrance. Take your

Prices for a three-course dinner per person without drinks and taxes:
$$$$= S$45 and above
$$$= S$30–$45
$$= S$20–$30
$= under S$20

pick from kaiseki, robatayaki, sashimi, teppanyaki and shabu shabu. Round up with sake in the garden.

The Civic District
CHINESE
Lei Garden
01-24 Chijmes, 30 Victoria Street; tel: 6339 3822; daily 11.30am–3pm and 6–11pm; $$$ (set lunch) $$$ (à la carte); MRT: City Hall; map p.136 B2
One of Singapore's best dim sum and Cantonese cuisine spots. The dim sum and healthful double-boiled soups, seafood dishes and various bird's nest concoctions are wonderful.

Royal China at Raffles
3/F, Raffles Hotel Shopping Arcade, 1 Beach Road; tel: 6338 3363; www.raffles.com; Mon–Sat noon–3pm, Sun 11am–2pm, daily 6–10.30pm; $$ (set lunch) $$$ (à la carte); MRT: City Hall; map p.136 B2
Run by the same people who operate London's most notable Cantonese restaurant, this is great for dim

sum. The wholesome double-boiled soups, lobster noodles and creative Chinese desserts will also leave you hankering for more.

INDONESIAN
Rendezvous
02-02/03 Hotel Rendezvous, 9 Bras Basah Road; tel: 6339 7508; www.rendezvous-hlk. com.sg; daily 11am–9pm; $$; MRT: Dhoby Ghaut; map p.136 A3
Its history stretches six decades. From an old steamy coffee shop, it has been transformed into a comfortable air-conditioned restaurant in Hotel Rendezvous. Still enduring are its fiery *nasi padang* favourites, including spicy thick curries and sambal seafood dishes. This will probably be your most expensive *nasi padang* meal in the city but it's worth every cent.

MODERN EUROPEAN
Equinox
1 and 69–72/F, Swissôtel The Stamford, 2 Stamford Road; tel: 6837 3322; www.equinox complex.com; Mon–Sat noon–2.30pm and 6.30–11pm, Sun 11am–2.30pm, daily 3.30–5pm and 6.30–11pm; $$$ (set lunch) $$$$ (à la carte); MRT: City Hall; map p.136 B2
At this complex of five restaurants and bars, start with drinks at the **New Asia Bar** on the 71st level while taking in stunning city views. Then descend one level to the swanky nouvelle-French restaurant **Jaan Par Andre**, helmed by Taiwanese chef Andre Chiang, who has been feted as the most exciting chef in the City, if not Asia, by many.
SEE ALSO NIGHTLIFE, P.96
Wild Rocket at Mount Emily
Hangout@Mt.Emily, 10A Upper Wilkie Road; tel: 6339 9448; www.wildrocket.com.sg; Tue–

For a detailed guide to the best restaurants in Singapore, pick up a copy of Singapore Tatler's *Singapore's Best Restaurants* or the local food magazine *Wine & Dine* from a major bookstore.

Sat noon–3pm and 6.30–11pm, Sun 11.30am–3pm and 6.30–10.30pm; $$$ (à la carte); MRT: Dhoby Ghaut; map p.136 A4
Lawyer-turned-chef Willin Low helms this breezy, stylish restaurant in a lovely hilltop location, scoring with refreshing Asian spins on European-style cuisine. Must-orders are the signature laksa pesto spaghetti with quail eggs, the juicy rib-eye and the divine strawberry cheesecake. End with drinks at **Wild Oats** bar next door (tel: 6336 5413).

THAI
Yhingthai Palace
36 Purvis Street; tel: 6337 9429; daily 11.30am–2pm and 6–10pm; $$; MRT: City Hall; map p.136 B2
There's nothing palatial about this place; in fact, the décor is uninspiring and it can be noisy. But it pleases with a bill of Thai-Chinese fare at reasonable prices. The olive fried rice and Thai fish cakes are particular favourites, as is

the grilled squid salad drenched in a piquant sauce.

Chinatown and the CBD
CHINESE
Majestic Restaurant
1/F, New Majestic Hotel, 31–37 Bukit Pasoh Road; tel: 6511 4718; www.restaurantmajestic.com; daily 11.45am–3pm and 6.30–11pm; $$$$ (à la carte); MRT: Outram Park; map p.138 B2
Arguably the hippest culinary address this side of town, this restaurant pairs refined modern Cantonese cuisine with an idiosyncratic décor. Savour elegant fare such as grilled rack of lamb in Chinese honey sauce with pan-fried carrot cake and braised lobster in a milk and lime sauce while you contemplate the view of swimmers in the pool above through ceiling portholes.
Silk Road
2/F, Amara Hotel, 165 Tanjong Pagar Road; tel: 6227 3848; www.silkroadrestaurants.com; daily 11am–3pm and 6–10pm; $$ (set lunch) $$$$ (à la carte); MRT: Tanjong Pagar; map p.138 B1
Delicious Chinese regional dishes from Beijing, Liaoning, Shaanxi and Sichuan cuisines. Everything else here is also refined, from the poem by Tang poet

Li Bai carved onto the entrance floor to the warm, contemporary décor.
Swee Kee Fishhead Noodle House
96 Amoy Street; tel: 6224 9920; www.ka-soh.com.sg; daily 11.45am–2.30pm and 5.30–10.45pm; $$; MRT: Raffles Place; map p.139 C3
The stern-looking waitresses will tell you their menu has not changed since the 1970s. So reliable it is that celebrities and politicians are known to drop by regularly for the creamy fish-head soup, prawn-paste chicken and pork ribs in a 'secret' sauce.

ITALIAN
Buko Nero
126 Tanjong Pagar Road; tel: 6324 6225; Fri–Sat noon–2pm, Tue–Sat 6.30–9.30pm; $$ (set lunch) $$$ (à la carte); MRT: Tanjong Pagar; map p.138 B2
The regularly changing menu reflects an Italian-Asian marriage, with signatures such as tofu and vegetable tower, spaghetti with spicy crabmeat and prawns, and Horlicks ice cream. The seven-table restaurant is always full. Call in advance for dinner.
Oso Ristorante
46 Bukit Pasoh Road; tel: 6327 8378; www.oso.sg; Mon–Fri noon–2.30pm, Mon–Sat 6.30–10.30pm; $$$$; MRT: Outram Park; map p.138 B2
This chic, cosy restaurant is recognised as one of the best in Singapore. It has a climate-controlled cheese and wine room, and the menu changes monthly. Order the rigatoni with rabbit and truffle puree.

JAPANESE
Marutama Ra-Men
03-90 The Central, 6 Eu Tong Sen Street; tel: 6534 8090; $$; daily 11am–10pm; MRT: Clarke Quay; map p. 138 C4

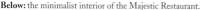

Below: the minimalist interior of the Majestic Restaurant.

The snaking queues that form outside its doors at mealtimes are evidence of this small restaurant's popularity. Its speciality is ramen served with one of four soup bases (chicken, spicy chicken, prawn or nuts). Don't forego the delicious side dishes like *kakuni* (thick wedges of stewed pork belly) and *dashimaki tamago* (a thick, pillowy omelette).

MODERN EUROPEAN
Ember

Hotel 1929, 50 Keong Saik Road; tel: 6347 1928; www.hotel1929.com; Mon–Fri 11.30am–2.30pm, Mon–Sat 6.30–10.30pm; $$$ (set lunch) $$$$ (à la carte); MRT: Tanjong Pagar; map p.138 B3

Chef-owner Sebastian Ng is one of Singapore's most talented young chefs. His modern European cuisine is delightfully robust yet refined, and sometimes comes with wonderful Asian accents. Everything is good really, but you should definitely have the slow-roasted lamb loin.

PERANAKAN
The Blue Ginger

97 Tanjong Pagar Road; tel: 6222 3928; www.thebluginger. com; daily noon–2.30pm and 6.30–10.30pm; $$$; MRT: Tanjong Pagar; map p.138 B2

This stylish, authentic Peranakan restaurant has been around for more than a decade. It serves satisfying offerings such as *ayam buah keluak* (stewed chicken with black nuts), *otak otak* (spicy fish mousse) and the must-have durian *cendol* (a dessert with green jelly).

THAI
Thanying

2/F, Amara Hotel, 165 Tanjong Pagar Road; tel: 6222 4688; daily 11am–3pm, 6.30–11pm; $$$ (à la carte); MRT: Tanjong Pagar; map p.138 B1

Thanying has a loyal following for its refined Thai cuisine. Whether it's the green curry or crispy grouper, every dish served in the elegant teak-panelled dining room is beautifully presented. The extensive menu is complemented by a Thai dessert buffet.

VEGETARIAN
Lingzhi

05-01 Liat Towers, 541 Orchard Road; tel: 6734 3788; www. lingzhivegetarian.com; daily 11am–3pm and 6–10pm; $$ (à la carte); MRT: Orchard; map p.134 B4

The vegetarian cuisine here is so good some would gladly give up meat for life. The goodness of soy, mushrooms, nuts and vegetables is creatively employed and the beautifully presented dishes complement the restaurant's understated elegance.

Orchard Road
CHINESE
Crystal Jade Palace

04-19 Ngee Ann City, 391 Orchard Road; tel: 6735 2388; www.crystaljade.com; Mon–Fri 11.30am–11pm, Sat 11am–3pm and 6–11pm, Sun 10.30am–3pm and 6–11pm; $$ (set lunch) $$$ (à la carte); MRT: Orchard; map p.134 C4

Crisp, contemporary décor – apart from the kitschy etched-glass windows. Excellent roast meat and seafood. Also runs **Crystal Jade La Mian Xiao Long Bao** (tel: 6238 1661) and **Crystal Jade Kitchen** (tel: 6238 1411) in the same building.

Din Tai Fung

B1-03/06 The Paragon, 290 Orchard Road; tel: 6836 8336; Mon–Fri 11am–9pm, Sat–Sun 10am–9.30pm; $$; MRT: Orchard Road; map p.135 C4

You notice the flurry of activity at the open-concept kitchen before you realise diners are watching the chefs in action and lining up for their *xiao long bao*, or steamed pork dumplings, that have exactly 18 pleats each. Fans sing praises of the chicken soup and humble fried rice, too.

Imperial Treasure Nan Bei

05-12/13 Ngee Ann City, 391 Orchard Road; tel: 6738 1238; Sun–Fri 11am–10pm, Sat 10.30am–10pm; $$$; MRT: Orchard; map p.134 C4

Left: some of the finest modern European food is at Ember.

Above: the Crustacean Bar at The Line at the Shangri-La.

Singaporeans make a beeline for luxurious hotel buffets. Offering some of the best are **Kopi Tiam** (tel: 6431 6156) at Swissôtel the Stamford, serving a wide variety of local dishes from Hainanese chicken rice to roti prata; and **The Line** (tel: 6213 4275) at The Shangri-La, named a 'Hot Table' of 2006 by *Conde Nast Traveler* magazine for its excellent international cuisine and chic interior.

The Imperial Treasure empire may have grown rapidly in a short period, but the standard has always been high. This outlet boasts top-grade Cantonese dishes, from roast goose and dim sum to comforting double-boiled chicken soup. The equally lauded **Imperial Treasure Teochew Cuisine**, one level down, serves fine Chaozhou dishes in plush surroundings (04-20A/21; tel: 6736 2118).

FRENCH
Au Jardin
The Corner House, Singapore Botanic Gardens, 1 Cluny Road; tel: 6466 8812; www.lesamis. com.sg; Fri noon–4pm, daily 7–midnight, Sun 11.30am–3pm; $$$$ (set dinner) $$$$ (à la carte); MRT: Orchard, then taxi; bus: 7, 105, 123 or 174

'Au Jardin', meaning 'in the garden', is set in a restored 1920s bungalow in the Botanic Gardens. The contemporary French flavours at this highly acclaimed restaurant are peerless. Choose the lavish nine-

Prices for a three-course dinner per person without drinks and taxes:
$$$$= S$45 and above
$$$= S$30–$45
$$= S$20–$30
$= under S$20

course dégustation menu or four-course *table d'hôte*.

Les Amis
02-16 Shaw Centre, 1 Scotts Road; tel: 6733 2225; www. lesamis.com.sg; Mon–Fri noon–2pm, Mon–Sat 7–9.30pm; $$$$ (set lunch) $$$$ (à la carte); MRT: Orchard; map p.134 C4

Flagship of the Les Amis Group, it is now helmed by chef Armin Leitgeb, who had stints at several Michelin-starred restaurants. The new décor exudes elegance and opulence; think chandeliers and velvety upholstery. Still boasting one of the city's best wine lists, this chichi restaurant understandably draws well-heeled regulars who appreciate contemporary French cuisine that's both delicate and flavourful.

INDONESIAN
The Rice Table
02-09/10 International Building, 360 Orchard Road; tel: 6835 3783; www.ricetable.com.sg; daily noon–3pm and 6–9.15pm; MRT: Orchard; map p.134 B4

For one price, you order as many Indonesian dishes as your stomach will allow. Try the *tahu telor*, a tower of bean curd with shredded cucumber and sweet sauce, the tender spicy beef *rendang* (dry curry) and grilled chicken. Don't be shy to ask for seconds.

INTERNATIONAL
Halia
Ginger Garden, Singapore Botanic Gardens, 1 Cluny Road; tel: 6476 6711; www.halia. com.sg; daily noon–5.30pm and 6.30–10.15pm; $$ (set lunch) $$$ (à la carte); MRT: Orchard, then taxi; bus: 7, 105, 123 or 174

To get to Halia ('ginger' in Malay), you walk past a ginger garden to find the restaurant nestled amid lush tropical foliage. It's so tranquil you will forget the city is just metres away. Lunch is a lighter menu of Western fusion delights. For dinner, there's a Continental menu of sublime ginger-inspired dishes.

mezza9
Grand Hyatt, 10 Scotts Road; tel: 6732 1234; www.singapore. grand.hyatt.com; Mon–Sat

Below: Au Jardin's trout with egg confit.

107

Above: stroll past a lush ginger garden to get to Halia in the Botanic Gardens *(see p.107)*.

noon–11pm, Sun 11.30am–11pm; $$ (set lunch) $$$$ (à la carte); MRT: Orchard; map p.134 B1

Conceptualised by international design firm 'Super Potato', this restaurant features show kitchens for sushi, yakitori, seafood, Western and Chinese dishes as well as deli and dessert counters and a **martini bar**. It's so cleverly designed you can sit anywhere and still watch the chefs in action.

SEE ALSO NIGHTLIFE, P.96

PS Café
03-41/44 The Paragon, 290 Orchard Road; tel: 6735 6765; www.pscafé.sg; daily 9.30am–10.30pm; $$; MRT: Orchard; map p.135 C4

The laid-back enclave of **Tanglin Village** is the latest hotspot for dining and wining. Tropical trees and colonial architecture lend a charming air to the achingly hip establishments housed in bungalows. Check out **Oosh** (Block 22 Dempsey Road; tel: 6475 0002) for Asian and Western food, **Hacienda** (Block 13A Dempsey Road; tel: 6476 2922) for drinks and bar snacks, and **PS Café** (Block 28B Harding Road; tel: 6479 3343) for light Australian-style food and yummy puddings.
(See also Nightlife, p.93, 94)

This trendy and perennially busy café has inspired East-West fusion dishes, sandwiches and scrumptious desserts. Favourites include the PS Caesar Salad and banana mango crumble. Another must-visit outlet, **PS Café**, is in Tanglin Village *(see box, below left)*.

JAPANESE
Akashi
1/F, Orchard Parade Hotel, 1 Tanglin Road; tel: 6732 4438; daily noon–3pm and 6.30–10.30pm; $$$; MRT: Orchard, then taxi; bus: 7, 105, 123 or 174; map p.134 A1

It's a good sign Akashi is well patronised by the expat Japanese community. The constant buzz, efficient service, and the food, especially the California roll, *ebi miso yaki* (grilled miso prawns) and smooth *tara inaniwa udon* noodles, all keep its regulars returning for more.

MODERN EUROPEAN
Iggy's
3/F, The Regent Hotel, 1 Cuscaden Road; tel: 6732 2234; www.iggys.com.sg; Mon–Fri noon–2pm, daily 7–9.30pm; $$$$ (set lunch and dinner); MRT: Orchard; map p.134 A1

With the British *Restaurant* magazine ranking it one of the world's top 100 restaurants in 2006, the 28-seat Iggy's is no longer the best-kept secret on Singapore's restaurant scene. Call ahead to enjoy degustation menus of inventive dishes, such as cappellini in scampi oil and scallop sashimi with foie gras and *yuzu*.

PERANAKAN
House of Peranakan Cuisine
10 Claymore Road; tel: 6831 6686; daily 6am–10.30am, noon–2.30pm and 6–10.30pm; $$; MRT: Orchard; map p.134 B1

The *Asian Wall Street Journal* once hailed its fish-head curry as the best dish in Singapore. Must-tries are the Blackmore full blood wagyu beef, braised duck, stewed pork and *ayam buah keluak* (stewed chicken with Indonesian black nuts), prepared from recipes that are three generations old.

SINGAPOREAN
Chatterbox
Mandarin Orchard, 333 Orchard Road; tel: 6831 6291; daily 6.30am–10.30am, Sun–Thur 11.30am–1am, Fri, Sat and eve of public holidays 24 hours; $$; MRT: Orchard; map p.135 C4

This coffee house is famed for its iconic but expensive chicken rice, often voted as the best in Singapore. Also check out the other local fare such as *nasi lemak* (rice cooked in coconut milk), lobster laksa and *bak kut teh* (pork rib soup).

Prima Taste
01-63/64 Centrepoint, 176 Orchard Road; tel: 6887 3786; www.pfs.com.sg; daily 10am–10pm; $; MRT: Somerset; map p.135 D4

When a restaurant calls itself a 'True Singapore restaurant', it usually spells tourist trap. Luckily Prima Taste isn't one of those. The tiny air-conditioned café is a hot lunch spot and locals happily tuck into its Hainanese chicken rice and *laksa*.

Little India and Kampong Glam

INDIAN
Ananda Bhavan
01-10 Block 663 Buffalo Road; tel: 6297 9522; www.anandabhavan.com; daily 7am–10pm; $; MRT: Little India; map p.132 C1

You order, take a queue number and wait for it to be called to collect your scrumptious South Indian meal. While waiting, read all about the virtues of vegetarianism posted on the wall. One of the vignettes reads 'the strength of an elephant is sustained on a vegetarian diet'. (Also at 58 Serangoon Road; tel: 6297 9522.)

Banana Leaf Apolo
54/56 Race Course Road; tel: 6293 8682; daily 10.30am–10.30pm; $$; MRT: Little India; map p.132 C1

Never mind the unimaginative, fluorescent-lit space. The busy restaurant fills up quickly. It is the place for spicy South Indian food served on banana leaves. Everything looks good and the efficient waiters are ever ready to help if you need recommendations. Musttries: masala prawns and

chicken. (Also at 01-32 Little India Arcade, 48 Serangoon Road; tel: 6297 1595.)

Komala Vilas
76/78 Serangoon Road; tel: 6293 6980; www.komalavilas.com.sg; daily 7am–10.30pm; $; MRT: Little India; map p.133 C1

This boisterous, charming Little India institution is the place for saffron rice accompanied by an array of vegetable curries, *vadai* (savoury fritters), and Indian breads such as wholewheat *bhattura* and *chappati* and rice flour-based *dosai*. Sauces and dips are replenished as desired and you should definitely eat with your fingers. (Also at 12/14 Serangoon Road; tel: 6293 3664.)

Muthu's Curry
138 Race Course Road; tel: 6392 1722; www.muthuscurry.com; daily 10am–10pm; $$; MRT: Farrer Park; map p.132 C1

Singaporeans are passionate about fish-head curry, and this inevitably comes up as one of the top places to sample the dish. It has served its award-winning version since 1969. The chicken, mutton and prawn dishes are also always good bets.

Below: flaky *roti prata* is a firm breakfast favourite.

Prices for a three-course dinner per person without drinks and taxes:
$$$$= S$45 and above
$$$= S$30–$45
$$= S$20–$30
$= under S$20

Singapore Zam Zam Restaurant
697–699 North Bridge Road; tel: 6298 6320; daily 8am–11pm; $; MRT: Bugis; map p.136 C4

A rough-and-ready place serving Indian Muslim specialities. The fragrant mutton or chicken *briyani* (saffron rice) is robustly spicy, as are the *prata* (flaky bread) and *murtabak* (flaky bread stuffed with minced meat) dipped in curry.

MALAY
Hajjah Maimunah Restaurant
11 & 15 Jalan Pisang; tel: 6291 3132; www.hjmaimunah.com; Mon–Sat 7am–8pm; $; MRT: Bugis; map p.136 C1

This self-service restaurant is always packed to the gills. Just point to the dishes you'd like and they will be served with fluffy rice. The tender and spicy beef *rendang* (dry curry) and *sotong bakar* (grilled squid) are heavenly.

MIDDLE EASTERN
Café Le Caire
39 Arab Street; tel: 6292 0979; www.cafelecaire.com; Sun–Thur 10am–3.30am, Fri–Sat 10am–5.30am; $; MRT: Bugis; map p.137 C4

Backpackers, creative types and students patronise this café run by a third-generation Arab Singaporean. It serves traditional dishes like kebabs, falafel and *mandi kharouf* (lamb served on rice). A wonderful selection of flavoured *shishas*; try the vanilla, caramel or apple.

109

Above: pizza at Trapizza.

Café Samar
27 Bali Lane; tel: 6398 0530;
daily 10am–6am; $ (set lunch)
$$$ (à la carte);
MRT: Bugis; map p.137 C4
This is a lovely spot to chill
out at after exploring Arab
Street. Its Middle Eastern
menu is small; try the
hummus with freshly baked
bread and the signature
mandhi lamb shank. You may
want to lie on the cushions
upstairs and smoke away on
colourful *shisha* pipes.
SEE ALSO NIGHTLIFE, P.93

Sentosa

ITALIAN
il Lido
Sentosa Golf Club, 27 Bukit
Manis Road; tel: 6866 1977;
www.il-lido.com; daily 11.30am–
2.30pm and 6.30–11pm; $$$
(set lunch); $$$$ (à la carte);
MRT: HarbourFront, then Sentosa Express from VivoCity
Chef Gianluca Visani serves
superb Italian cuisine in a
gorgeous setting. The balcony offers a beautiful sunset
view. Try the home-made
pasta with sea urchin, and
the squid ink tagliolini stuffed
with scallops. The classy **il
Lido Lounge Bar**'s designer
décor, champagne and DJ-
spun chill-out music make for
a posh finale to the evening.

Trapizza
Siloso Beach; tel: 6376 2662;
Mon–Fri 11am–10pm, Sat–Sun
11am–11pm; $$$; MRT: Har-
bourFront, then Sentosa Express
from VivoCity or Shangri-La's
Rasa Sentosa shuttle bus from
HarbourFront Centre
This Italian-style family
restaurant sits on Siloso
Beach next to a trapeze. On
a hot day, nothing beats a
scoop of mango sorbet and a
mug of cold beer. Wait for the
sun to set and wind down
with hearty salads, delicious
pastas and excellent pizzas
from the wood-fired oven.

SEAFOOD
The Cliff
The Sentosa, 2 Bukit Manis
Road; tel: 6371 1425; www.
thesentosa.com; daily 6.30–
10pm; $$$$; MRT: HarbourFront,
then The Sentosa shuttle bus
from VivoCity
One of Singapore's most
beautiful and dramatic
restaurants, The Cliff sits at
the edge of a cliff and offers
a view of lovely, lush
surroundings and the South
China Sea. In fact, the artful
and sensuous Yasuhiro
Koichi-designed restaurant
and Chef Shawn Armstrong's
elegant contemporary
seafood-inspired dishes
seem a perfect marriage.
There are eight varieties of
oysters, which can be pre-
pared in four different ways.

Southern and Western Singapore

CHINESE
Imperial Herbal Restaurant
03-08 VivoCity Lobby G, 1 Har-
bourFront Walk; tel: 6337 0491;
www.imperialherbal.com; daily
11.30am–2.30pm and 6.15–
10pm; $$$ (set lunch) $$$ (à la
carte); MRT: HarbourFront
From ministers and visiting
VIPs to celebrities and the

who's who of Singapore – all
have dined here. Why?
Perhaps the presence of a
Chinese herbal doctor helps.
Consult him before you tuck
into curative double-boiled
soups. If you're feeling
adventurous, try the black
ants on shredded potato or
the deep-fried scorpions.

Min Jiang
5 Rochester Park; tel: 6774 0122;
daily 11am–2.30pm and
6–10.30pm; $$$$; MRT:
Buona Vista
Long acclaimed for its refined
food at Goodwood Park
Hotel (tel: 6737 7411), Min
Jiang now has a second
home – a conserved colonial-
style bungalow in Rochester
Park. The repertoire here
extends beyond Sichuan
fare. There are dishes from
various Chinese regions, and
the highlight is the Peking
duck with eight different
condiments. It's also the first
Chinese restaurant in Singa-
pore to have a Peking duck
oven – a chef was specially
flown in from China to over-
see the whole building
process.

Tung Lok Signatures
01-57 VivoCity, 1 HarbourFront
Walk; tel: 6376 9555; www.
tunglok.com; Mon–Sat 11.30am–
3pm, Sun 11am–3pm, daily
6–10.30pm; $$$$;
MRT: HarbourFront
You will not be disappointed
when the name says 'Tung
Lok'. This outlet, done up in
minimalist white décor,
serves the most memorable
dishes from the group's sta-
ble of outstanding Hunanese,

Prices for a three-course
dinner per person without
drinks and taxes:
$$$$= S$45 and above
$$$= S$30–$45
$$= S$20–$30
$= under S$20

Fashionable eating and drinking establishments have gathered in far-flung enclaves in recent years. One example is **Rochester Park**, in western Singapore, which was once the home and haunt of British officers. Now their black-and-white colonial-era bungalows have been taken over by hip restaurants and bars, whose alluring ambience amid lush gardens draw gastronauts who do not mind the trek out of the city centre.

Cantonese, seafood and other restaurants. There are classic Chinese dishes, healthful double-boiled soups and exquisite dim sum.

FRENCH
Bistro Petit Salut
01-54 Block 44 Chip Bee Gardens, Jalan Merah Saga, Holland Village; tel: 6474 9788; www.aupetitsalut.com; Mon–Sat 11.30am–2.30pm and 6.30–10.30pm; $$ (set lunch) $$$$ (à la carte); MRT: Buona Vista
Petite this French restaurant may be, but it is big on flavours. Chef Jason Wong brings diners traditional French cuisine with contemporary touches. Signatures include oven-baked portobello mushroom with mixed greens and melted comté cheese.

ITALIAN
Da Paolo La Terazza
01-56 Block 44 Chip Bee Gardens, Jalan Merah Saga, Holland Village; tel: 6476 1332; www.dapaolo.com.sg; Wed–Mon 11.30am–2.30pm and 6.30–10.30pm; $$; (set lunch) $$$$ (à la carte); MRT: Buona Vista
Despite Da Paolo's expansion in recent years, its outlets are as stylish as ever. This outlet

oozes sophistication yet remains laid-back. Chef-owner Paolo Scarpa's pastas are always excellent – you won't go wrong with any of the pasta dishes on the menu.
Michelangelo's
01-60 Block 44 Chip Bee Gardens, Jalan Merah Saga, Holland Village; tel: 6475 9069; www.michelangelos.com.sg; Mon–Fri, Sun 11.30am–3pm, daily 6–11pm; $$ (set lunch) $$$ (à la carte); MRT: Buona Vista
It's been more than a decade since Michelangelo's opened, but it is still one of the best around. Chef-owner Angelo Sanelli is like your big Italian mama – fastidious, funny and an accomplished chef. His food is Italian with Australian and Asian accents, fine examples of which are the penne vodka and fettuccine di Angelo.
Sistina Ristorante
01-58 Block 44 Chip Bee Gardens, Jalan Merah Saga, Holland Village; tel: 6476 4261;

www.michelangelos.com.sg; Mon–Fri 3–10.30pm, Sat 11.30am–2.30pm and 6.30–10.30pm, Sun 11.30am–10.30pm; $$$; MRT: Buona Vista
The humble pizza is transformed into a high-cuisine treat. There are over 50 types of toppings, including scallops, oysters, goat cheese and rosemary-infused lamb for your regular or thin-crust gourmet pizza. An extensive list of New World wines.

MEDITERRANEAN
Original Sin
01-62 Block 43 Chip Bee Gardens, Jalan Merah Saga, Holland Village; tel: 6475 5605; www.originalsin.com.sg; daily 11.30am–2.30pm and 6–10.30pm; $$ (set lunch) $$$ (à la carte); MRT: Buona Vista
Whether you're on an ovo-lacto diet, a vegan or just plain health-conscious, chef-owner Marisa Bertocchi ensures there's something

Below: The Cliff has been voted one of the most romantic dining spots in Singapore.

R

If you like your food organic, **Bunalun** (01-70 Block 43 Chip Bee Gardens, Jalan Merah Saga; tel: 6472 0870; www.bunalun.com.sg; daily 9am–9pm) is the place. A chic, breezy organic café that dishes up delicious gourmet meals and ready-to-go salads, crab cakes and pastries. The retail section stocks a good range of organic produce as well as home and beauty products under the Bunalun label.

imaginative for everyone. Her mezze platter, moussaka, Sicilian pizza and tiramisu would win over even the most hardened meat lover.

MEXICAN
Cha Cha Cha
32 Lorong Mambong, Holland Village; tel: 6462 1650; daily 11.30am–11pm, Fri–Sat 11.30am–midnight; $$$; MRT: Buona Vista

This is a subdued little spot where you will find good south-of-the-border food – chimichangas, fajitas, burritos – along with a relaxed atmosphere and great margaritas.

MODERN EUROPEAN
Graze
4 Rochester Park; tel: 6775 9000; www.graze.sg; Mon–Sat noon–4pm (open all day for drinks), Tue–Fri 6pm–midnight, Sat 6pm–2am, Sun 9.30am–4pm, 6–11pm; $$$$; MRT: Buona Vista
Owned by the same people behind the hip JIA boutique hotels, this stylish restaurant is housed in a beautiful pre-war black-and-white bungalow. The cuisine is modern Western–Asian cuisine, and at weekends, a hearty breakfast and brunch is also served. After dinner, chill out in its lounge bar with an outdoor terrace.

The East Coast
AMERICAN
Bernie's BFD
Marine Cove, 1000 East Coast Parkway, tel: 6244 4434; Mon–Fri 5pm–midnight, Sat–Sun noon–midnight; $$$; MRT: Bedok, then bus: 16, 31 or 196
With its beachfront location, an energetic band, intoxicating margaritas, and over-sized burgers and steaks, it's little wonder Bernie's is such a hit.

INDIAN
Vansh
01-04 Singapore Indoor Stadium, 2 Stadium Walk; tel: 6345 4466; www.vansh.com.sg; daily noon–2.30pm and 6–10.30pm; $$ (set lunch) $$$$ (à la carte); MRT: Kallang, then taxi
The setting is so bold, yet so sexy, you may just want to sip the Kamasutra cocktail horizontally – on the low lounge chairs around the open tandoor kitchen. Modern Indian cuisine means everything is individually plated and creatively presented.

PERANAKAN
Guan Hoe Soon
38/40 Joo Chiat Place, 214 Joo Chiat Road; tel: 6344 2761; www.guanhoesoon.com; Wed–Mon 11am–2.30pm and 6–9.30pm; $$; MRT: Paya Lebar, then taxi or MRT: Bedok, then bus: 33
Singapore's oldest Peranakan restaurant was a mere coffee shop when it was founded in 1953. Despite some attempts at modernisation in the 1980s, its old-world ambience is still palpable. You can't go wrong with traditional dishes such as *satay babi* (pork satay curry),

Left: a sexy décor at Vansh to go with its modern Indian cuisine.

nogh hiang sausage and ayam tempra (chicken stew).

True Blue
49 Armenian Street; tel: 6440 0449; daily 11am–2pm and 6–9.30pm; $$$$; MRT: City Hall; map p.136 A2
The food here is good, but it's very expensive. Be prepared to pay for every cup of tea that's poured and every miniscule saucer of chilli belachan you ask for. Ask for the ayam buah keluak (chicken with Indonesian black nuts). While waiting for your food, feast your eyes on owner Benjamin Seck's personal collection of Straits Chinese antiques.

SEAFOOD
East Coast Seafood Centre
1202–1206 East Coast Parkway, near car park E1; $$$; MRT: Bedok, then bus: 31, 196 or 197
A collection of casual seafood restaurants, located by the beach, which fill up at weekends. These are good spots for Singapore-style seafood, including **Red House** (tel: 6442 3112), **Jumbo** (tel: 6442 3435) and **Long Beach** (tel: 6448 3636).

Hua Yu Wee
462 Upper East Coast Road; tel: 6442 9313; daily 5.30–11.30pm; MRT: Tanah Merah, then bus: 14
Chinese families flock in droves to this nondescript restaurant for its Singapore-style seafood. Its chilli and pepper crabs, butter prawns and seafood rolls are highly recommended.

SINGAPOREAN
Marine Parade Laksa
Nan Sin Food Centre, 57/59 East Coast Road; daily 9am–6pm, closed alternate Tue; $; MRT: Paya Lebar, then taxi or MRT: Tanah Merah, then bus: 12
Laksa is noodles in a curry-

Above: chilli crab is a must-try in Singapore; one of the best places to have it is the East Coast Seafood Centre.

like, coconut-based soup. This particular stall is said to have pioneered Katong laksa, the now-famous variety that has even warranted a story in The New York Times. You can ask for clams (or without) and you eat the short noodles with your spoon – no chopsticks required.

Central and Northern Singapore
FRENCH
Vis-A-Vis
12 Chun Tin Road; tel: 6468 7433; www.vis-a-vis.com.sg; daily 11.30am–2.30pm and 6.30–10.30pm; $$$$ (à la carte); MRT: Newton, then taxi; bus: 66, 67, 170, 171
Reward yourself with a lobster thermidor (by special request only) after a rigorous trek at the nearby Bukit Timah Nature Reserve. This has a seasonal menu offering snails, quail, foie gras and all things French, along with a reasonably good wine list.

PERANAKAN
Ivins
4 Jalan Leban, Upper Thomson Road; tel: 6451 4622; www.

ivins.com.sg; Fri–Wed 11am–3pm and 6–10pm; $ (set lunch) $$ (à la carte); MRT: Ang Mo Kio, then taxi; bus: 169 or 265
Delicious Peranakan fare at down-to-earth prices. A lavish meal of chilli prawns, spring rolls, honey pork and stewed chicken with Indonesian black nuts can be had for a song.

SINGAPOREAN
The Roti Prata House
246M Upper Thomson Road; tel: 6459 5260; daily 24 hours; $; MRT: Ang Mo Kio, then taxi; bus: 132 or 165
Enjoy your roti prata bread crispy or paper thin, with cheese or filled with chicken, mutton, sardines or vegetables. Then work off the calories at the MacRitchie Reservoir Park, just 15 minutes' walk away.

Prices for a three-course dinner per person without drinks and taxes:
$$$$= S$45 and above
$$$= S$30–$45
$$= S$20–$30
$= under S$20

113

Shopping

For Singaporeans, shopping is right up there with eating – they love it; they live for it. This might explain the large number of malls in the city, both downtown and in the suburbs. Orchard Road and Marina Bay are Singapore's style headquarters, filled with mall-crawling shoppers any time of the day and week. Beyond the malls and department stores are idiosyncratic shops hidden in little enclaves such as Ann Siang Hill, just a stone's throw from Chinatown, and Haji and Bali lanes in Kampong Glam. In the flea markets and ethnic neighbourhoods, cultural finds and arts and crafts quietly wait to be discovered.

Department Stores

DFS Galleria
25 Scotts Road; tel: 6229 8100; www.dfsgalleria.com; Sun–Thur 10am–10pm, Fri–Sat 10am–10.30pm; MRT: Orchard; map p.134 B1
Shop duty-free at this temple to consumerism, with high-end clothing, kitschy tourist souvenirs and fine wines.

Mustafa Centre
145 Syed Alwi Road; tel: 6295 5855; www.mustafa.com.sg; daily 24 hours; MRT: Farrer Park; map p.133 D2
An institution in Singapore, selling just about everything under the sun. Luggage, jewellery, electronics, power tools, you name it – if no one else stocks it – Mustafa probably does The prices here are great, too. But be warned: like everywhere in Little India, this place is packed on Sunday.

Robinsons
05-05 Centrepoint, 176 Orchard Road; tel: 6733 0888; www.robinsons.com.sg; daily 10.30am–10pm; MRT: Somerset; map p.135 D3
Robinsons dates back to the 1850s. When its owners tried to sell it in 2003, infuriated shoppers petitioned against the sale – such is the loyalty it enjoys. It has the nicest sales staff around, and its biannual sales are eagerly awaited. (Also at Raffles City; tel: 6216 8388.)

TANGS
310 Orchard Road; tel: 6737 5500; www.tangs.com.sg; Mon–Thur 10.30am–9.30pm, Fri–Sat 10.30am–11pm, Sun 11am–8.30am; MRT: Orchard; map p.134 C4
This well-loved icon was founded by C.K. Tang, who made his fortune by peddling China-made lace from house to house in the early 1900s. It is particularly noted for its cult skincare labels and kitchen gadgets. (Also at VivoCity; tel: 6303 8688.)

Left: some malls focus on streetwear for the youth market.

Left: colourful fabrics in Little India.

transformed into this mall of glassed-in shophouses housing boutiques.

Far East Plaza
14 Scotts Road; tel: 6732 6266; www.fareast-plaza.com; daily 10am–10pm; MRT: Orchard; map p.134 B1

Don't let the slightly decrepit exterior put you off. Shops here sell great streetwear. There is a host of tattoo parlours and cheap and good food on the upper levels.

The Heeren Shops
260 Orchard Road; tel: 6733 4725; www.heeren.com.sg; daily 10am–11pm; MRT: Somerset; map p.135 D4

The mall of choice for younger shoppers, with shops selling trendy threads.

ION Orchard
2 Orchard Turn; tel: 6238 8228; www.ionorchard.com; daily 10am–10pm; MRT: Orchard; map p.134 C4

The latest darling of Singapore's glitzy malls, ION Orchard is laid out like the Borobudur of shopping with mass labels and eateries built four floors underground, while the bigger designer names are spread across four floors up from the street level.

Marina Square
6 Raffles Boulevard; tel: 6339 8787; www.marinasquare.com.sg; daily 10am–10pm; MRT: City Hall; map p.136 C1

This shiny mall has plenty of hip boutiques, eateries and a cineplex. Check out Cathay Photo in the basement for affordable photo equipment.

Ngee Ann City
391 Orchard Road; tel: 6506 0461; www.ngeeanncity.

All of Singapore (and the region) comes out to shop during the Great Singapore Sale from end May to early July. *(See Festivals and Events, p.58)*

Yue Hwa
70 Eu Tong Sen Street; tel: 6538 4222; www.yuehwa.com.sg; Sun–Fri 11am–9pm, Sat 11am–10pm; MRT: Chinatown; map p.138 B3

All things Chinese, from silk products to herbs and health tonics, can be found here.

Shopping Malls

313@Somerset
313 Orchard Road; tel: 6496 9300; www.313somerset.com.sg; daily 10am–11pm; MRT: Somerset; map p.135 D3

Recently built, this mall offers a decidedly girl-oriented shopping experience with three floors of American label Forever 21 and a host of other ladies boutiques including Spanish label Zara. It also boasts the largest food court in Singapore.

Bugis Junction
200 Victoria Street; tel: 6557 6557; www.bugisjunction-mall.com.sg; daily 10am–10pm; MRT: Bugis; map p.136 B3

Bugis Street was once famous for the transvestites and transsexuals who plied the area. Today it has been

Left: exploring VivoCity could take days *(see p.116)*.

Above: fashion-shopping hot spot Wisma Atria.

com.sg; daily 10am–9.30pm; MRT: Orchard; map p.134 C4

Locals like to refer to it as 'Taka' (its anchor tenant is Takashimaya Shopping Centre), and love the **Books Kinokuniya** store on the third level and the food hall in the basement.

SEE ALSO LITERATURE, P.77

The Paragon

290 Orchard Road; tel: 6738 5535; www.paragonsc.com.sg; daily 10am–9.30pm; MRT: Orchard; map p.135 C4

Sleek high-fashion boutiques from Gucci to Prada, younger brands like Miss Sixty and home-grown label Project Shop, with a gourmet super-market and eateries in the mix.

Raffles Hotel Shopping Arcade

Raffles Hotel, 1 Beach Road; tel: 6337 1886; www.raffles.com; daily 10.30am–7pm; MRT: City Hall; map p.136 B2

You can lodge complaints against errant retailers with the **Singapore Tourism Board** (tel: 1800-736 2000; www.visitsin gapore.com) or the **Small Claims Tribunal** (tel: 6435 5946; www.smallclaims.gov.sg).

Luxury labels (think Tiffany & Co., Swarovski, Louis Vuitton), bespoke tailors and antiques stores pepper this mall within the legendary Raffles Hotel.

Suntec City Mall

3 Temasek Boulevard; tel: 6825 2667; www.sunteccity.com.sg; daily 10am–10pm; MRT: City Hall; map p.136 C2

It is easy to get lost in this veritable city with over 350 shops and a whole lot of restaurants and eateries. Until VivoCity was built, Suntec City was the largest mall on the island.

VivoCity

1 HarbourFront Walk; tel: 6377 6860; www.vivocity.com.sg; daily 10am–10pm; MRT: HarbourFront

This is so huge that most visitors never make it to the second floor on their first visit. Spread over one million square foot, it has a cineplex, a hypermart and hundreds of shops and restaurants, some of which overlook Sentosa.

Wisma Atria

435 Orchard Road; tel: 6235 8177; www.wismaonline.com; daily 7.30am–11pm; MRT: Orchard; map p.134 C4

Wisma Atria has European high-street boutiques aplenty – Warehouse, FCUK, the Gap and Mango.

Markets

Chinatown Night Market

Pagoda, Trengganu and Sago streets; Sun–Thur 5–11pm, Fri–Sat 5pm–1am; MRT: Chinatown; map p.138 B3/C3

Over 200 stalls selling trinkets, tourist souvenirs and traditional Chinese goods like calligraphy and masks.

MAAD

red dot design museum, 28 Maxwell Road; tel: 6534 7209; www.maad.sg; 1st weekend of the month 11am–7pm; MRT: Tanjong Pagar; map p.138 C2

On Saturday nights, many stores in Orchard Road malls such as Wisma Atria and Heeren are open until 11pm.

The Market of Artists and Designers is a bazaar with t-shirts, bags, home accessories and more crafted by local emerging talents.

SEE ALSO MUSEUMS AND GALLERIES, P.86

Sungei Market (Thieves' Market)

Sungei Road; daily 11am–7pm; MRT: Bugis; map p.133 D1

Broken radios, chipped crockery and vinyl records might not be the sort of things you would want to buy, but this market, busiest at weekends, offers an insight into the city's underbelly.

Tanglin Mall

163 Tanglin Road; tel: 6736 4922; www.tanglinmall.com.sg; daily 10am–10pm; MRT: Orchard, then taxi, or bus: 7, 105, 123 or 174; map p.134 A1

Stalls at the biggest flea market in Singapore sell rare toys, comics and second-hand clothes.

What to Buy

ANTIQUES

Lopburi Arts & Antiques

01-04 Tanglin Place, 91 Tanglin Road; tel: 6738 3834; daily 11am–7pm; MRT: Orchard, then taxi; map p.134 A1

Shipping and certificates of authenticity are provided for its Buddhist art and antiques.

Pagoda House

143/145 Tanglin Road, Tudor Court; tel 6732 2177; www.pagodahouse.com; Mon–Sat 11am–7pm, Sun 11am–5pm; MRT: Orchard, then taxi; map p.134 A1

Specialises in antique furniture from Europe, North Asia and Southeast Asia. It also custom-makes furniture and offers a selection of home

Above: Pluck, a fashion and home accessories store on Haji Lane.

accessories and arts objects.

Renee Hoy Fine Arts
01-44 Tanglin Shopping Centre, 19 Tanglin Road; tel: 6235 1596; Mon–Sat 10.30am–6.30pm, Sun by appointment only; MRT: Orchard, then taxi; map p.134 A1
Antique furniture from China, Korea, Japan and other Asian countries. It takes orders for reproductions as well.

ELECTRONICS
Funan DigitaLife Mall
109 North Bridge Road; tel: 6336 8327; www.funan.com.sg; daily 10.30am–8.30pm; MRT: City Hall; map p.136 A1
Check out **South Asia Computer** (03-01; tel: 6337 0871) and **Challenger Superstore** (06-00; tel: 6339 9008) for computer accessories and MP3 players. For photographic equipment, try **John 3:16** (05-46; tel: 6337 2877).

Sim Lim Square
1 Rochor Canal Road; tel: 6332 5839; www.simlimsquare.com.sg; daily 10.30am–9pm; MRT: Bugis or Little India; map p.136 B4
A crowded mall dedicated to electronics. You must compare prices and haggle here – otherwise, you'll be ripped off hard. That said, there are some good deals to be had.

HOME ACCESSORIES AND SOUVENIRS
Egg 3
01-10/12, 33 Erskine Road, tel: 6536 6977; eggthree.com; Mon–

Sat 10am–8pm, Sun 10am–7pm; MRT: Chinatown; map p.138 C3
Quirky homeware and graphic T-shirts.

Lim's Arts & Living
02-01 Holland Road Shopping Centre, 211 Holland Avenue; tel: 6467 1300; www.lims.com.sg; daily 10am–8.30pm; MRT: Buona Vista
A wide selection of ethnic items and handicrafts.

Pluck
31/33 Haji Lane; tel: 6396 4048; www.pluck.com.sg; Tue–Sat 11am–8pm, Sun 1–7pm; MRT: Bugis; map p.136 C3
This has girly soft furnishings, vintage clothes and a little ice cream parlour.

Risis
Singapore Botanic Gardens, 1 Cluny Road; tel: 6475 5104; www.risis.com.sg; daily 8.45am–5.45pm; MRT: Orchard, then taxi; bus: 7, 105, 123 or 174
Gold-plated orchid blooms are crafted into jewellery. (Also at Suntec City Mall; tel 6338 8250 and Centrepoint; tel: 6235 0988.)

Salad
25 Haji Lane; tel: 6299 5805; Mon–Sat 1–8pm; MRT: Bugis; map p.136 C3
Stocks slightly pricey home accessories like mirrors and picture frames and a range of affordable clothes.

The Shop
The Arts House, 1 Old Parliament Lane; tel: 6337 1086; www.theartshouse.com.sg; Mon–Sat 10am–8pm; MRT:

City Hall; map p.139 D4
Inspired homeware, jewellery, pottery and illustrations from local artists and designers.

Style: Nordic
39 Ann Siang Road; tel: 6423 9496; www.stylenordic.com; Mon–Sat noon–8pm, Sun noon–5pm; MRT: Chinatown or Tanjong Pagar; map p.138 C2
Lifestyle boutique with Scandinavian furniture from OFFECCT, David Design and Nola. There are also Nordic fashion labels like Nudie Jeans and Filippa K.

ORIENTAL CARPETS
Oriental carpets, from tribal rugs to silk carpets, come from China, India, Iran, Turkey or Pakistan. The following has good selections:

Amir & Sons
36 Kandahar Street; tel: 6734 9112; Mon–Sat 11am–7pm, Sun 1–6pm; MRT: Bugis; map p.137 C4

Eastern Carpets
03-21C Raffles City Shopping Centre, 252 North Bridge Road; tel: 6338 8135; www.eastern carpets.com.sg; daily 10.30am–9pm; MRT: City Hall; map p.136 B2

Jehan Gallery
03-08 Tan Boon Liat Building, 315 Outram Road; tel: 6334 4333; www.jehan.com.sg; daily 10am–7pm; MRT: Outram Park

Below: a poster for the MAAD weekend market.

Sport

Perhaps it is the country's miniscule size and population, or the fact that its people place an intense focus on academic education for its younger generation, but Singapore doesn't have a robust sporting culture. Its athletes tend to be stronger in only a few activities, such as bowling, table tennis, swimming, *wushu* (Chinese martial arts) and sailing, and have made their country-men proud by taking top honours at international competitions. Efforts to promote a healthier appetite for sport among the people have led to a sound infrastructure and an event-packed calendar, which visitors are welcome to enjoy.

Adventure

Forest Adventure

825 Bedok Reservoir Road, Bedok Reservoir Park; tel: 8100 7420; www.forestadventure. com.sg; Tue–Sun 10am–6pm; MRT: Bedok, then bus: 18 or 28

Drum up some of that city-slicker courage for this camp. You'll go through a safety briefing and initiation course before plunging into the two-hour 'Grand Course', where you climb, crawl, swing from tree to tree, and swoop down on ziplines in mid air across water to fine views of the Bedok Reservoir. There's also a less challenging kids' course for the little ones.

Golf

Several of Singapore's golf courses are world class, attracting such international tournaments as the **Johnnie Walker Classic**. Private golf courses offer limited access to non-members while public courses have no restrictions on visitors. Green fees range from S$40 for a nine-hole course on a weekday to S$450 for a full round on a championship course at the weekend. Some clubs ask for a proficiency certificate. Call ahead for tee times.

Green Fairways Golf Course

60 Fairways Drive; tel: 6468 7233; daily 6.30am–5.30pm (golf course), 7am–10.30pm (driving range); MRT: Orchard, then taxi

Only 10 minutes by taxi from Orchard Road, this has a 62-bay driving range and a nine-hole public course.

Raffles Country Club

450 Jalan Ahmad Ibrahim; tel: 6861 7655; www.rcc.org.sg; daily 7am–6.30pm; MRT: Joo Koon, then taxi

Widely regarded as the most scenic course in Singapore. Two 18-hole courses skirt a reservoir and offer lovely views of Malaysia.

Seletar Country Club

101 Seletar Club Road; tel: 6481 4812; www.seletarclub.com.sg; Mon 11am–7.30pm, Tue–Sun 7am–7.30pm; MRT: Khatib, then taxi

Formerly known as the Sele-tar Base Golf course, this challenging 18-hole course has the scenic Lower Seletar Reservoir as its backdrop.

Sentosa Golf Club

27 Bukit Manis Road, Sentosa; tel: 6275 0090; www.sentosa golf.com; MRT: HarbourFront, then taxi or Sentosa Express from VivoCity

Home to two of Singapore's best courses with views of the South China Sea. The Tanjong course and the more difficult Serapong course offer challenging layouts and are impeccably maintained.

Below: sailing off Changi.

Left: beach volleyball action on Sentosa.

Offers windsurfing, kayaking and laser sailing courses. Rental fees for equipment will apply.

Ski360 Cableski Park
1206A East Coast Parkway; tel: 6442 7318; www.ski360degree.com; Mon–Thur 10am–10pm, Fri 10am–midnight, Sat 9am–midnight, Sun 9am–10pm; MRT: Bedok, then bus: 197 or 401 (weekends only)

Wakeboarders and water-skiers can practise on a 'track' pulled by cables here. It is a lot harder to learn wakeboarding this way, as the cables move at a predetermined speed, which may be too quick for learners. It's best to learn behind a boat.

Venue

Singapore Indoor Stadium
2 Stadium Walk; tel: 6344 2660; www.sis.gov.sg; MRT: Kallang, then taxi

This seats 13,000 and has played host to sporting events like the the the AVIVA Badminton Open. It is also the home venue of the Singapore Slingers, which plays in the Australian National Basketball League. At other times it hosts big-name concerts.

Below: hiking in Sungei Buloh Wetland Reserve.

Beach volleyball is gaining popularity in Singapore. The best place to play and watch it is the white-sand Siloso Beach on Sentosa island. The beach also hosts beach volleyball championships and clinics regularly. See www.sentosa.com.sg for event schedules.

Hiking

Despite the heat and humidity, hiking is one of Singapore's most attractive outdoor pursuits. The **Bukit Timah Nature Reserve**, **Sungei Buloh Wetland Reserve**, **Central Catchment Nature Reserve** and **Pulau Ubin** are popular trekking areas.

SEE ALSO BEACHES AND ISLANDS, P.33; WALKS AND VIEWS, P.128, 131

Spectator Sport

Among the most followed are cricket, rugby and field hockey, matches of which you might chance to see at the **Padang** (see p.101), especially at the weekends. The annual Singapore Cricket Club International Rugby 7s tournament

(www.sccrugbysevens.com) is also held at the Padang.

Singapore also has its own football league, the **S-League**, in which local and international teams play at stadiums around the island. Check www.sleague.com for match schedules.

Watersport

Changi Sailing Club
32 Netheravon Road; tel: 6545 2876; www.csc.org.sg; MRT: Tampines, then bus: 29

Singapore's only sailing club that offers courses in dinghy, catamaran and keelboat sailing for non-members.

Marina Country Club
600 Punggol Avenue Seventeenth Avenue; tel: 6385 6166; www.marinacountryclub.com.sg; MRT: Punggol, then shuttle bus

The watersport that has captured popular interest is wakeboarding. Several operators here offer boat and board rentals. Try **Waketime** (tel: 6387 1997; www.waketime.com.sg).

SAFYC Sea Sports Centre
110 Tanah Merah Coast Road; tel: 6758 3032; ww.safyc.org.sg; MRT: Tanah Merah, then taxi

119

Theatre

Major foreign and local theatre works with an Asian focus often premiere in Singapore, especially at the Singapore Arts Festival *(see Festivals and Events, p.57)*. Long-running Broadway favourites like *Les Misérables*, *Oliver!* and *Phantom of the Opera* also frequently make appearances. All these are showcased alongside a very healthy local English-language theatre scene populated by professional and amateur companies. These perform foreign and locally written works, including those that attempt to push boundaries and test the state's OB (out-of-bound) markers for politics, sexual content and more.

Major Companies

ACTION Theatre
42 Waterloo Street; tel: 6837 0842; www.action.org.sg; MRT: Dhoby Ghaut or City Hall; map p.136 A3

The creator of *Chang & Eng*, Singapore's longest-running home-grown musical. This company presents original works and has staged some of the country's most acclaimed plays in its 30 years of operation. On its premises is a 100-seat studio theatre.

The Necessary Stage
B1-02 Marine Parade Community Building, 278 Marine Parade Road; tel: 6440 8115; www.necessary.org; bus: 15, 31, 36, 48 or 76

For over 20 years, TNS has consistently created some of the island's most provocative works, depicting the marginalised and repressed. It also runs the annual M1 Singapore Fringe Festival, in which its theatre section features local and foreign companies. Smaller productions are held in its 80-seat black box.

Singapore Repertory Theatre
20 Merbau Road; tel: 6221 5585; www.srt.com.sg; MRT: Clarke Quay, then taxi; bus: 32, 64, 123, 143 or 195; map p.135 D1

SRT is most associated with Broadway-scale productions that have brought together talented Asian stars like David Henry Hwang and Lea Salonga and award-winning directors, playwrights and designers. Its star musical *Forbidden City: Portrait of an Empress*, about the scheming Qing-dynasty Empress Dowager Cixi, returned for a second sell-out season in 2006. It has its own theatre, the DBS Arts Centre, on its premises.

TheatreWorks
72-13 Mohamed Sultan Road; tel: 6737 7213; www.theatreworks.org.sg; MRT: Clarke Quay, then taxi; bus: 32, 54, 139 or 195; map p.135 D1

Singapore's top theatre company thrives under the artistic direction of Ong Keng Sen, most known for his edgy productions that turn tradition on its head with a mosaic of cultural interpretations. The group has its own warehouse performance space near the Singapore River.

Event listings can be found in the newspapers or in listings magazines like *I-S* and *Arts Beat*, available free at restaurants and shops all over Singapore. For ticketing, check out **SISTIC** (tel: 6348 5555; www.sistic.com.sg) or **Tickets.com** (tel: 6296 2929; www.tdc.sg).

Toy Factory Productions
15A Smith Street; tel: 6222 1526; www.toyfactory.com.sg; MRT: Chinatown

One of the country's leading bilingual (English and Mandarin) theatre companies. Among its repertoire are sell-out favourites like *Titoudao*, which is inspired by the life story of its chief artistic director's mother who was a famous Chinese opera performer, as well as some of the most risqué shows possible in Singapore, including the raunchy *Cabaret*, *Bent*, and *Shopping & F*cking*.

Wild Rice
3A Kerbau Road; tel: 6292 2695; www.wildrice.com.sg; MRT: Little India

Wild Rice creates 'glocal'

Left: the Singapore Repertory Theatre's *Forbidden City – Portrait of an Empress*.

Theatre Studio are the city's premier performance spaces for drama.

SEE ALSO ARCHITECTURE, P.27; DANCE, P.47; MUSIC, P.90

Jubilee Hall
3/F, Raffles Hotel Shopping Arcade, 328 North Bridge Road; tel: 6412 1340; MRT: City Hall; map p.136 B2

It's easy to imagine what watching a performance in the Jubilee Hall was like in the old days with its chandeliers, red velvet curtains and ceiling cornices. It is limited to smaller performations.

The Substation
45 Armenian Street; tel: 6337 7535; www.substation.org; MRT: City Hall; map p.136 A2

The late Kuo Pao Kun, doyen of Singapore theatre, turned this former power station into the country's first independent contemporary arts centre in 1990. The Substation is a real bare-bones kind of place, but therein lies the charm of its bohemian atmosphere. Small performances are held at its Guinness Theatre.

works inspired by Singapore society and universal issues. It has played to sell-out crowds at the New Zealand International Festival, with a distinctly and disturbingly Singaporean adaptation of George Orwell's *Animal Farm*. Its founding artistic director Ivan Heng is something of an institution himself in Singapore – a wonderful actor, writer and director, he has won international awards for his solo performances as *Emily of Emerald Hill*.

Venues

The Arts House
1 Old Parliament Lane; tel: 6332 6900; www.theartshouse.com.sg; MRT: City Hall; map p.139 D4

Housed in the former Parliament House, this stages a monthly programme of small performances and exhibitions.

SEE ALSO FILM, P.61

Drama Centre
3/F, National Library, 100 Victoria Street; tel: 6837 8400; MRT: Bugis; map p.136 B3

Once a decrepit venue behind the original National Library on Stamford Road, the Drama Centre has gained a fresh lease of life in its new location within the new National Library building. It now has a main space that seats 615 and a black box that can accommodate 120.

Esplanade Theatres
Esplanade – Theatres on the Bay, 1 Esplanade Drive; tel: 6828 8377; www.esplanade.com; MRT: City Hall; map p.136 B1

The Esplanade's Theatre and

Right: one of Toy Factory's hits, *Titoudao*.

Transport

Singapore is easily accessible from just about every city in the world. More than 80 airlines operate over 4,000 flights a week to the Singapore Changi Airport. The city is linked by rail to Malaysia and Thailand, and by cruise services to Southeast Asia. Singapore is also an excellent base from which to explore the Southeast Asian and Australasian region, especially with the proliferation of budget airlines in recent years. Within Singapore, a modern, efficient and clean public transport system helps visitors get to wherever they want with minimal fuss.

Getting There

BY AIR

Singapore Changi Airport is frequently rated the best in the world. It is so efficient that one can hop into a taxi – after clearing immigration and customs and retrieving bags – within 15 minutes of landing. Its four terminals – Terminal 1 (T1), Terminal 2 (T2), Terminal 3 (T3) and the Budget Terminal – have a total handling capacity of about 70 million passengers a year.

The main terminals are linked to one other by the Sky Train. Passengers can shuttle between the Budget Terminal and the main terminals by the BT Shuttle Service.

The airport has been conceived for maximum comfort and convenience, with a wide range of services and shops. Everything from post offices to free broadband Internet access to a transit hotel is available to make waiting time at the airport enjoyable.

If you need help, look out for the Information and Customer Service counters in the terminals or the 24-hour help phones. These phones will link you to the appropriate customer service officers.

Singapore is an ideal jumping-off point to Southeast Asian destinations like Bali, Phuket, Koh Samui, Langkawi, and Siem Reap, many of which are served by Singapore Airlines' sister airline **SilkAir** (www.silkair.com). Budget carriers like **AirAsia** (www.airasia.com), **Jetstar Asia** (www.jetstar.com) and **Tiger Airways** (www.tigerairways.com) also fly out of Singapore to regional tourism centres.

For more information on airport services, contact **Changi Airport Customer Service** (tel: 6595 6868; www.changiairport.com.sg). For information on flight arrival and departure times, dial tel: 1800-542 4422.

Flying from the UK and the US

The national carrier Singapore Airlines (www.singaporeair.com) is based at the Changi Airport and flies to over 60 cities in 34 countries.

There are regular daily flights out of London and major European cities direct to Singapore. Flying time is

Below: the Changi Airport's facilities, such as the orchid garden pictured here, keep passengers suitably entertained.

Left: Singapore's MRT system is reliable and speedy.

such as Star Cruises, and by many large cruise liners stopping over on their long voyages around the world.

Tanah Merah Ferry Terminal (tel: 6545 2048), located near the Changi Airport, handles boat traffic to the resorts on Indonesia's Bintan island as well as Tanjung Pinang, its capital, and to Nongsa, on neighbouring Batam island. Ferries to Malaysia's Sebana Cove also depart from here.

Changi Ferry Terminal (tel: 6214 8031), also near the Changi Airport, handles regular ferry services to Tanjung Belungkor, on Malaysia's east coast.

BY TRAIN

Coming by train through Malaysia and then across the Causeway at Woodlands in the north of Singapore is a leisurely way to arrive. Malaysia's **Keretapi Tanah Melayu** (KTM) has two lines: one links Singapore to Kuala Lumpur, Butterworth, Alor Setar and north across the Thai border to Bangkok, and

between 12 and 13 hours. Many UK and European travellers heading to Australia and New Zealand often use Singapore as a transit point to break the long journey. From Singapore, it is another 4½ hours to Perth, 7½ hours to Sydney and Melbourne, and 10 hours to Auckland.

Flying from the US takes longer; a flight from Los Angeles or San Francisco, which crosses the Pacific Ocean, takes about 16 to 18 hours with a stop in Seoul, Taipei or Tokyo en route. From New

York, flight time is about 22 hours, including transit time.

Singapore Airlines offers non-stop flights from Los Angeles and New York to Singapore. These flights typically shave two to four hours off flying time.

BY SEA

Most visitors arrive at the **Singapore Cruise Centre** (tel: 6513 2200; www.singapore cruise.com) located at the HarbourFront Centre. The facility is also used by several regional cruise operators,

Below: travelling is a doddle at the efficient Changi Airport.

If money is no object, consider the **E&O Express** (tel: 6392 3500, www.orient-express. com), the ultimate re-creation of a bygone age of romantic Asian rail travel. The train carries a maximum of 132 passengers on the three-night trip from Bangkok through southern Thailand, Butterworth and Kuala Lumpur to Singapore. This luxury does not come cheap; the one-way, 50-hour Singapore–Bangkok trip starts from S$1,780 per person (twin share), inclusive of meals.

the other branches off at Gemas and connects to Tumpat, near Kota Bharu on Malaysia's east coast.

Both Malaysian and Singapore immigration facilities are located at Woodlands. For more information, call the **Tanjong Pagar Railway Station** (tel: 6222 5165; www.ktmb.com.my). Located on Keppel Road, the station is a 20-minute walk from the Tanjong Pagar MRT station.

BY COACH/BUS

There are good roads down the west and east coasts of Peninsular Malaysia, crossing either the Causeway in Woodlands or the Second Link in Tuas into Singapore. The Second Link is far less prone to the frequent congestion that the Woodlands checkpoint experiences.

Private air-conditioned buses run from Hat Yai in Thailand and many towns in Malaysia to Singapore. The ride from Hat Yai takes about 14 hours with stops for refreshments and arrives in Singapore at Golden Mile Complex on Beach Road. Call **Grassland** (tel: 6293 1166) for bus tickets to Hat Yai.

Hasry (tel: 6294 9306; www.hasryexpress.com) has buses that connect Singapore to key Malaysian cities like Kuala Lumpur, Penang and Melaka. Buses arrive at and leave from its Lavender Street office.

Other coach operators such as **Five Stars** (Kuala Lumpur: 03-2142 0877, Singapore tel: 6533 5555), **Plusliner** (Kuala Lumpur tel: 03-2272 3646, Singapore tel: 6256 5755; www.plusliner.com), **Aeroline** (Kuala Lumpur tel: 03-2164 9611, Singapore tel: 6341 9338; www.aeroline.com.my) and **Airebus** (Kuala Lumpur tel: 03-2287 9200, Singapore tel: 6737

6535) offer the more luxurious and roomier 26-seater, executive-class coaches. These link Kuala Lumpur and other major Malaysian cities to Singapore.

Getting Around

FROM THE AIRPORT

Changi Airport is linked to the city centre by the East Coast Parkway (ECP) and to the other parts of Singapore by the Pan-Island (PIE) and Tampines (TPE) expressways. There are four types of transport from the airport – taxi, bus, airport shuttle and MRT.

By Taxi

At the airport terminals, the taxi stands are situated on the same level as the arrival halls. A surcharge of S$3 (or S$5 from 5pm to midnight Fri–Sun) applies in addition to the fare shown on the taxi meter. Two other surcharges are added to the fare where applicable: for rides between midnight and 6am and for ERP (Electronic Road Pricing) tolls. The taxi trip to the city centre takes about 20–30 minutes and costs S$16–25, excluding surcharges.

By Bus

In the basements of the terminals are public bus depots. Buses depart between 6am and midnight daily, and information on bus routes is available at the bus stands. Service No. 36 gets you directly into the city. You'll need the exact fare as no change is given on board. The bus stops closest to the Budget Terminal are a 15-minute walk away on Airport Boulevard. It is easier to take the BT Shuttle Service to Terminal 2 to transfer to MRT service or to any of the terminals for the bus service to the city.

By Airport Shuttle

A shuttle bus service operates between the airport and major hotels in the city, with flexible alighting points within the CBD. Tickets at S$9 for adults and S$6 for children are available at the shuttle counters located at the terminals.

By MRT

The MRT link to the Changi Airport is located underground next to Terminal 2 and Terminal 3. A ride to the city centre takes about 30 minutes and costs S$1.70. Note that trains do not go directly to the city so you have to switch lines at the Tanah Merah MRT station.

Below: the city is served by an excellent MRT network and infrastructure of roads.

124

Fares are cheap (maximum S$1.90 on air-conditioned buses) and calculated based on the number of sectors. Have loose change ready; bus drivers are generally helpful and will tell you the exact fare on boarding. Fare information is also clearly displayed at bus stops. Tickets are issued by automatic dispensers on board.

For convenience, buy an ez-link card or a tourist pass (see left).

Above: the City Hall MRT interchange is always a bustle of activity at any time of the day.

The first train arrives at about 5.30am, and the last train departs at 11.18pm.

CITY TRANSPORT Information

A helpful source for information on the use of public transport is the **'Travel with Ease' Public Transport Guide for Tourists**, which is available at Singapore Visitors Centres and MRT stations. This guide gives travel directions to major tourist spots.

Ez-link Card

If you are going to be moving around a lot by public transport, it is convenient to buy a **TransitLink ez-link card**, which is a stored-value card for use on the MRT, LRT and buses. This card is available from all Transit Link offices in MRT stations and bus interchanges for S$15, of which S$5 is a non-refundable deposit. To use this card, tap it on the electronic reader located at MRT turnstiles or the entrances of buses. The electronic reader will automatically deduct the maxi-

Call TransitLink (tel: 1800-225 5663) for public transport information.

mum fare. When exiting from an MRT station and bus, tap the card again against the electronic reader and the unused portion of the fare is credited back to your card. You can top up the value of your card when it runs low.

Singapore Tourist Pass

An excellent deal for tourists is the Singapore Tourist Pass. For just S$8 a day, you can use this pass (with 1-, 2- and 3-day options) for unlimited rides on the public transport system. Functioning like an ez-link card, it can be purchased at Singapore Visitors Centres at the airport and on Orchard Road as well as TransitLink Ticketing offices in selected MRT stations.

Buses

Around 11,000 buses operated by **Singapore Bus Service** (SBS) and **SMRT Buses** ply about 260 routes, covering practically every corner of the island. Buses (single and double deckers with or without air-conditioning) run from around 5.30am to 11.30pm, and some services have an extension of about half an hour for both starting and ending times at weekends and on public holidays.

Taxis

More than 23,000 taxis stalk the roads. Singapore's taxis are clean and generally in good condition. Most drivers speak or understand English.

All taxis are metered with a flagfall of S$2.80 to $5 for the first kilometre (0.6 miles) and 20 cents for every 385m (1,263ft) thereafter or less for a trip of up to 10km (6.2 miles), or every 330m (1,083ft) thereafter or less after 10km, or every 45 seconds or less of waiting time.

A string of surcharges apply: 50 percent extra from midnight to 5.59am; S$3 surcharge for trips hired in the CBD Mon–Sat 5pm–midnight; 35 percent extra

Below: bus numbers and bus-route information are clearly displayed at bus stops.

125

Above: all taxis in Singapore are metered, but watch out for the surcharges, which can add up.

during peak hours; S$1 on public holidays; for bookings *(see below)*; Electronic Road Pricing (ERP) fees *(see Environment, p.48)*; and trips from the airport. Tipping is not necessary.

Most taxi stands are found outside shopping centres, hotels and other public buildings. In the CBD and downtown areas, taxis can only pick up passengers at taxi stands, even when on call booking. Elsewhere, you can flag one down on the road. But be warned that during morning and evening rush hours and when it rains, it can be difficult to get one if you haven't booked ahead.

To book a taxi, contact:
Comfort/CityCab
Tel: 6552 1111
SMRT Taxi
Tel: 6555 8888
Premier Taxi
Tel: 6363 6888
Smart Cab
Tel: 6485 7777
Trans Cab
Tel: 6555 3333

Booking fees apply: S$3.50 for peak-hour current bookings; S$2.50 for off-peak current bookings; and S$5.20 when booking at least half an hour in advance.

DRIVING

Car rental is not cheap. Rates start from S$175 for a 1.3-litre car to S$295 for a two-litre car per day, including mileage but not insurance. These rates are only applicable for driving in Singapore; taking the car to Malaysia will cost extra.

Before you head out, stock up on parking coupons, available from petrol stations and convenience stores, and make sure you have a complete understanding of the Electronic Road Pricing (ERP) system *(see Environment, p.48)*. A valid driver's licence from your country of residence or an international driver's licence is required for driving in Singapore. Driving is on the left, and the wearing of seatbelts and the use of special child seats is compulsory. Speed limits are 60–70km/h (37–44 miles/h) in residential areas and 80–90km/h (50–56 miles/h) on expressways.

Contact any of the following car rental companies:
Avis
Tel: 6737 1668;
www.avis.com.sg
Hertz
Tel: 1800-734 4646 ;
www.hertz.com.sg

Tours

East West Executive Traveller
12-05 Suntec Tower 5, 5 Temasek Boulevard; tel: 6438 6722; www.ewet.com; MRT: City Hall; map p.136 C3
Excellent for customised tours, such as the *Traders Trail* tour where guests travel around the city on bumboats, trishaws, buses, the MRT and on foot, in a treasure-hunt-style adventure.
Original Singapore Walks
Tel: 6325 1631; www.singapore walks.com
There's no need for bookings; just visit the website for tour schedules and turn up at the

Below: view the city skyline from a Singapore River cruise.

designated MRT station. These entertaining guided walking tours are a great way to see Singapore's heritage areas, from Chinatown and Little India to Fort Canning Hill and the Changi Chapel and Museum. The *Tipple Exchange* tour, albeit more suitable for adults, deserves a mention. It is held at the Singapore River on Tuesday; guides tell stories of the river's glories and scandals at sunset over pints of beer.

Perspective Journeys
Mobile tel: 8127 2723;
www.perspectivejourneys.com
Who better to give insight into Chinese culture in Singapore than an anthropologist? Mr C.W. Chan offers in-depth cultural tours like *Dreams of a Sojourner*, which traces the footsteps of Chinese immigrants, and one that looks at the various schools of Buddhism that coexist in Singapore. Tours last three to four hours.

SH Tours
Tel: 6734 9923;
www.asiatours.com.sg
This offers a whole host of options, including a *feng shui* tour and an *Eastern Heartlands* tour that visits Geylang Serai, Changi Chapel and Museum and Tampines town. If you want a guided glimpse of Singaporean suburban life, this is

Transit passengers at the Changi Airport who have a minimum of five hours' layover time before catching their connecting flight can book a two-hour **Free City Tour**. Bookings can be made at the Singapore Visitors Centre counters at the main terminals, which open for registration from 8am to 4.25pm daily. Six tours are available 10am–5pm on a first-come-first-served basis.

Above: touring the city on trishaws.

it. There are also city tours offered in German (six persons minimum).

Singapore River Cruise
Tel: 6336 6111;
www.rivercruise.com.sg
Hop on an old bumboat and see the city from the water for a languid 30 minutes. Tickets are available from any of the nine jetties along the Singapore River – the Esplanade, Merlion Park, Fullerton, Boat Quay, Raffles' Landing Site, Riverside Point, Liang Court, Robertson Quay and Grand Copthorne Waterfront Hotel. Boats run daily from 9.30am to 10.30pm.

Singapore Trolley
Tel: 6339 6833;
www.singaporeexplorer.com.sg
Operates tram buses that ply past major hotels and landmarks in Orchard Road, the Civic District, Chinatown and around the Singapore River area daily, making 17 stops along the route. Daily, unlimited-ride tickets can be purchased from your hotel concierge or the trolley driver.

Tour East Singapore
Tel: 6238 2893;
www.toureast.net
Its half-day city tour is always popular. Also consider *Affairs of the Arts* that tours the Esplanade theatres and concert hall and the Ng Eng Teng Gallery at the National

University of Singapore Museums before culminating in a traditional Malay dance performance. Other options include an ethnic tour and a Changi/East Coast tour. Call for pick-up details.

Trishaw Tours
Alphaland Travel Services mobile tel: 9100 4276; Singapore Explorer tel: 6339 6833; Trishaw Tours tel: 6545 6311; Triwheel Tours tel: 6336 9025
The quaint trishaw, a bicycle with a sidecar, has almost disappeared from Singapore's streets. Today it exists only for tourists who want to experience something of the old days. Most tours operate around Chinatown, Little India and the Civic District and last 30–45 minutes. Tickets cost S$25. Don't flag down a trishaw on the street unless you want to be ripped off.

Watertours
1/F, HarbourFront Centre, 1 Maritime Square; tel: 6533 9811; www.watertours.com.sg; MRT: HarbourFront
Hop on its ornate replica of a Ming-dynasty Chinese junk and take a leisurely cruise around Sentosa and the southern islands of St John's, Sisters' and Kusu. Day cruises with high tea are at 10.30am and 3pm, while dining cruises set off at 3pm and 6.30pm.

Walks and Views

With Singapore's excellent transport system, it's easy to just hop on a bus, train or taxi and sightsee your way around the island. But if you don't mind the tropical heat and humidity, get out on foot, and the city will surprise you. A few of the walks recommended here involve more strenuous climbs and trails in delightful pockets of green in the suburbs, while others are simply idyllic strolls in charming neighbourhoods. It is best to embark on walks in the early morning or late evening, when the air is fresher and the weather is cooler. Wear good walking shoes and bring along plenty of water.

Bukit Timah Nature Reserve

Entrance at Hindhede Drive; tel: 6468 5736; www.nparks. gov.sg; daily 6am–7pm (night walks not encouraged); bus 67, 75, 170, 171, 173, 184, 852 or 961

Located 12km (7.5 miles) from the city, in the middle of the island, this is most easily reached by taxi. If you are taking the bus, alight along Upper Bukit Timah Road, opposite Bukit Timah Shopping Centre, or along Jalan Anak Bukit, opposite Courts furniture store, and walk to the end of Hindhede Drive.

The reserve includes Singapore's highest hill, Bukit Timah, at a mere 164m (538ft),

and protects 163 hectares (403 acres) of the nation's only virgin lowland rainforest. Despite its diminutive size, the number of plant species in the reserve exceeds that found in all of North America. Make your way to the hilltop, which is a good place to wait for white-bellied sea eagles or brahminy kites. The besotted birdwatcher can take the challenge of identifying at least nine species of swifts and swallows. The view over the protected forest of several water reservoirs makes you forget you are in one of the world's most densely populated cities.

There are five walking trails, all clearly marked and

with varying levels of difficulty, taking from 45 minutes to 2 hours to complete. There is also a challenging 6-km- (3.7-mile-) long mountain-bike trail for enthusiasts. Brochures and trail maps are available at the Visitor Centre. The hill gets crowded at weekends – if you're planning a trek, weekdays are your best bet.

Kampong Glam

MRT: Bugis

Start your stroll at **Arab Street**, where you can shop for batiks, baskets of every shape and size, leatherware, ethnic jewellery and alcohol-free perfume. At the end of Arab Street is **Beach Road**. Turn left past the fishing tackle shops – a reminder that this was once the seafront – and turn left again at **Bussorah Street**, which during the Ramadan fasting month before the Muslim celebration of Hari Raya Puasa is filled with street vendors peddling delicacies for Muslims breaking their fast at sunset. From here, gaze at the great golden dome of **Sultan Mosque**, which dates back to 1924.

Below: a common treeshrew at the Bukit Timah Nature Reserve.

Left: the Treetop Walk at the Central Catchment Reserve.

further along **Victoria Street**, opposite Jalan Kledek.

Finally, end your walk at Singapore's very own Leaning Tower, the **Hajjah Fatimah Mosque**, built circa 1846, located behind Jalan Sultan and off Beach Road. SEE ALSO CHURCHES, MOSQUES AND TEMPLES, P.41, 43, 44; MUSEUMS AND GALLERIES, P.85; SHOPPING, P.117

Katong

Eastern Singapore; MRT: Eunos, then taxi or MRT: Bedok, then bus: 31, 32, 40

Begin at the unofficial start of Katong, near the **Holy Family Church** (6 Chapel Road), where Catholics in the area have worshipped for decades. Walk down the same side of the street, towards **Katong Village** (86 East Coast Road). This former police station, built in 1928, is a hub of restaurants and pubs that come alive in the evening.

Across the road is **Katong Antique House** (No. 208), where Peranakan artefacts are on display (tel: 6345 8544;

Among the shops that sell Asian and Muslim-inspired crafts on Bussorah Street are also Arabic-style cafés and restaurants serving Middle Eastern cuisine, a magnet for young urban Malays in the evenings.

Two streets down, on **Haji Lane**, the hip quotient rises. There are arty venues like the indie film gallery **Pitch Black** (63 Haji Lane) and the style emporium-cum-ice cream parlour **Pluck**. The cool vibe continues on **Bali Lane**, where cafés like **Blu Jaz** (11 Bali Lane) have local musicians performing during dinner.

At the very heart of the district, at 85 Sultan Gate, is **Istana Kampong Gelam**, once the palace of the Malay royal family who ruled the island before Raffles arrived, which has now been converted into the **Malay Heritage Centre**.

Wander towards the corner of Jalan Sultan and Victoria Street and you'll find the blue mosaic-tiled **Malabar Muslim Jama-Ath Mosque**, a quiet place of worship that is as old as Kampong Glam.

> Arabic architectural influences are the most resplendent in Bussorah Street, which used to house *haj* pilgrims travelling to Mecca in the early days. Today the Arabic-style cafés and restaurants serving Middle Eastern cuisine attract a more secular crowd of patrons.

The islands's oldest Muslim cemetery lies beneath fragrant frangipani trees a little

Below: basketware spills over onto the street in Arab Street.

Above: a morning walk in the MacRitchie Reservoir Park.

viewing by appointment only; entrance charge to gallery). This century-old shophouse has been home to five generations of Peranakan families. The gallery on level two showcases the owner's collection of porcelain, beaded slippers, *kebaya* (traditional embroidered blouses) and silver jewellery.

Further down the road, **Glory** (No.139) is best known for its pineapple tarts and traditional Peranakan confectionery, while **Kim Choo Kueh Chang** (No.109/111) sells delicious rice dumplings wrapped in fragrant pandan leaves. Two doors away is **Rumah Bebe** (No.113), a trove of Peranakan artefacts in a 1928 shophouse. Check out the lovely bridal chamber on level two. Peranakan culinary classes are also offered here. Peranakan fare is in fact Singapore's very own fusion cuisine, blending Chinese and Malay cooking styles and ingredients with flair.

If you don't fancy a heavy meal, walk down towards Ceylon Road to the *Katong laksa* (rice noodles in curried coconut gravy) stalls situated at the start of the lane. The lively hawkers will yell for your custom.

The ornate **Sri Senpaga Vinayagar Temple** (daily 5.55am–11pm) sits at 19 Ceylon Road. An important place of worship for Hindus in the East Coast, it dates back to the 1850s. The present building, completed in 2003, features a five-tier, 21-m (69-ft) *rajagopuram* (royal entrance tower) sculpted according to Indian Chola traditions. The *dwarapalakas* (gatekeepers) at the base tier of the tower are not found anywhere else in Asia. The temple is also capped by a golden dome.

MacRitchie Reservoir Park, Central Catchment Nature Reserve

Enter via MacRitchie Reservoir or Venus Drive off Upper Thomson Road; tel: 1800 471 7300; www.nparks.gov.sg; Tue–Fri 9am–5pm, Sat, Sun and public holidays 8.30am–5pm; free; MRT: Ang Mo Kio, then bus: 166

Several hiking routes in the **MacRitchie Reservoir Park**, which is located in the Central Catchment Nature Reserve, take visitors through mature secondary forest. Among these trails, the **HSBC Treetop Walk** is the most interesting. This free-standing suspension bridge is the first of its kind in Singapore and the region, connecting the two highest points of MacRitchie and offering a spectacular panorama of the forest canopy. The walkway is 250m (820ft) long, and its highest point is at 25m (82ft).

Getting to the Treetop Walk is a trek in itself. Enter through MacRitchie Reservoir Park via the **MacRitchie Nature Trail**. It's a 4.5km (2.8 mile) walk (about 1.5–2 hours) where you'll encounter interesting flora like the pitcher plant and ant plant, and catch a glimpse of the myriad forest birds and animals like the racket-tailed drongo, clouded monitor lizard and black bearded dragon. A round trip by this route, including the Treetop Walk, takes about 3–5 hours (7–10km/4.3–6.2 miles), depending on your pace.

The shorter route to the Treetop Walk is a 2.5-km (1.5 mile) walk (approximately 1 hour) from **Venus Drive** off Upper Thomson Road, along a stream. A round trip by this route takes about 3 hours.

Do note that the walk has been graded as moderate to difficult, so it may not be suitable for young children and the elderly. As an alternative,

Below: living room display at Rumah Bebe.

try the boardwalk trails, which also offer rewarding experiences. They are accessible from the MacRitchie Reservoir Park.

Mount Faber
MRT: HarbourFront

Mount Faber offers both a lovely walking route and some of the island's best views. The sprawling rainforest-covered park, which surrounds Mount Faber, is one of the oldest in Singapore. During your walk, be sure to stop at the various lookout points for panoramic views of the city and the port area.

There are several well-defined footpaths that visitors can take, the best beginning at Kampong Bahru Road. A large stone sign marks the start of your 10–15-minute walk up. Along the way, sneak a peek at the *keramat* (Muslim shrine) built in honour of Radin Ayu Mas, a Javanese princess who sacrificed herself to save her father. She is buried at the foot of Mount Faber.

The Jewel Box on the summit is worth a stopover. Wind down with fine food and drinks at one of its restaurants or bars and take in fantastic vistas. From here, you can also hop on a cable car ride to Sentosa, with a fine view of the harbour (tel: 6377 9688; daily

Get an unobstructed bird's-eye view of Singapore, Malaysia and Indonesia on a 37-minute ride on the 165-m- (541-ft-) high **Singapore Flyer** observation wheel. Located at Marina Bay, it is unabashedly touted as Singapore's version of the London Eye (tel: 6734 8829; www.singaporeflyer.com.sg; daily 8.30am–10.30pm; entrance charge).

8.30am–9pm; entrance charge; www.mountfaber.com.sg).

Early mornings and evenings are the best times to take this walk. At daybreak, the song of birds and the cool morning air make for a delightful experience. At night, the view of lights twinkling in the distance is just dazzling, especially with a cold cocktail in hand.
SEE ALSO NIGHTLIFE, P.94

Sungei Buloh Wetland Reserve
301 Neo Tiew Crescent; tel: 6794 1401; www.sbwr.org.sg; Mon–Sat 7.30am–7pm, Sun and public holidays 7am–7pm; free except on Sat, Sun, public and school holidays; MRT: Kranji, then taxi or bus: 925

On the extreme northwestern coast of Singapore is the Sungei Buloh Wetland Reserve, remarkable for its abundant and diverse birdlife – over 212 species of birds can be seen here. A boardwalk guides visitors through part of the reserve, with hides at regular intervals from where birds can be observed and platforms at vantage points. There are three trails, which last from one to five hours, including one through

Below: the Singapore Flyer.

Above: Sungei Buloh Wetland Reserve is also a nesting ground for animals.

a mangrove. The Visitor Centre has more details on these and also screens an informative 10-minute audio-visual show at its theatrette at scheduled times.

The old ponds still remain, surrounded by mangroves. Plenty of fish and prawns still thrive, and with the farmers long gone, birds have a field day. Collared as well as white-throated kingfishers sit on the low stakes by the bunds waiting to swoop while cinnamon and yellow bitterns stalk the reedy edges.

But it is the migrating waders, of which more than 20 species have been sighted feeding on exposed mud beds, that are the stars of the reserve. From September to March, large flocks of plovers, sandpipers, stints, curlews, godwits and egrets gather to feed on the mud exposed by the ebbing tide.

With the rapid reclamation of other coastal areas in Singapore, this sanctuary now stands out as the last significant, sizeable feeding ground for migrating wading birds. It is the birds' last stopover on the migration path before the thrust to regions further south.

131

A   **B**

Chinese
Seventh-Day
Adventist Church

Novena
Church

Tan Tock Seng
Hospital

Tunggal Road

Abdul Hamid
Mosque

Gentle Road

4

Gilstead Road

NOVENA

Novena Terrace

Sinaran

Novena
Square 2

Jln Tan Tock Seng

Mandalay Road

Thomson Road

Moulmein Rise

Moulmein

Revival
Centre
Church

Church
of Christ

Road

Buckley Road

Newton Road

Goldhill
Plaza

Goldhill
Centre

Leong Wah
Chan Si

Sathya
Sai Baba
Centre

Kuang Chee
Tng Buddhist
Temple

Khiang Guan Avenue

Goldhill
Plaza

Shrewsbury

Royal

Buckley Road

Newton Road

Surrey Road

United
Square

Essex Road

Debn Rd

Expressway

Road

Cambridge Road

Qin
De

Evelyn Road

Lincoln Road

Wee Nam Road

Jln
Korma

Derb Rd

3

The Church
in Singapore

Norfolk Road

Carlisle Rd

Carlisle Road

Truro Road

Road

Suffolk Walk

Singapore
Thompson Road
Baptist Church

Cambr
Rd

Camb

Newton
Circus

Newton Road

Newton Life
Church

Suffolk Rd

Hong Leng
Yien Temple

Cambridge Road

Hentford Road

Bristol Rd

Dorset

Truro Road

Keng Lee Road

Rochor Canal Road

Singapore Baptist
Church

Tasek Utara
Mosque

Kampong

Java Road

Farrer Park
Tennis Centre

Newton
Food Centre

Bukit

Mekeway Ave

Jln

Keng Lee Road

Kg. Java Road

FAR

Makepeace Rd

Javia Rd

Halifax Road

Parish of
Christ Church

PA

2

Madrasah
Al-Irsyad
Al-Isiamiah

Timah

Monk's Hill Ter.

Hooper Road

Cavenagh Road

KAMPONG
JAVA PARK

Rutland

PP
Swimming
Complex

FIE

Monk's Hill Road

W. Dr.

Winstedt Dr.

Road

KK Women's
& Children's
Hospital

Java Road

Hampshire Road

Clemenceau Avenue North

Winstedt Road

Road

Bt. Timah
Water Works

Land Transport
Authority

Shree Laksh
Naray
Kerba

1

| 0 | 50 | 100 | 150 | 200 m |
| 0 | 50 | 100 | 150 | 200 yds |

Cavenagh Road

Bukit

Bukit Timah Road

Mack Rd

Alfa
Centre

Tan Kong
Tien Building

Tekka Lane

Buffalo

LITTLE
INDIA

Istana
(President's Residence)

The Free Christ
Church of Singapore

Boon Siew
Building

Rex
House

Tekka
Centre

MacKenzie

Maye Road

Litt

p132 | **p133**

p134 | **p135** | **p136** | **p137**

p138 | **p139**

RESTRICTED AREA

MT
EMILY
PARK

Mount Emily Road

The

A   135   **B**   136

132

Hai
ple

Cao Da Bo
ong Gong Temple
ality

Balestier Road

7th-Day
Adventist
Church

Jln Kebun Limau

Towner

May

Road

Road

Sungei Whampoa

Road

Serangoon

BOON KENG

Central Sikh
Gurdwara

Bendemeer
Shopping Mall

4

Eye Hospital

Ceylon
Sports Club

Balestier Road

McNair

Singapore Indian
Association

Road

Kwong Wai
Shiu Hospital

Road

Boon

Keng

Kempas Rd

Jalan Lembah Kallang

Chew
Road

Rangoon Lane.

Rangoon

Road

Ji De Tang

Singapore Chinese
Recreation Club

CSC Tessensohn
Clubhouse

Singapore Khalsa
Association

Beo San Hood
Chor Temple

Long Shan
Tang Temple

Road

Fu Xi Tang Temple

Tronoh

Kempas

Road

Bendemeer

3

Road

Sing Ave.

Sing

Joo Avenue

Leong
San See

Sri Vadapathira
Kaliamman

Lavender

Singapore Indian
Fine Arts Society

Sing

Avenue

Sing Joo Walk

Hock
Siew
Tong

Course

Sakya Muni
Buddha Gaya
'Temple of 1000 Lights'

Cactus

Jalan Besar

Hindu
Centre

Starlight

Tessensohn

Ter.

Sri Srinivasa
Perumal

Rangoon

Road

Rangoon

Rawe

Perumal

Road

Marne

Sturdee

Beatty

Road

Kam Leng

Eminent
Plaza

Street

Worcester

Road

Road

Road

Road

Petain

Road

Road

Lavender
Food Square

Foot

Beatty

Toothpick

Kallang

FARRER
PARK

Course

Farrer Park
Station Road

Serangoon

Road

Owen

Road

Kitchener

Hamsrs
Square

Sturdee

Sturdee

Road

Jalan Besar

Road

Road

Road

Tyrwhitt

Kallang Bahru
Complex

Roberts Lane

Birch Road

Fortuna

Claremont

Burman

Road

Kitchener

Kitchener Link

Owen

City Square
Mall

Allenby

Horne

Holy
Trinity
Church

Hamilton

Road

Hamilton

Hotel 81
(Violet)

Cavan

Road

Lavender Street

Kinta Road

eland Road

Peace Course

Asia
Star

Anguilla
Mosque

Desker

Lembu

Mustafa
Centre

Serangoon
Plaza

Parkroyal on
Kitchener Road

Tai Hoe

Verdun

Road

Syed

Sam Leong Road

Light of Christ
City Church

Plumer

Tyrwhitt

Road

Road

Cavan

Avenue

Hotel 81
(Lavender)

King
George's
Building

2

Tan Tans
Niah
House

Broadway

Grandmax

Aliwi

Road

Royal
India

Alexandra

Classique
Jalan Besar
Plaza

Hing Hwa
Methodist Church

Road

George's

Road

Cathedral
of Glory Church

Road

Renhas

Home

Road

Road

ist

Baboo Lane

Hindoo

Road

Road

Maude

Syed

Kitchener Rd

King

Road

French

Road

Jellicoe

Road

Road

Little India
Guest House

Sri
Veeramakaliamman

Norris Rd

Veerasamy Rd

Bussorah

Kelantan Lane

Townshend Road

Road

Berseh

Rochor

Road

Kallang

LAVENDER

Kerbau Inn

Cuff Road

Kampong Kapor
Methodist Church

Chitty Rd

Kelantan

Jalan

Jalan

ICA Building
(Immigration)

1

ngo St.

Dickson

Upper Weld

Road

Perak

Pitt

Sungei Market
(Thieves' Market)

Lane

Pasar

Old Malay Cemetery
Kampong Glam

Victoria

Rochor

Road

Malabar
Muslim
Jama-Ath
Mosque

Crawford

Lane

Madras

Dunlop St

Dickson
Court

Boon Wah

Haising

Rochor

Canal

MUSLIM
CEMETERY

Road

Crawford
Centre

Madras

Abdul
Gaffoor Mosque

136

D

137

MUSLIM
CEMETERY

E

133

Ming Arcade

Forum *Hilton*

HPL House

Four Seasons

Far East Shopping Centre

International Building

Liat Towers

Shaw House

Shaw Centre   Scotts Square

Marriott

ORCHARD   TANGS

Cuscaden   Road

Cuscaden Walk

Wheelock Place

ION Orchard

Argullia Park

Gra Hy

Orchard

See map be

4

Tourism Court

Orchard Boulevard

Rochalle Drive

Grange   Road

Grange Garden

Tomlinson   Road

Lengkok   Merak

One Tree Hill

Jalan   Amap

Jalan Kelawar

Argullia Park

Paterson

Orchard

Orchard Turn

Orchard Turn

W

3

Chatsworth Road

Jalan   Amap

Stamford Canal

Grange   Road

Lengkok Angsa

Paterson   Hill

Paterson   Road

Grange   Roa

Leonie   Hill

Bo

2

Metro Y Lodge

Stevens Rd   Balmoral

Sloane Court

Dalvey Rd

Robin

Balmoral Park

Park

Balmoral   Road

Fernhill   Road

Stevens   Road

Pinetree Club

River   Valley

Fernhill

Fernhill   Cres

Orange Grove Road

RELC International

Walshe   Road

Anderson Road

Stevens   Road

Stevens Road

Goodwood Hill

River   Gr

Fernhill   Road

The Shangri-La

Orange

Anderson Road

Ardmore Point

Ardmore Park

Draycott Park

Draycott   Park

Tanglin Club

Great World City

Kim   Seng   Road

Kin Sen Pla

Lady   Hill Road

Grove

Ardmore   Park

Draycott   Drive

American Club

Kin Se Pla

Nassim   Road

Claym Rd

Orchard

Orchard Parade

Meritus Negara

Claym Rd

Thong Teck Building

DFS Galleria

Claymore   Hill

Scotts Rd

Zion   Road

1

Nassim   Road

Nassim Hill

Sexton Close

Sekar Walk

Tanglin   Road

Delfi Orchard

Royal Plaza on Scotts

Claym Rd

Claym Rd

Far East Plaza

St. M St St. Martin's Dr

Tudor Ct S. Gallery

St Regis Singapore

Tanglin S.C.

Ming Arcade

HPL House

Orchard Twrs

Palais Renaissance

Forum *Hilton*

Orchard Rd

Int'l Bldg

Pacific Plaza

Shaw Centre

Grand Hyatt

TANGS

Haveock   Link

Havelock Road

Giok Hong Tian

Tanglin Mall

Regent

Traders

Tanglin Rd   Grove Rd

Cuscaden

Four Seasons

Boulevard

Far East S.C.

Liat Towers

Lido

Marriott

ORCHARD

TANGS

Ho Atrium Sing Concord Shoppin

Boulevard

Orchard   Boulevard

Wheelock Place

Paterson

ION Orchard

0   200 m

0   200 yds

D

E

Malabar Muslim
Jama-Ath Mosque

Crawford
Centre

Crawford St

Rochor

Crawford
Lane

Road

Sultan

Bridge

Road

Textile Centre

Plaza
Cinema

Aliwal Pk

Golden Sultan
Theatre

GC

Sultan
Plaza

Jalan Sultan

Golden Mile
Food Centre

Hajjah
Fatimah
Mosque

Army
Market

Minto Rd

Beach

Road

Golden
Mile Complex

Highway

STM Video Theatre

Golden Theatre

Golden Mile
Tower

p132 p133

p134 p135 p136 p137

p138 p139

4

ana
mpong
lam

Pahang St

Keypoint

Baghdad St
rah St

Sultan Gate

Beach Road

The Concourse

Nicoll

Avenue

MARINA PROMENADE

Oasis
Building

Kallang
Basin

3

Plaza
Parkroyal

The Plaza

ateway

Republic

NICOLL
HIGHWAY

Tanjong Rhu

Rhu

View

Cross

Tanjong Rhu Road

Republic

MARINA

East Coast Parkway

2

EAST COAST PARK

Centennial
Tower

nia

Millenia
Tower

illenia
lections

PROMENADE

PROMENADE

Boulevard

Bridge

Boulevard

Sheares

arlton
nia

Avenue

Avenue

Raffles

PROMENADE

Benjamin

PARK

Singapore
Flyer

0   50   100 150 200 m

0   50   100 150 200 yds

1

D

E

137

A   135   B   135

WaterFront Plaza
River View
Havelock
Road
Holiday Inn Atrium Singapore & Concord Shopping Centre
Miramar
Copthorne King's
Jalan Minyak
Jalan Kukoh
Thong Chai Building

Tan Si Chong Su
Havelock
Upper
Riverside Point
Read Bridge
Magazine Rd
Cumming St
Fisher St
Keng Cheow St
Merchant Rd
Read Cres
Swissôtel Merca
Omar Kampung Melaka Mosque
Market Rd
Central Mall
Ministry of Manpower
Subordinate Courts
Havelock
Thong Ch Medical S
Apollo Centre
Furama City Centre
Bridge Rd
Picke

YORK HILL ESTATE
Furama Riverfront Singapore
Outram Road
Outram Road
The Jubilee Presby Church
York Hill
Swee
San Centre
Pearl's Hill Road
Cross
HAVELOCK SQUARE
People's Park Centre

Ho Lim Kong Temple
Outram Hill
Swee
Terrace
PEARL'S HILL
Pearl Rd
OG Bldg
Majestic Mall
Ywe Hwa Emporium
Hotel 81
New Bridge Rd
Chinatown Point
Hong Lim Compl
Upp

Qi Tian Gong Temple
Chin
Central Expressway
Pearl's Hill Reservoir
CITY PARK
Police National Service H.Q.
CHINATOWN
People's Park Complex
Lucky Chinatown
Mosque St
Pagoda St
CHINATOWN
Chinatown Point
Street

Outram
Chin
Outram Park
Pearl Bank
Central Police Station
New Bridge Centre
Smith
The Inn
Yes Chinatown
Chinatown Heritage Centre
Temple St
Jamae Mosque
Mosq
Sri Mariamma
Outram Flyover
Avenue
Oriental Plaza
Chinatown Complex
Trengganu St
Buddha Tooth Relic Temple & Museum
Lai Chun Yu
College Road
Hospital
Third
Avenue
Yangtze Theatre
Pearl's Centre
Eu Tong
Bridge
Kreta
Kreta Ayer People's Theatre
Sago St
Banda St
Sago Lane
A Siang Hill
Scarlet
OUTRAM PARK
Layan Sithi Vinayagar Temple
The Keong Saik
Hotel 1929
Keong Saik
Smith St
Dickenson
Hill Rd
South
Erskine Road
Maxwell Food Centre

Singapore National Eye Centre
HSA
Royal Peacock
Tropical
Chinatown
Bukit
Spring
Kadoorie
Siar
Singapore General Hospital
Hospital
Third Hospital Avenue
Second Hospital Avenue
National Dental Centre
OUTRAM PARK
New Majestic
New Bridge Rd
Hong
Teck Lim Rd
Keong Saik Rd
Jinriksha Station
Murray
Maxwell
Street
Singapore City Gall
URA
MN

Hospital Drive
Central Circus
First Hospital
Sen Bridge
Street
DUXTON PLAIN PARK
Chinatown Plaza
Duxton
Berjaya Duxton
Maxwell Hse
Cook St
red dot design museum

Bus Terminal
Hospital Dr.
Eu Tong Sen
New Bridge
St Matthew's Church
Neil
Cantonment
Tanjong Pagar Conservation Area
Duxton Road
Craig
Road
Pagar
Tras
Wallich St
TAN PA

Baba House
Neil Road
Everton
Everton Park
Phoo Thor Jee
Wallich St
Choon Guan Stre
International Plaza

Kampong Bahru Rd
Blair Road
Everton Road
Maritime House
VANDA MS JOAQUIM PK
Tanjong Pagar Plaza
Gopeng St
Seng Wong Beo
Springleaf T
MAS
Anson Centre

SPOTTISWOODE PARK
Spottiswoode Park
Everton Road
Cantonment Link
Yan
Kee Seng St
Tanjong Pagar
Amara
Tras
Lim Huat Building
Union Building
Anson House
Raeburn Park
Spottiswoode Park Road
South Point
Keppel Towers
Hoe Chiang Rd
GE Tower
Enggor St
Realty Centre
Bernam St
76
Shentor
M Hotel
78
Anson Road

Tanjong Pagar Railway Station
Singapore Railway Station
Euro-Asia Centre
Lim Teck Kim Rd
Singapore Technologies Building
Jit Poh Building
RCL Centre
80 Anson Road
Shenton Way

Keppel Road
Ayer Rajah Expressway
Keppel Road
Tanjong Pagar Complex

A   B

138

LARKE
QUAY

The
Riverwalk

Upp. Circular Rd

North Boat Quay

Elgin
Bridge

enter Street

Parliament
House

The Arts
House

Singapore
Cricket Club

Queen Elizabeth Walk

Anderson B. Dr

Esplanade – Theatres
on the Bay

Esplanade
Mall

MARINA
PROMENADE
PARK

Circular

Road

ong St

Bridge

Canal

Boat
Quay

Road

Lor Teluk

Canton Street

South Canal Rd

Bonham Street

Fullerton Rd

Esplanade

Esplanade
Bridge

The Float @
Marina Bay

Victoria Concert
Hall & Theatre

Lim Bo Seng
Memorial

Sir Stamford
Raffles Statue

Raffles'
Landing
Site

Asian
Civilisations
Museum

Cavenagh
Bridge

Merlion

MERLION
PARK

Art Science
Museum

One
George
Street

South Canal Road

OCBC
Centre

UOB Plaza

Chulia Street

Bank of
China

The
Fullerton

Fullerton Rd

Raffles
Place

One Fullerton

Fullerton
Square

Marina Bay

Yueh Hai
Ching
Temple

Capital
Square

Church St

OUB
Centre

Market Street

RAFFLES PL.

Malacca St

Clifford
Centre

One on
the Bund

The Fullerton
Bay Hotel

Marina Bay Sands

Far
East
Square

Pekin St

The Arcade

Ch Ch St

D'Almeida St

Republic
Plaza

China
Square

De Souza St

Ocean
Building

Marina Bay
Casino

Fu Tak Chi
Museum

Cecil

Street

China St

Market St

Telegraph St

Finlayson
Green

Collyer Quay

Customs Harbour
Division H.Q.

Baylront Avenue

gore
a Shrine

Thian Hock
Keng

Hong Leong
Building

One
Raffles
Quay

Marina

Boulevard

Sands Expo &
Convention
Centre

Abrar
sque

Business
District

Lau Pa
Sat

Raffles

Street

The Sail @
Marina Bay

McCallum

Link

Central

Marina Sands Hotels
& Skypark

k Ayer Chinese
hodist Church

Shenton Way

Asia Square
(under construction)

Boulevard

Robinson

Maxwell

DBS
Bldg

U.I.C.
Bldg

Shenton
House

Parkway

pital
wer

DBS
Auditorium

MARINA
BAY

Coast

GARDEN BY THE BAY
AT MARINA SOUTH

Maxwell

Road

Way

Singapore
Conference Hall

East

nton
Shenton

Yess

Prince
Edward St

Marina Station Road

Marina Street

Marina Place

Edward

Rd

Prince Edward
Road

Telok Ayer
Flyover

Avenue

i Muhd
leh Mosque

k Teck See
er Road

r Rd

Shenton Way
Bus Terminal

Finger Pier Building

Pagar

Terminal

Docks

Finger
Pier

Tanjong

| 0 | 50 | 100 | 150 | 200 m |

| 0 | 50 | 100 | 150 | 200 yds |

	p132	p133	
p134	p135	p136	p137
	p138	p139	

D

E

Selective Index for Street Atlas

140

Index

143

Insight Smart Guide: Singapore
Compiled and updated by: Annette Tan
Edited by: Low Jat Leng and
Sarah Sweeney

Photography by: Jonathan Koh/Apa and
Vincent Ng/APA, except: Alain Compost
128b; 67b; Amara Sanctuary Sentosa
Resort 75; Apa Archives 40b; Aramsa
Spa 98/99t; Archipalego 94; Asian Civilisations Museum 82b; Au Jardin 102/
103t, 107b; Bettmann/Corbis 68br, 69tl;
Chijmes 78b; Civil Aviation Authority of
Singapore 123b; David Henley/Apa 19b;
Denise Tackett/Apa 33; Escape Theme
Park 36b; Front Row 54b, 54t; The
Fullerton Hotel 28, 93b; The Gallery
Hotel 70b; Halia 108; Hotel 1929 73l,
106; Jack Hollingsworth/Apa 2/3t; 7t,
10, 11b, 12, 15b, 17l&r, 21b, 42, 43t, 44,
45b, 48/49t, 49b, 51b, 58t, 76b, 79b, 80,
81b, 100b, 129b, 130t; Jamie Koh 26/
27t; Jon Hicks/Corbis 52b, 69bl; Kazbar
95b; Las Vegas Sands Corp/Handout/
epa/Corbis 69br; Lifebrandz 96, 97b;
Low Jat Leng 110; Luke Duggleby/ona-
sia 127; Tiffany Koh 93; Marina Mandarin 102b; Mary Evans Picture Library
68bl; Maximilian Weinzierl/Alamy 122/
123t; National Arts Council 57b; National
Museum of Singapore 5cl, 86; National
Orchid Garden 101b; National Parks
Board 128/129t; New Majestic Hotel
70/71t, 73r, 105; Hansel 52-53,53b;
Nick Hanna/Alamy 122b; Night Safari

5cr, 37b; NUS Museums 87b; Javad
Namazie/Pluck 117t; Photobank Singapore 68tl; Raffles Hotel 72; Rang Mahal
103b, 112; red dot design museum 87t,
117b; Reuters/Corbis 69tr; Rex Butcher/
Jon Arnold Images/photolibrary 81t;
Roslan Rahman/afp/Getty Images 66/
67t; Royal Plaza on Scotts 74; Sentosa
18, 19t, 32/33t, 35b,85, 118/119t; The
Sentosa Resort & Spa 98b, 99b; The
Shangri-La 107t; Singapore Art Museum
82/83t, 88; The Pond Photography/Sin-
gapore Dance Theatre 46/47t, 46b; Sin-
gapore Flyer Pte Ltd 131b; Singapore
Repertory Theatre 120/121t; Singapore
Tourism Board 100/101t, 113; SPP
Images/Alamy 76/77t; Swissôtel The
Stamford 104; T'ang Quartet 91b; Tan
Kok Yong 5c, 26, 29, 30, 31b, 38b, 116,
131t; Timbre 97t; Topham 68tr; Toy Fac-
tory Productions 120b; Thumper 92/93t;
Tony Ying 40/41t, 56b, 59t&b; WOMAD
Singapore 90/91t; Zhaowei Films
60/61t, 61b

Maps: Neal Jordan-Caws,
James Macdonald
Picture Manager: Steven Lawrence
Series Editor: Jason Mitchell

Second Edition 2010
First Edition 2008

© 2010 Apa Publications GmbH & Co.
Verlag KG Singapore Branch, Singapore.
Printed by CTPS-China

Worldwide distribution enquiries:
Apa Publications GmbH & Co. Verlag KG
(Singapore Branch) 38 Joo Koon Road,
Singapore 628990; tel: (65) 6865 1600;
e-mail: apasin@signet.com.sg
Distributed in the UK and Ireland by:
GeoCenter International Ltd
Meridian House, Churchill Way West,
Basingstoke, Hampshire RG21 6YR;
tel: (44 1256) 817 987;
e-mail: sales@geocenter.co.uk
Distributed in the United States by:
Langenscheidt Publishers, Inc.
36–36 33rd Street 4th Floor, Long Island
City, NY 11106; tel: (1 718) 784
0055; e-mail: orders@langenscheidt.com

Contacting the Editors
We would appreciate it if readers would alert
us to outdated information by writing to:
Apa Publications, PO Box 7910, London
SE1 1WE, UK; fax: (44 20) 7403 0290;
e-mail: insight@apaguide.co.uk
No part of this book may be reproduced,
stored in a retrieval system or transmitted
in any form or by any means (electronic,
mechanical, photocopying, recording or
otherwise), without prior written permission
of Apa Publications. Brief text quotations
with use of photographs are exempted for
book review purposes only. Information has
been obtained from sources believed to be
reliable, but its accuracy and completeness,
and the opinions based thereon, are
not guaranteed.

MRT & LRT System

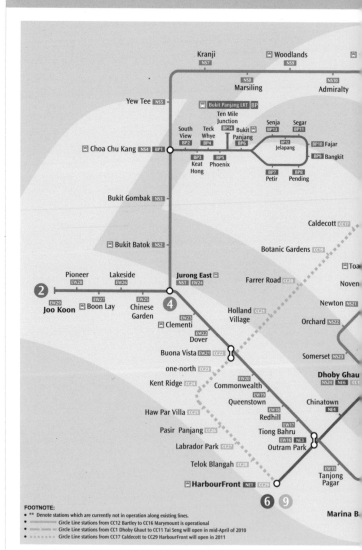

Kranji **NS7**

☐ Woodlands **NS9** ☐

NS8 Marsiling

NS10 Admiralty

Yew Tee **NS5**

🚈 Bukit Panjang LRT **BP**

Ten Mile Junction **BP14** Bukit ☐ Panjang **BP6**

South View **BP2**

Teck Whye **BP4**

Senja **BP13**

Segar **BP11**

BP12 Jelapang

BP10 Fajar

BP9 Bangkit

☐ Choa Chu Kang **NS4** **BP1**

BP3 Keat Hong

BP5 Phoenix

BP7 Petir

BP8 Pending

Bukit Gombak **NS3**

Caldecott **CC17**

☐ Bukit Batok **NS2**

Botanic Gardens **CC19**

☐ Toa

Pioneer **EW28**

Lakeside **EW26**

Jurong East ☐ **NS1** **EW24**

Farrer Road **CC20**

Noven

EW29 Joo Koon

☐ Boon Lay **EW27**

EW25 Chinese Garden

❹

Newton **NS21**

❷

Holland **CC21** Village

Orchard **NS22**

EW23 Clementi

EW22 Dover

Buona Vista **EW21** **CC22**

Somerset **NS23**

one-north **CC23**

Dhoby Ghau **NS24** **NE6** **CC1**

Kent Ridge **CC24**

EW20 Commonwealth

EW19 Queenstown

Chinatown **NE4**

Haw Par Villa **CC25**

EW18 Redhill

Pasir Panjang **CC26**

EW17 Tiong Bahru

Labrador Park **CC27**

EW16 **NE3** Outram Park

Telok Blangah **CC28**

EW15 Tanjong Pagar

☐ HarbourFront **NE1** **CC29**

❻ ❾

Marina B

FOOTNOTE:
- ** Denote stations which are currently not in operation along existing lines.
- ▬▬▬ Circle Line stations from CC12 Bartley to CC16 Marymount is operational
- ▬ ▬ ▬ Circle Line stations from CC1 Dhoby Ghaut to CC11 Tai Seng will open in mid-April of 2010
- ▪▪▪▪▪ Circle Line stations from CC17 Caldecott to CC29 HarbourFront will open in 2011